THE DEFINITIVE MIDDLE SCHOOL GUIDE

A Handbook For Success

by Imogene Forte & Sandra Schurr

Incentive Publications, Inc.
Nashville, Tennessee

Edited by Jan Keeling
Cover: a collaborative effort of the creative KIDS' STUFF™ crew!

Library of Congress Catalog Card Number: 93-077473
ISBN 0-86530-270-7

Overview

PREFACE...13

NUTS AND BOLTS OF MIDDLE GRADES EDUCATION.................................15

INTERDISCIPLINARY TEAMING..73

ADVISORY...115

COOPERATIVE LEARNING..157

CREATIVE AND CRITICAL THINKING SKILLS...................................191

ASSESSMENT...257

INTERDISCIPLINARY INSTRUCTION...299

BIBLIOGRAPHY AND INDEX..341

Table Of Contents

Preface 13

NUTS AND BOLTS OF MIDDLE GRADES EDUCATION

Nuts And Bolts Of Middle Grades Education Overview.............................17

Ten (Plus Three) Important Nuts And Bolts Questions To Find Answers For............18

Ten (Plus Five) Terms Essential To Middle Level Education Success 19

Ten (Plus One) Findings From The Published Literature About
    Needs And Characteristics Of Early Adolescence And Adolescent Programs 21

Ten (Plus Fifteen) Needs/Characteristics Of Young Adolescents................26

Ten Traits Of Young Adolescents To Keep In Mind When Planning Lessons
    And Activities..27

Ten Characteristics Of An At-Risk Student
    And Ten Characteristics Of Schools That Meet Needs Of At-Risk Students 28

Ten (Plus Thirteen) Indicators Of A Gifted/Talented Student.....................29

Ten (Plus Ten) Characteristics Of Exemplary Middle School Programs 30

Ten (Plus Three) Major Distinctions Between
    The Middle School And The Junior High School 31

Ten Contributions To The Middle School From The Junior High School 32

Ten (Minus Two) Recommendations For Transforming
    Middle Level Schools In Accordance With The Carnegie Report...............33

Ten Points To Consider When Developing A School Mission Statement 34

Ten Things To Look For In A Good Middle School 35

Ten (Plus Four) Essential Elements
    For Developing A Positive Middle School Climate 36

Ten (Plus Three) Ideas For Developing A Positive Middle School Climate 37

Ten Suggestions For Facility Requirements For Middle Schools 38

Ten Suggestions For Organizing Space And Enhancing Classroom Climate 39

Ten Ways To Use Bulletin Boards 40

Ten Ways To Differentiate Instruction And Five Examples Of Each Way 41

Ten Curriculum Priorities To Use To Develop A Balanced
    Middle Grades Program (Annotated Curriculum Checklist) 43

Ten Factors To Consider When Selecting Instructional Materials 44

Ten Questions For Teachers To Ask When Planning A Lesson 45

Ten Ways To Respond To Incorrect Student Answers 46

Ten (Minus One) Things To Think About
    When Putting Together A Middle School's Master Schedule 47

Ten High-Priority Areas To Consider When Setting Up A Master Schedule 48

Ten Advantages Of The Block Schedule 49

Ten Reasons To Flex The Block 50

Ten (Minus One) Ways To Flex A Block Schedule 51

Ten (Minus One) Sample Schedules 54

Ten (Times Three) Suggested Middle School Exploratory Offerings 63

Ten Suggested Mini-Courses 64

Ten (Minus Six) Assumptions About Ability Grouping
    And What The Research Shows About Ability Grouping 65

Ten (Plus Two) Things School Practitioners Can Do About Ability Grouping 66

Ten Creative Approaches To A Positive Classroom Climate 67

Ten Guidelines For Developing A Discipline Program 68

Ten (Plus Twelve) Planning Strategies 69

Ten Teacher Timesavers And Stress Reducers And Twelve Teacher Time Wasters 70

Ten (Plus Three) Ways To Inform Parents And Caregivers
    And Involve Them In Their Middle Grader's School Progress 71

Nuts And Bolts Of Middle Grades Education—Teacher's Wrap-Up, À La Bloom
    (Teacher's Check-Up According To Bloom's Taxonomy) 72

INTERDISCIPLINARY TEAMING

Interdisciplinary Teaming Overview 75

Ten Important Interdisciplinary Teaming Questions To Find Answers For 76

Ten Definitions Essential To Teaming Success 77

Ten Findings From The Published Literature
About Teaming In The Middle School...78

Ten (Plus Four) Things To Remember When Developing Teams 82

Ten Pieces of Data To Consider When Forming Teams 83

Ten Decisions For Teachers To Make When Organizing Teams..............................84

Ten Possible Team Member Traits To Consider 85

Ten (Minus Six) Teaching Dilemmas: What Would You Do? 87

Ten (Plus Fifteen) Criteria
To Determine How Well You Would Fit Into The Teaming Concept 88

Ten Ways To Rate Yourself As An Effective Team Builder 90

Ten (Plus Four) Roles And Responsibilities Of A Team Leader 91

Ten (Plus One) Things On Which Team Members Should Agree............................92

Ten (Plus Twenty) Tools For Building A Team Identity....................................93

Ten Things That Great Teams Do 94

Ten More Things That Great Teams Do 95

Ten Barriers For Effective Teams To Overcome 96

Ten Ideas For Developing A Team Handbook 98

Ten (Plus Two) Ways To Use Common Planning Time 100

Ten (Minus Three) Guidelines For Setting Team Discipline Rules......................101

Ten Steps For An Effective Parent Conference 102

Ten (Plus Ten) Techniques For Effective Team Meetings 103

Ten (Plus Two) Characteristics Of Effective Teaming.....................................104

A List Of Advantages And Disadvantages Of Varying Team Sizes......................105

A Working Definition Of A Flexible Block Master Schedule 107

Sample Interdisciplinary Team Assignment Data Sheet 108

Sample Interdisciplinary Team Evaluation Report 109

Ten (Plus One) Questions To Use During A Team Interview.............................110

A Sample Team Self-Evaluation Checklist 111

Teacher's Interdisciplinary Teaming Wrap-Up, À La Bloom
(Teacher's Check-Up According To Bloom's Taxonomy).................................114

ADVISORY

Advisory Concept Overview..117

Ten Important Advisory Questions To Find Answers For 118

Ten (Plus One) Definitions Essential To Advisory Success................................119

Ten (Plus Two) Findings From The Published Literature
To Document The Need For An Advisee/Advisor Program 121

Ten Characteristics Of A Quality Advisory Program..................................127

Ten (Plus Two) Decisions To Be Made Regarding An Advisory Program 128

Ten Responsibilities Of An Advisor..130

Ten Ways Teachers Can Prepare Themselves For The Role Of Advisor 131

Ten (Plus Ten) DOs And Ten DON'Ts For Advisors 132

Advisory Program Scheduling..134

Overview Of One Model For A Complete Middle Grades Advisory Program
(Excerpts From *Advisory*™ Middle Grades Advisee/Advisor Program) 136

    Scope And Sequence Charts..137

    Table Of Contents For Three Levels..138

    Investigation Tasks For Three Levels 139

    Sample Lesson Plan Level I 140

    Sample Lesson Plan Level II 141

    Sample Lesson Plan Level III 142

Ten (Plus Two) Children's Picture Books To Use To Help Students In Transition
Express And Understand Feelings And Emotions...............................143

Sample Lesson Plan For Using A Picture Book To Explore Behaviors.......................145

Sample Lesson Plan For Using A Picture Book To Develop
Appreciation Of Differences In People...146

Ten (Plus Ten) Springboards For Discussion Starters And
Journal Writing In Advisory 147

Ten (Plus Ten) Possible Advisory Activities
In Addition To Regular Curriculum Activities..................................148

Ten (Plus One) Quotations From Well-Known Figures
To Use As Discussion Sparkers 149

Sample Student Interest Inventory..150

Sample Student Advisory Questionnaire 151

Sample Instrument For Evaluating An Advisory Program's Effectiveness
(The Teacher Self-Checklist) 152

Sample Instrument For Evaluating An Advisory Program's Effectiveness
(The Advisory Class Observation Form) 153

Instrument For Evaluating An Advisory Program's Effectiveness
(Teacher Interview Form)..154

Selected Resources For Discussion Starters And Session Sparkers
For Advisory Sessions..155

Advisory Teacher's Wrap-Up, À La Bloom
(Teacher's Check-Up According To Bloom's Taxonomy)............................156

COOPERATIVE LEARNING

Cooperative Learning Overview..159

Ten Important Cooperative Learning Questions To Find Answers For.....................160

Ten Definitions Essential To Cooperative Learning Success.....................................161

Ten (Plus One) Findings From The Published Literature
To Document The Need For Cooperative Learning...162

Cooperative Learning And Global Education..168

Ten Often-Used Student Roles For Cooperative Learning Groups...........................169

Ten Pitfalls To Avoid When Moving Into Cooperative Learning..............................170

Ten Creative Methods For Grouping Students...171

Ten (Plus Ten) Social/Process Skills To Work On In Learning Groups....................172

Ten Affective Activities For Nurturing Group Cohesiveness....................................173

Ten (Minus Two) "Warmup" Activities For Cooperative Learning.............................176

    Send The Message...177

    Biographical Beginnings..178

    In Pursuit Of Trivia..179

    Bee Sharp...180

    A Different Drummer..180

    For Good Measure...181

Group Plan At A Glance (For Teacher And Student Use)...182

Off To A Good Start (Student Planning Worksheet)..183

Behavior Checklist For Observing A Cooperative Learning Activity........................184

Ten Discussion Questions For Assessing Social Skills In Group Work.....................185

Ten (Plus One) Ways To Look At Members In My Group...186

Ten (Plus Four) Student Measures Of Success..187

Cooperative Learning Post-Test (Sample Student Evaluation)................................188

Teacher's Cooperative Learning Wrap-Up, À La Bloom
(Teacher's Check-Up According To Bloom's Taxonomy).....................................190

CREATIVE AND CRITICAL THINKING SKILLS

Thinking Skills Overview 193

Ten Important Thinking Skills Questions To Find Answers For 194

Ten (Plus Ten) Definitions Essential To Success With Thinking Skills 195

Ten Findings From The Published Literature
    To Document The Need For Higher-Order Questioning And Thinking Skills.......197

Ten Characteristics Of Intellectual Growth In Students.......................................201

Ten Guidelines For Making The "Lecturette"
    A Thinking Time And Learning Tool For Students 202

Ten (Plus One) Points To Ponder When Setting Up
    A Classroom Discussion To Promote Thinking Skills 203

Ten Teacher Responses To Incorrect Answers That Encourage Student Thinking.......204

Ten (Plus Ten) Examples Of Questions For Student Journal Writing That Are
    Transitions For Thinking Activities And Follow-up Thinking Lessons..............205

Ten (Plus One) Guidelines For Developing Simulation Games
    To Encourage The Use Of Thinking Skills 206

Ten Selected Models For Teaching Thinking Skills In The Classroom

    Model One: Bloom's Taxonomy Of Cognitive Development 207

    Model Two: Williams' Taxonomy Of Divergent Thinking And Feeling.................211

    Model Three: The Web...213

    Model Four: Research, Write, And Create Model 214

    Model Five: Chart For Making Quality Decisions..215

    Model Six: The Thinktrix 217

    Model Seven: Thinking On Your Feet...219

    Model Eight: Using A Pattern For Problem-Solving Tasks 221

    Model Nine: The Why Model..222

    Model Ten: Starter Statements...223

Ten Ways To Use Questions To Develop Higher-Level Thinking Skills.....................225

Ten Questions To Use To Assess Creativity In Your School....................................226

Ten (Minus Two) Ways To Foster A Creative Climate In The Classroom..................227

Ten Strategies For Smuggling Thinking Skills Into Your Subject Area

    Strategy One: Think Smart Task Cards..228

    Strategy Two: Independent Study Sheets 232

    Strategy Three: Commercial Posters...234

    Strategy Four: Reports 236

    Strategy Five: Investigation Kits..238

Strategy Six: Desktop Learning Stations..239

Strategy Seven: Fact And Activity File Folders..241

Strategy Eight: Learning Logs And Dialogue Diaries................................245

Strategy Nine: Interdisciplinary Units 246

Strategy Ten: Games 253

Ten Characteristics Of Five Varied Learning Styles...................................254

Teacher's Thinking Skills Wrap-Up, À La Bloom
(Teacher's Check-Up According To Bloom's Taxonomy)..........................256

ASSESSMENT

Assessment Overview 259

Ten (Plus Ten) Important Assessment Questions To Find Answers For 260

Ten Definitions Essential To Assessment Success 262

Ten (Minus One) Findings From The Published Literature
To Document The Need For Alternative Assessment Methods..................263

Ten Commandments Of Testing In Middle Grades.....................................267

Ten Questions Students Need To Have Answered Before A Test
And Ten Ways Students Can Use Test Time Wisely................................268

Ten Guidelines For Improving Teacher-Made Tests 269

Ten Things For Teachers To Consider When Evaluating A Lesson Plan......270

Ten Guidelines To Consider When Writing Quality Test Items 271

Ten (Plus Five) Hints For Writing Better Objective Test Items 272

Ten (Plus Ten, Plus Ten) Essay Direction Words 274

Ten Ways To Prepare Middle Level Students For Taking Essay Tests........277

Ten Good Starter Verbs/Behaviors For Assessing Student Achievement
Using The Levels Of Bloom's Taxonomy...278

Ten Characteristics Of Authentic Tests 279

Ten (Minus Two) Guidelines For Realizing The Power Of The Portfolio.....280

Ten (Minus Five) Decisions To Be Made For Portfolios
Plus Five Reasons To Consider Portfolio Assessment 282

Ten Reasons Student Products Are Good Assessment Tools 283

Bloom Project Chart..284

Ten Steps For Designing Performance Tests In Core Curricular Areas 285

Ten Benefits Of Self-Evaluations For Students 286

Ten (Plus One) Types Of Questions To Ask When Gathering Assessment Data........287

Ten Guidelines To Follow When Organizing A Student Study Group 290

Sample Student Study Guide 291

Ten (Plus Two) Informal Methods Of Assessing Student
    Understanding Of Material Covered During Instruction..............................292

Ten (Plus Three) Statements To Assess "The House We Live In" 297

Teacher's Assessment Wrap-Up, À La Bloom
    (Teacher's Check-Up According To Bloom's Taxonomy)............................298

INTERDISCIPLINARY INSTRUCTION: A MODEL FOR SUCCESS

Interdisciplinary Instruction Overview 301

Ten Important Interdisciplinary Instruction Questions To Find Answers For 302

Ten Definitions Essential To Interdisciplinary Instruction Success 303

Ten Findings From The Published Literature
    About Interdisciplinary Instruction In The Middle School 304

Ten (Minus Four) Myths About Interdisciplinary Instruction 308

Ten (Minus Five) Reasons To Integrate The Disciplines 309

Ten Things To Think About When Selecting A Unit Theme 310

Ten Steps For Beginning To Integrate The Disciplines 311

Ten Points For Teachers And Teams To Ponder
    When Defining Interdisciplinary Curriculum And Instruction 313

Building An Interdisciplinary Planning Matrix 314

Ten (Plus One) Springboards For Intersection Of Curriculum Themes
    With Personal And Social Concerns 315

Ten Essential Elements Of An Interdisciplinary Unit.............................316

Ten Elements That Make A Great Interdisciplinary Unit 317

Ten (Plus Ten) Favorite Themes For Interdisciplinary Units 318

Ten (Plus Eight) Sample Tasks/Assignments
    For An Interdisciplinary Unit On Measurement 319

Ten Views For Integrating The Curricula 321

Ten (Plus Six)-Item Team Checklist For Evaluating
    The Interdisciplinary Unit And Development Process 322

The Interdisciplinary Team (IDT) Test...323

Interdisciplinary Unit: A Model For Success ("The Future Is News To Me")............324

Teacher's Interdisciplinary Instruction Wrap-Up, À La Bloom
    (Teacher's Check-Up According To Bloom's Taxonomy)........................340

BIBLIOGRAPHY 343

INDEX...347

PREFACE

The concept of the Middle School became a reality when educators became convinced that *student-centered education* is the most effective approach to meeting young adolescents' needs and that grouping these youngsters together in a supportive environment provides the best climate for learning and growing.

The Definitive Middle School Guide is a substantial collection of relevant information concerning the middle school philosophy and its essential program components. It is intended to serve as a combination encyclopedia, dictionary, and almanac so that readers can quickly and easily find out "everything they ever wanted to know about middle schools." The book features self-contained modules arranged in a sequence designed to present the evolution of an effective middle school organizational pattern. Each module may also stand on its own to be used independently of the other modules should the need arise. For example, if the reader has a great deal of knowledge of interdisciplinary teaming or cooperative learning, but wants to learn more about advisory programs, he or she can go directly to the advisory module without first working through the previous sections. It should also be noted that a "TOP TEN" format has been utilized to allow the user to unearth major concepts without having to sift through extraneous information. The authors have spent considerable time researching and synthesizing the literature on middle schools so that it can be presented in an orderly and timely fashion to meet the needs of the busy teacher, administrator, or others needing "fingertip information" essential to middle school understanding and success.

Educators responsible for setting up or conducting workshops or in-service programs will be delighted to discover that the common format for each of the seven modules provides a complete and workable training package:

- A one-page overview.

- A set of meaningful questions that serve as learning goals as well as pre- and post-tests of the material addressed in the module.

- A glossary of key terms.

- A collection of findings from the published literature to provide motivation and support for the implementation of significant changes in schooling at the middle grade level.

- A series of "Top Ten" pages that present the most important and germane material on the module's topic or theme in the form of lists, descriptions, references, tools, and techniques.

- "Teacher's Wrap-Up À La Bloom": a page of activities, one at each level of Bloom's Taxonomy, that will help the reader wrap up and make use of the information, concepts, and ideas included in the module.

Major topics include:

Nuts and Bolts of Middle Grades Education
- Needs and characteristics of young adolescents
- Basic elements of the exemplary middle school
- School climate
- Facility requirements
- Flexible block scheduling
- Exploratory and mini-class offerings
- Classroom management tips

Interdisciplinary Teaming
- Forming teams
- Roles and responsibilities of team members
- Ways to build team identity
- Developing a team handbook
- Evaluating a team's effectiveness

Advisory
- Characteristics of high-quality advisory programs
- Responsibilities of advisors
- Ways to schedule advisory time
- Sample advisory activities
- Instruments for evaluating an advisory program's success

Cooperative Learning
- Methods for grouping students
- Assigning student roles and rules
- Elements of cooperative learning
- Social processing skills
- Sample lesson plans and activities

Creative and Critical Thinking Skills
- Intellectual growth in students
- Suggestions for conducting group discussions and "lecturettes"
- Models for teaching thinking skills
- Strategies for integrating thinking skills into the curriculum

Assessment
- Improving teacher-made tests
- Helping students become test-wise
- Characteristics of authentic tests
- Examples of performance, product, and portfolio assessment measures

Interdisciplinary Instruction: A Model For Success
- A model interdisciplinary unit
- Special challenges of an interdisciplinary team
- Designing and implementing an effective curriculum
- The module from which you can launch your successful program!

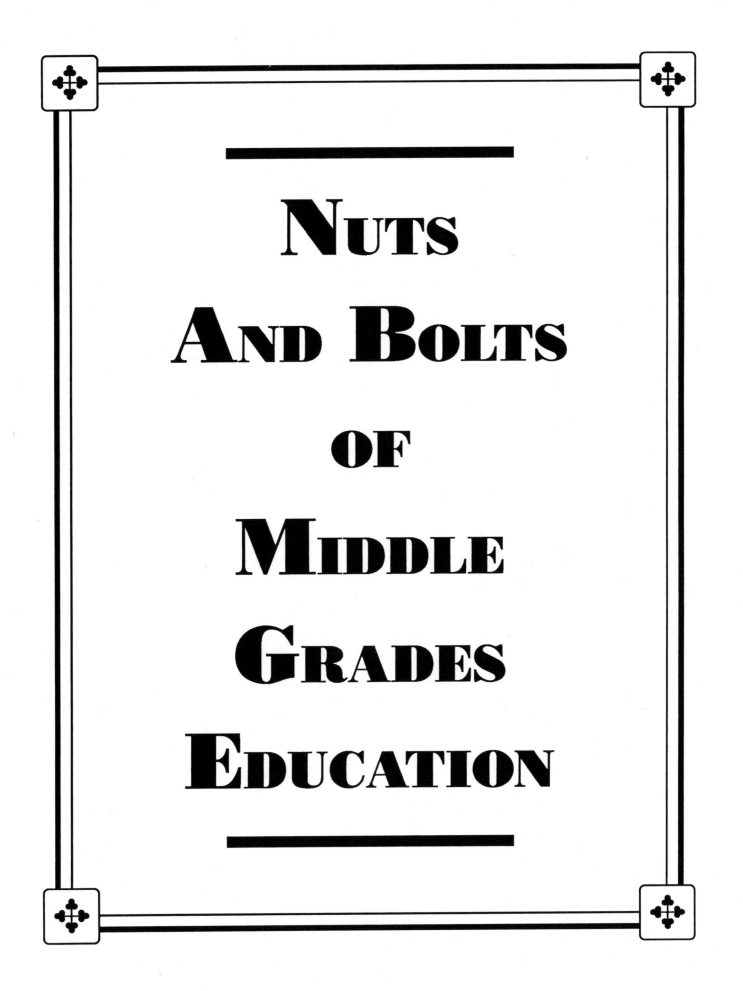

NUTS

AND BOLTS

OF

MIDDLE

GRADES

EDUCATION

Nuts And Bolts Of Middle Grades Education Overview

THE PHILOSOPHY OF AN EFFECTIVE MIDDLE SCHOOL:
- It is based on the unique needs and characteristics of the young adolescent. These needs encompass physical, psychological, intellectual, social, and moral and ethical needs. The entire program is developed around these needs.
- It is student-centered rather than subject-centered.
- It includes provision for both pre-service and in-service teacher training to meet the widely-varying exceptionalities in interests, abilities, and experiences of students in transition.
- It accepts and respects each student and teacher as an individual of worth and dignity in his or her own right; it celebrates differences and encourages creativity and freedom of expression in keeping with ethnic genealogy and background experiences.
- It requires the *same* teachers to share the *same* students over the *same* block of time in the *same* part of the building.

ADVANTAGES OF THE MIDDLE SCHOOL ORGANIZATIONAL PATTERN:
- Articulation between the elementary school and the middle school is enhanced through increased communication and a student-centered focus. Articulation between the middle school and the high school is also an important aspect of the program.
- Flexible block scheduling allows for varied learning activities, grouping and regrouping students for instruction, and common planning time for teachers.
- Interdisciplinary approaches in all disciplines are encouraged. This provides for integration of the curricular areas.
- A varied range of exploratory opportunities for students is presented.
- Opportunities for focusing on affective education are built into the daily schedule.
- An emphasis is placed on intramural rather than interscholastic athletics. Cooperation and participation, not just winning, are stressed.
- The educators have been especially trained to work with middle level students and are committed to the education of the young adolescent. They have knowledge of needs and characteristics of the age and have mastered varied teaching strategies which promote active rather than passive activities.

IN SUMMARY:
The successful middle school program is forward thinking, outcome-based, and devoted to excellence in classroom instruction, student motivation, and the quest for life skills, broad-based learning, and creative thinking.

10 PLUS 3

Important Nuts And Bolts Questions To Find Answers For

1. How should the physical plant best be arranged to facilitate the middle school philosophy and program?

2. What are the unique needs and characteristics of the middle grade student?

3. What are some guidelines for establishing a student-centered rather than subject-centered middle school mission statement?

4. What advantages are afforded through flexible block scheduling?

5. Why are interdisciplinary approaches to curriculum and instruction desirable?

6. How can successful practices and strategies in effective middle school classrooms be identified and how can teachers, students, and administrators work together to nurture and maximize these characteristics for the good of all students?

7. What are some ways that parents and caregivers can be involved in the decision-making and day-to-day operations of the middle school program?

8. What is a good definition of a mini-course? Give two or three good examples of interesting mini-course titles and descriptions.

9. How would you define an authentic exploratory offering? Give examples of five to ten content areas in which exploratory offerings could be developed.

10. What are some ways to differentiate instruction? Give one good example.

11. What are some ways middle grades teachers can save time and reduce stress, and what are some time-wasters and stress-producers to avoid?

12. What are some steps middle grades teachers can take to be more effective as positive rather than negative disciplinarians?

13. Why have young adolescents in our society today been labeled as "Kids Caught In The Middle"?

10

PLUS 5

Terms Essential To Middle Level Education Success

1. **Advisory Time:** A regularly-scheduled period each day/week in which students interact with peers/teachers about both personal and school-related concerns.

2. **Block/Flexible Schedule:** Organization of the school day into large units of time that may be utilized in varied and productive ways by the school staff.

3. **Common Planning (Team Duty) Time:** Regularly-scheduled time during the school day during which a given team of teachers who are responsible for the same group of students is available for joint planning, parent conferencing, and/or lesson preparation.

4. **Core Curriculum:** The basic subject areas of math, science, social studies, and reading/language arts.

5. **Early Adolescence:** The stage of development between ages 10 and 14 when the student begins to reach puberty.

6. **Exploration:** Regularly-scheduled curriculum experiences designed to help students discover and/or examine learning related to their changing needs, aptitudes, and interests. Often referred to as the "wheel" or mini-classes.

7. **Heterogeneous Grouping:** Grouping of students that does not divide learners on the basis of ability or academic achievement.

8. **Homogeneous Grouping:** Grouping of students that divides learners on the basis of specific levels of ability, achievement, or interest. Sometimes referred to as tracking.

9. **Interdisciplinary Program:** Instruction that integrates and combines subject matter ordinarily taught separately into a single organizational structure.

10. **Interdisciplinary Team:** An instructional organization of two to five teachers representing varied disciplines that pool their resources, interests, expertise, and knowledge of students to jointly take the responsibility for meeting educational needs of a common group of students.

11. **Interscholastic:** Athletic activities or events whose primary purpose is to foster competition between schools and school districts. Participation usually limited to students with exceptional athletic ability.

12. **Intrascholastic or Intramural:** Athletic activities or events held within the school day, or shortly thereafter, whose primary purpose is to encourage all students to participate regardless of athletic ability.

13. **Mini-Courses:** Special interest activities of short duration that provide learning opportunities for students based on student interest, faculty expertise, and community involvement.

14. **Metacognition:** The process by which individuals examine their own thinking processes.

15. **Transescence:** The stage of development which begins prior to the onset of puberty and extends through the early stages of adolescence.

10 PLUS 1

Findings From The Published Literature About Needs And Characteristics Of Early Adolescence And Adolescent Programs

1. FINDING

Alexander and George state: Regardless of what we call middle-schoolers, there are common developmental tasks that each one will encounter, is currently encountering, or has just encountered. Usually a middle-schooler will become involved with most if not all of these tasks while in the middle school, but not necessarily at the same time. Thornburg's designation of seven developmental tasks is a useful one to note as we turn to a brief identification of some major characteristics of the age group:

1. Becoming aware of increased physical changes
2. Organizing knowledge and concepts into problem-solving strategies
3. Learning new social/sex roles
4. Recognizing one's identification with stereotypes
5. Developing friendships with others
6. Gaining a sense of independence
7. Developing a sense of morality and values

Reference: Alexander, William M. and George, Paul S. The Exemplary Middle School. New York: Holt, Rinehart and Winston, 1981, p. 5.

2. FINDING

Donald H. Eichhorn emphasized: More and more professional literature is offering evidence that the junior high school concept is being seriously challenged. Usually, however, the suggested remedies take the form of treating the ills of the present structure rather than proposing an attack at the root causes of the problem. Substantiated assumptions of this study indicate that the root of the problem be attacked through an altered school district organization pattern. One way would be to initiate a new pattern: an elementary unit of grades kindergarten through five, a middle school grouping of grades six through eight, and a high school unit of grades nine through twelve.

Reference: Eichhorn, Donald H. The Middle School. National Association of Secondary School Principals, Reston, Virginia, and National Middle School Association, Columbus, Ohio, Special Printing, 1987, p. 104.

3. FINDING
John H. Lounsbury writes:

There is considerable consensus about the educational ideas and ideals that are inherent in the so-called middle school concept, all of which grow out of the unique nature of this age group and their needs. While there is no single model, no "right" curriculum, no complete orthodoxy, there is widespread agreement on the basic principles of transescent education and the conditions which gave rise to it. Some of these views and conditions are summarized as follows:

• The middle school is an educational response to the needs and characteristics of youngsters during transescence and, as such, deals with the full range of intellectual and developmental needs.

• Young people going through the rapid growth and extensive maturation that occurs in early adolescence need an educational program that is distinctively different from either the elementary or the secondary model.

• Existing programs for this age group have all too often lacked focus on transescent characteristics and needs.

• Educators, school board members, parents, and citizens generally need to become more cognizant of this age group and what an effective educational program for this group requires.

• No other age level is of more enduring importance because the determinants of one's behavior as an adult, self-concept, learning interests and skills, and values are largely formed in this period of life.

• The developmental diversity of this age group makes it especially difficult to organize an educational program that adequately meets the needs of all.

• The academic needs of middle school students are affected greatly by their physical, social, and emotional needs which also must be addressed directly in the school program.

Reference: Lounsbury, John, Editor. Perspectives. National Middle School Association, Columbus, Ohio, 1984.

4. FINDING
Van Hoose and Strahan stress:

Personal needs can be summarized with three words: security, support, and success. While young adolescents often seem self-assured, interviews and survey responses indicate that most of them need to feel secure. Among top fears are the loss of a parent and disease. As children, they may have known these fears. As adolescents, they often dwell on them.

Reference: Van Hoose, John and Strahan, David. Young Adolescent Development and School Practices: Promoting Harmony. National Middle School Association, Columbus, Ohio, 1988, p. 23.

5. FINDING
Johnston and Markle point out:

Effective middle school teachers . . .
1. have positive self-concepts.
2. demonstrate warmth.
3. are optimistic.
4. are enthusiastic.
5. are flexible.
6. are spontaneous.
7. accept students.
8. demonstrate awareness of developmental levels.
9. demonstrate knowledge of subject matter.
10. use a variety of instructional activities and materials.
11. structure instruction.
12. monitor learning.
13. use concrete materials and focused learning strategies.
14. ask varied questions.
15. incorporate indirectness in teaching.
16. incorporate "success-building" behavior in teaching.
17. diagnose individual learning needs and prescribe individual instruction.
18. listen.

Reference: Johnston, J. Howard and Markle, Glenn C. What Research Says to the Practitioner. National Middle School Association, Columbus, Ohio, 1986, pp. 16–18.

6. FINDING
NASSP's Council on Middle Level Education discusses client-centeredness:

Client Centeredness: The most successful schools are those that understand the unique needs of their clients and fill those needs quickly and effectively. Most important, effective schools understand the relationship of development to learning so that students are not asked to violate the dictates of their development in order to participate fully in the educational program.

Reference: Arth, Alfred A., et. al. An Agenda For Excellence. National Association of Secondary School Principals, Reston, Virginia, 1985, p. 20.

7. FINDING

NASSP's Council on Middle Level Education communicates:
All effective organizations have a clear sense of their mission. From the largest corporations to the smallest clubs or special interest groups, a clear mission helps members of the organization decide on goals, set priorities, and monitor behavior.

All of the recent literature on organizational effectiveness starts with the premise that without a mission statement that is widely accepted by everyone in the organization, any improvement efforts are doomed from the outset. This involvement of all stockholders in defining mission has long been a premise of effective collaborative planning.

School improvement literature offers the same conclusions. Schools with a clear understanding of their unique missions are more effective than schools that lack a sense of mission. Fortunately, mission statements can be developed and used by schools interested in improving.

Reference: Arth, Alfred A., et. al. Developing a Mission Statement for the Middle Level School. National Association of Secondary School Principals, Reston, Virginia, 1987, pp. 1–2.

8. FINDING

Alexander and McEwin state:
Since 1986, the middle school has been recognized as the bridge school between elementary and high school. Both this study (comparing middle level schools in 1968 and 1988) and a recent ASCD study show that the schools with grades 6–8 are more likely to feature the following:

1. An interdisciplinary organization with a flexibly scheduled day.
2. An adequate guidance program, including a teacher advisory plan.
3. A full scale exploratory program.
4. Curricular provision for such goals and curriculum domains as personal development, continued learning skills, and basic knowledge areas.
5. Varied and effective instructional methodology for the age group.
6. Continued orientation and articulation for students, parents, and teachers.

Adapted from: Alexander, William M. and McEwin, C. Kenneth. Schools in the Middle: Status and Progress. National Middle School Association, Columbus, Ohio, 1989.

9. FINDING

Lounsbury states:

Since the 1990s appear to be the time for more fully implementing the middle school concept, here are some tips that individual teachers might use to strengthen the goals of a middle school:

1. Increase personal interaction with students. Talk to students as much as possible on an informal basis, especially the at-risk student.
2. Allow students to become more involved in their studies. Provide opportunities for them to plan and develop activities.
3. Stress critical thinking for all students. Push students to think, to ask "why" and "so what" as well as who, what, where, and when.
4. Share the content, topics, and skills to be taught among team teachers, as well as other staff members involved with teaching the same set of students.

Reference: Lounsbury, John H. "As I See It—Strike While The Iron Is Hot," Middle School Journal. November, 1989, p. 39.

10. FINDING

George states three lessons American middle level educators can learn from the Japanese Junior High:

1. We must teach our students a sense of reality and a new vision. We must teach our students to be ready and aware of our changing position in the world.
2. The skills of tomorrow—learning to work effectively in groups and developing consensus-building skills—must be a vital part of our instructional strategies.
3. More money is not the answer to a better educational program in America. The Japanese educate their students well with far less spent on buildings and equipment than in America. Commitment to a quality education by everyone—parents, educators, business community—is the key.

Adapted from: George, Paul S. The Japanese Junior High School: A View From the Inside. National Middle School Association, 1989, pp. 31–34.

10 PLUS 15

Needs/ Characteristics Of Young Adolescents

Physical Needs/Characteristics

1. Experience irregular growth spurts in physical development
2. Experience fluctuations in basal metabolism causing restlessness and listlessness
3. Have ravenous appetites
4. Mature at varying rates of speed
5. Highly disturbed by body changes

Intellectual Needs/Characteristics

6. Are highly curious
7. Prefer active over passive learning experiences
8. Relate to real-life problems and situations
9. Are egocentric
10. Experience metacognition (the ability to analyze complex thought processes)

Psychological Needs/Characteristics

11. Are often erratic and inconsistent in behavior
12. Are highly sensitive to criticism
13. Are moody, restless, and self-conscious
14. Are optimistic and hopeful
15. Are searching for identity and acceptance from peers

Social Needs/Characteristics

16. Are rebellious toward parents and authority figures
17. Are confused and frightened by new school/social settings
18. Are fiercely loyal to peer group values
19. Are often aggressive and argumentative
20. Need frequent affirmation of love from adults

Moral and Ethical Needs/Characteristics

21. Are idealistic
22. Have strong sense of fairness
23. Are reflective and introspective in thoughts and feelings
24. Confront moral and ethical questions head on
25. Ask large, ambiguous questions about the meaning of life

Adapted from *Advisory Middle Grades Advisee/Advisor Program* by Imogene Forte and Sandra Schurr. Nashville, TN: Incentive Publications, 1991. Used by permission.

10 Traits Of Young Adolescents To Keep In Mind When Planning Lessons And Activities

As you plan activities, develop lessons, and deliver instruction, keep this information in mind:

1. Young adolescents have unique interests and varied abilities. They need opportunities to express their creativity.

2. Young adolescents identify with their peers and want to belong to the group. They must have opportunities to form positive peer relationships.

3. Young adolescents reflect a willingness to learn new things they consider to be useful; therefore, they require occasions to use skills to solve real-life problems.

4. Young adolescents are curious about their world. They need varied situations for exploration and extension of knowledge.

5. Young adolescents experience rapid and sporadic physical development. They require varied activities and time to be themselves.

6. Young adolescents are self-conscious and susceptible to feelings of low self-esteem. They need opportunities for success and recognition.

7. Young adolescents are at a time in their lives when they need adults but don't want to admit it. They need caring adult role models and advisors who like and respect them.

8. Young adolescents want to make their own decisions. They need consistency and direction.

9. Young adolescents prefer active over passive learning activities. They need hands-on and cooperative learning experiences.

10. Young adolescents are idealistic and possess a strong sense of fairness; therefore, they require situations appropriate for sharing thoughts, feelings, and attitudes.

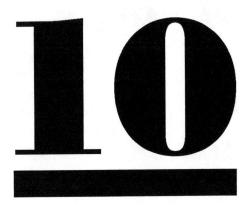

Characteristics Of An At-Risk Student And Ten Characteristics Of Schools That Meet Needs Of At-Risk Students

STUDENT CHARACTERISTICS

An at-risk student:

1. . . . demonstrates academic learning and achievement problems.

2. . . . tends to be inattentive.

3. . . . is easily distracted.

4. . . . displays short attention span.

5. . . . has low self-esteem.

6. . . . lacks social skills.

7. . . . reflects narrow range of interests.

8. . . . fears failure.

9. . . . lacks structure and organization.

10. . . . avoids responsibility and independence.

SCHOOL CHARACTERISTICS

A school that meets needs of at-risk students:

1. . . . focuses on kids.

2. . . . challenges the regularities.

3. . . . collaborates with parents/ guardians.

4. . . . avoids reforms that intensify or perpetuate impediments.

5. . . . decentralizes instructional decisions.

6. . . . promotes success.

7. . . . reduces negative effects of large school size.

8. . . . values differences in students.

9. . . . minimizes mistakes and failures.

10. . . . adopts a "whatever it takes" stance.

10 PLUS 13

Indicators Of A Gifted/Talented Student

1. Is an avid reader

2. Is outstanding in science, math, or literature

3. Has a wide range of interests

4. Is anxious to try new things

5. Seems very alert and gives rapid answers

6. Is self-motivated and needs little outside control

7. Tends to dominate peers or situations

8. Has self-confidence

9. Is sensitive to situations or the feelings of others

10. Can solve problems ingeniously

11. Has creative thoughts, ideas, or innovations

12. Is anxious to complete tasks

13. Has a great desire to excel

14. Is very expressive verbally

15. Tells imaginative stories

16. Has a mature sense of humor

17. Is inquisitive; examines things closely

18. Can show relationships between apparently unrelated things or ideas

19. Shows excitement about discoveries and is eager to share them

20. Tends to lose awareness of time

21. Is adept with the art of visual expression

22. Exhibits very expressive body/facial gestures

23. Likes to work alone

Adapted from *What To Do With The Gifted Child* by Judith Cochran. Nashville, TN: Incentive Publications, 1992. Used by permission.

10 PLUS 10

Characteristics Of Exemplary Middle School Programs

1. A philosophy based on the unique needs and characteristics of the young adolescent
2. Educators knowledgeable about and committed to the young adolescent
3. A balanced curriculum between the cognitive (subject-centered) and affective (student-centered) needs of the young adolescent
4. Teachers who use varied instructional strategies
5. A comprehensive advisor/advisee program
6. An interdisciplinary team organization at all grades
7. A flexible block master schedule
8. A full exploratory program
9. Both team planning and personal planning for all teachers
10. A positive and collaborative school climate
11. Shared decision-making in which the people closest to the "client" are involved in the decision-making process of the school
12. A smooth transition process from elementary to middle school and from middle school to high school
13. A high-quality extracurricular program including intramurals, interest-based mini-courses, clubs, and social events
14. A physical plant where teams are housed together for core classes and large areas for full team sessions
15. A commitment to the importance of health and physical fitness for all students on a regular basis
16. A commitment to regular involvement of families in the education of young adolescents by keeping them informed of student progress and school programs and by giving them meaningful roles in the schooling process
17. A positive connection between school and the community through student service projects, business partnerships, and use of community resources within the school curriculum
18. Consistent use of cooperative learning strategies in the classroom
19. An emphasis on the use of higher-order thinking skills and hands-on instructional strategies
20. Empowerment of students whenever possible

From *How To Evaluate Your Middle School* by Sandra Schurr. Columbus, OH: National Middle School Association, 1992. Used by permission.

10 PLUS 3 Major Distinctions Between The Middle School And The Junior High School

MIDDLE SCHOOL	JUNIOR HIGH SCHOOL
1. Is student-centered	Is subject-centered
2. Fosters collaboration and empowerment of teachers and students	Fosters competition and empowerment of administrators
3. Focuses on creative exploration and experimentation of subject matter	Focuses on mastery of concepts and skills in separate disciplines
4. Allows for flexible scheduling with large blocks of time	Requires a regular six-period day of 50- to 55-minute periods
5. Varies length of time students are in courses	Offers subjects for one semester or one year
6. Encourages multi-materials approach to instruction	Depends on textbook-oriented instruction
7. Organizes teachers on interdisciplinary teams with common planning period	Organizes teachers in departments with no common planning period
8. Arranges work spaces of teamed teachers adjacent to one another	Arranges work spaces of teachers according to disciplines taught
9. Emphasizes both affective and cognitive development of student	Emphasizes only cognitive development of student
10. Offers advisor/advisee teacher-oriented guidance program	Offers study hall and access to counselor upon request
11. Provides high-interest "mini-courses" during school day	Provides highly-structured activity program after school
12. Uses varied delivery systems with high level of interaction among students and teachers	Uses lecture styles a majority of the time with high percentage of teacher talk time
13. Organizes athletics around intramural concept	Organizes athletics around interscholastic concept

10 Contributions To The Middle School From The Junior High School

1. The original goal of the junior high school was to provide a separate transition between the elementary school and the high school.

2. Another initial goal was to provide a basis for the scientific study of adolescence.

3. A new grade level pattern (7-8-9 in the case of junior high schools) was implemented to meet the social and physical needs of the age group.

4. The junior high school successfully expanded and enriched the curriculum for young adolescents.

5. A variety of exploratory programs became available to seventh and eighth graders.

6. Guidance-oriented homeroom programs were developed and put into operation.

7. Clubs and student activities based on special interests and needs were provided.

8. Junior high schools became centers for experimentation with curriculum and scheduling.

9. Opportunities for students to discover and explore special interests and aptitudes for future vocational decisions were provided.

10. The possibilities for careers in the major fields of learning were revealed to students.

10 MINUS 2

Recommendations For Transforming Middle Level Schools In Accordance With The Carnegie Report

1. **Create small communities for learning** where stable, close, mutually respectful relationships with adults and peers are considered fundamental for intellectual development and personal growth. The key elements of these communities are schools-within-schools or houses, students and teachers grouped together as teams, and small group advisories that ensure that every student is known well by at least one adult.

2. **Teach a core academic program that results in students who are literate,** in the sciences as well as in the other disciplines, and who know how to think critically, lead a healthy life, behave ethically, and assume the responsibilities of citizenship in a pluralistic society. Youth service to promote values for citizenship is an essential part of the core academic program.

3. **Ensure success for all students** through the elimination of tracking by achievement level and promotion of cooperative learning, flexibility in arranging instructional time, and adequate resources (time, space, equipment, and materials) for teachers.

4. **Empower teachers and administrators to make decisions about the experiences of middle grade students** through creative control by teachers over the instructional program linked to greater responsibilities for students' performance, governance committees that assist the principal in designing and coordinating schoolwide programs, and autonomy and leadership within subschools or houses to create environments tailored to enhance the intellectual and emotional development of all youth.

5. **Staff middle grade schools with teachers who are expert at teaching young adolescents** and who have been specially prepared for assignment to the middle grades.

6. **Improve academic performance through fostering the health and fitness** of young adolescents by providing a health coordinator in every middle grade school, access to health care and counseling services, and a health-promoting school environment.

7. **Re-engage families in the education of young adolescents** by giving families meaningful roles in school governance, communicating with families about the school program and student's progress, and offering families opportunities to support the learning process at home and at the school.

8. **Connect schools with communities,** which together share responsibility for each middle grade student's success, through identifying service opportunities to ensure student's access to health and social services, and using community resources to enrich the instructional program and opportunities for constructive after-school activities.

Adapted from *Turning Points: Preparing American Youth for the 21st Century.* Carnegie Corporation of New York: Carnegie Council On Academic Development. June, 1989.

10 Points To Consider When Developing A School Mission Statement

1. A school mission statement is a brief but essential sentence that clearly communicates the overall intent and focus for the schooling process in a given educational setting.

2. A school mission statement is important to a school because it very clearly communicates the teaching and learning priorities which a school has established for its "work."

3. A school mission statement is developed through the collaborative efforts of a team that includes representatives from the administrative staff, the faculty, the student population, the parents, and the business community it serves.

4. A school mission statement must reflect the diverse cultures, beliefs, values, and purposes of the entire school population.

5. A mission statement should evolve from a series of data-gathering activities that includes surveys or questionnaires, interviews, discussions, town meetings, and/or forums.

6. A mission statement draft should be written to reflect the input from the various stakeholders represented in the data-gathering process.

7. A mission statement draft should be circulated throughout the school community to elicit recommendations for revisions.

8. A final school mission statement should be written to represent the "best thinking" of all stakeholder groups in the school.

9. A sample middle school mission statement might read as follows: "The mission of XYZ Middle School is to provide our students with the opportunities, resources, and environment to be lifelong learners and productive, responsible citizens in a changing, global society."

10. A school mission statement should be evaluated on a regular basis to determine the effect it is having on school practices and individual behavior of those associated with the school.

10 Things To Look For In A Good Middle School

1. Eliminates the middle grades as a mini- or junior high school organization by providing its own identity as a middle level school.

2. Places students together who are more alike in their needs and characteristics through a 6–8 grade configuration rather than a 7–9 grade configuration.

3. Creates "smallness within bigness" by forming teams of teachers and students into surrogate families.

4. Provides a logical transition from the self-contained classroom of the elementary school setting to the departmentalization of the high school setting.

5. Expands guidance and counseling services through the teacher-as-advisor concept.

6. Promotes the integration of subject matter through the interdisciplinary team and common planning period concepts.

7. Removes the constraints and limitations of a rigid schedule and bell system to a flexible block schedule with no predetermined time periods.

8. Empowers both teachers and students to make decisions.

9. Discourages the "winner/loser" or "star" system through emphasis on cooperation and collaboration.

10. Provides variety through alternative delivery systems, multi-media resources, and exploratory offerings.

10 PLUS 4

Essential Elements For A Positive Middle School Climate

Research on effective schools has established the following elements as essential to building a positive climate in the middle school setting:

1. Clear academic and behavioral goals

2. Order and discipline

3. High expectations for students and teachers

4. Rewards and incentives for students and teachers

5. Positive (not remedial) school environments

6. Constructive administrative leadership

7. Community and parental support

8. Concentration on academic learning time

9. Frequent, monitored homework

10. Regular and frequent monitoring of student work

11. Well planned and integrated curriculum

12. Variety of teaching strategies and delivery systems

13. Opportunities for student responsibility

14. Teacher efficacy

10

PLUS 3

Ideas For Developing A Positive Middle School Climate

1. Develop a school motto and logo and use them widely.

2. Develop a referral to the office for positive student recognition.

3. Reinforce good attendance at all school functions through individual and group incentives.

4. Display student work in all classrooms and throughout the building on a large scale.

5. Use marquees, school windows, and lobby showcases to convey positive messages.

6. Designate and maintain quality teacher, student, and parent lounges as "time in" rooms.

7. Take care when stating or promoting school rules so they take on a positive rather than a punitive flavor.

8. Support and encourage an active student council/government and parent advisory groups.

9. Seize opportunities to augment school life with extracurricular activities.

10. Form an "academic boosters" group to promote academics within the school.

11. Issue many invitations and encourage people to visit your school.

12. Draw attention to personal and professional growth of staff members.

13. Develop a positive marketing plan for your school that includes a multi-media presentation, regular newspaper/radio/television promotions, and parent communications.

10 Suggestions For Facility Requirements For Middle Schools

1. Team classrooms should be in proximity to one another. This will make for instant communication and will cut down on time required for students to travel from one classroom to another.

2. These classrooms should adapt easily for grouping and regrouping of students. It may be necessary to vary class size, learning experiences, and delivery systems.

3. The environment at all times must be safe and secure for students and staff. This issue is of great concern to parents.

4. The furniture and equipment in classrooms should be functional, movable, and size-appropriate. Remember that flexibility is the "key" in middle school.

5. The media center should be the center of all curriculum and instruction, not just a library with books. The media specialist is the "expert" in curriculum, materials, equipment, and information.

6. The physical plant should be aesthetically pleasing and attractive. This enhances the setting for learning.

7. A large well-lighted (with shades if necessary) group instruction/meeting area should be made available for use by all teams. A good plan is to have a sign-up sheet posted on or near the entrance to the room and to ask team leaders to sign up in ink for no more than two consecutive days at a time.

8. It is recommended that teachers have an assigned team meeting room for their use. A round table, comfortable chairs, and a bulletin board with a calendar enhance team meeting space.

9. Plan effective traffic patterns so that the minimum number of students is changing classes at one time. The environment (both inside and outside of classrooms) should reflect the physical needs of students.

10. If lockers are provided, consider height and size. Assign lockers to students whose team classrooms are in the same area.

10 Suggestions For Organizing Space And Enhancing Classroom Climate

1. Keep traffic lanes clear.

2. Plan seating and furniture arrangements with instructional goals and activities in mind.

3. Be sure window and door exits are unobstructed.

4. Plan room's overall appearance to be attractive and inviting.

5. Decorate classroom with attractive, interactive bulletin boards.

6. Personalize classroom with plants, posters, maps, personal artifacts, floor pillows, or lofts.

7. Make sure students can see displays, screens, and presentations from desks or tables.

8. Be sure student work areas are visible to the teacher.

9. Provide opportunities for youngsters to move around and work in different areas of the classroom.

10. Make storage space, supplies, and materials easily accessible.

10 Ways To Use Bulletin Boards

A bulletin board can be used . . .

1. . . . to display student work.

2. . . . to enhance and provide motivation for an interdisciplinary topic.

3. . . . as an interactive learning center.

4. . . . as a visual springboard for problem-solving and creative writing.

5. . . . to share school and team information.

6. . . . to provide enrichment and extra credit activities.

7. . . . to display examples of students' interests and hobbies.

8. . . . to keep students aware of current events in the world, the nation, the state, the community.

9. . . . to create a positive, healthy classroom climate.

10. . . . to provide ownership for students as they create original bulletin board displays.

10 Ten Ways To Differentiate Instruction And Five Examples Of Each Way

D IFFERENTIATE...

1. ...assessment data.
   a. interest surveys
   b. learning style inventories
   c. left/right brain indicators
   d. skill competency checklists
   e. pre- and post-test results

2. ...the content level of the material.
   a. different levels of textbooks
   b. different levels of resource materials
   c. textbook(s) on audiotape
   d. manipulatives
   e. audio/visual presentations

3. ...the complexity of learning tasks.
   a. Bloom's Cognitive Taxonomy
   b. Williams' Creative Taxonomy
   c. Krathwohl's Affective Taxonomy
   d. Kohlberg's Stages of Moral Development
   e. Maslow's Hierarchy of Needs

4. ...the kinds of resources.
   a. peer and volunteer resources
   b. library books and reference materials
   c. audio-visuals
   d. computers
   e. laserdisc and CD-ROM technologies

DIFFERENTIATE...

5. ...the instructional delivery systems.
a. games and simulations
b. learning/interest centers
c. cooperative learning activities
d. individual inquiry and study packages
e. investigation cards

6. ...the duration of learning activities.
a. division of task into two or more sessions
b. allowing students time to infuse personal interests
c. reteaching as needed
d. allowing for student choice
e. providing enrichment

7. ...the degree of student involvement in planning.
a. development of organizational skills
b. development of time management strategies
c. establishment of goal-setting methods
d. creation of feeling of ownership
e. maintaining motivation

8. ...the expected outcomes.
a. gearing standards to individual abilities
b. gearing standards to individual interests
c. gearing standards to group norms
d. setting criteria for quality of work
e. setting criteria for quantity of work

9. ...the evaluation process.
a. self-evaluation
b. portfolio evaluation
c. product evaluation
d. performance evaluation
e. paper/pencil evaluation

10. ...the types of recognition used in the classroom.
a. a quiet pat on the shoulder
b. papers displayed
c. a rousing cheer and round of applause
d. a happy-gram
e. a personal note/stamp on the paper

10 Curriculum Priorities To Use To Develop A Balanced Middle Grades Program

Teacher _____ Grade Level _____

1. _____ **Reading, Writing, Speaking, and Listening**
Knowledge, appreciation, and skill in the language arts.

2. _____ **Arts**
Visual and performing arts, music, and literature.

3. _____ **Self-Awareness**
Sense of self; self-confidence, self-esteem, and discipline; moral character; development of unique talents and abilities.

4. _____ **Health and Physical Fitness**
Nutrition, exercise, alertness, endurance, skill in sports and games.

5. _____ **Science and Math**
Knowledge in math and science.

6. _____ **Critical and Creative Thinking**
Curiosity, inquisitiveness, creativity, and decision-making skills.

7. _____ **Home Relations**
Ability to communicate, cooperate, respect differences, and get along with others.

8. _____ **Social Sciences**
Knowledge, appreciation, and understanding of geography, history, economics, sociology, and anthropology.

9. _____ **Work Habits**
Initiative and motivation; organizational, directional, objectivity, and evaluation skills; quest for excellence.

10. _____ **Environment**
Knowledge, appreciation, and commitment to respect, enjoy, protect, and share the world's natural resources.

10 Factors To Consider When Selecting Instructional Materials

1. Higher level critical thinking skills are included.

2. Cooperative learning strategies are suggested.

3. An interdisciplinary approach is stressed.

4. The materials are free of bias (culture, gender, racial, religious).

5. The materials offer optional delivery systems.

6. Illustrations and examples are appropriate for the age.

7. The materials meet required instructional objectives.

8. Alternative activities for learning styles are infused.

9. Materials are appropriate for heterogeneous classroom use.

10. Materials are enhanced by use of multimedia technology.

10 Questions For Teachers To Ask When Planning A Lesson

1. Are my objectives relevant and realistic in terms of intent and number?

2. Have I planned a varied delivery system to accommodate different learning modalities?

3. Have I organized my lesson into the quartile system (one fourth of the class period each for direct instruction, class discussion, cooperative group work, and independent time)?

4. Are my directions clear and to the point?

5. Have I selected questions and activities representative of different levels of the cognitive and creative taxonomies?

6. What method of assessment best suits this lesson?

7. How and what will I need to differentiate (content level, learning tasks, resources, delivery systems) to meet my students' needs?

8. Have I provided alternatives to the textbook (posters, learning centers, audio visuals, technology, etc.)?

9. Does the pacing fit into the planned time frame?

10. What materials, supplies, manipulatives, and resources do I need?

10 Ways To Respond To Incorrect Student Answers

1. If the answer is incomplete, provide a hint or clue.

2. Rephrase the question in case it was not understood.

3. Supply the correct answer and discuss it with the student.

4. Give examples of possible answers in a positive way.

5. Tell the student where the answer may be found.

6. Ask the student to determine the question that he or she actually answered.

7. Ask a classmate to determine the question that the student actually answered.

8. Next time, after questioning, be sure to allow "wait time" for all students to think.

9. State reasons that the answer seemed logical.

10. Ask the student to explain his or her reasoning.

10 MINUS 1

Things To Think About When Putting Together A Middle School's Master Schedule

1. Every schedule for every school is unique because the demographics of every school vary.

2. Set priorities for scheduling and accept the fact that every schedule has its share of trade-offs or compromises.

3. The more single or special classes/programs you have, the more conflicts will surface during the scheduling process.

4. Limit or, if possible, eliminate prerequisite courses in the exploratory areas.

5. Don't depend on computer services and/or scheduling software packages to solve your scheduling problems.

6. The master schedule must serve the students first, the teachers second, and the administrators third.

7. One must have the courage to try new paradigms when setting up the schedule. Try something different.

8. One must live a master schedule to realize its limitations, advantages, and possibilities.

9. Keep a sense of humor.

10 High-Priority Areas To Consider When Setting Up A Master Schedule

1. Build in an advisory program for 20–30 minutes daily.

2. Provide common planning time for interdisciplinary teams.

3. Place all core teachers on a single academic team with no cross teaming.

4. Maintain a student-teacher ratio of 150 students per four-person team.

5. Allow students to have options in choosing exploratory classes.

6. Offer a co-curricular program.

7. Plan for multi-age groupings in electives and mini-classes.

8. Organize electives and academic classes on a trimester schedule.

9. Program reasonable times for lunch periods.

10. Encourage a "school within a school" concept or a multi-age pilot team.

10 Advantages Of The Block Schedule

1. Time is available at the beginning of the day for the advisor/advisee program.

2. All teachers have a common team planning and conference time.

3. Every teacher has a duty-free lunch.

4. Physical education and exploratory classes are shorter than core subject area classes.

5. Interdisciplinary teams have the flexibility and autonomy to schedule classes around curriculum needs.

6. Students can be grouped and regrouped for instruction.

7. Teachers can team teach in any given subject area.

8. Teachers can more easily integrate the disciplines.

9. Teachers can vary the instructional periods on an hourly, daily, or weekly basis.

10. Teachers can more easily schedule field trips, speakers, and community involvement projects.

10 Reasons To Flex The Block

A flexible block schedule can have the following beneficial results.

1. The total team can test during the same time period to accommodate best testing time and better use of class time.

2. A film/video can be shown to a total team to make better use of instructional time.

3. A teacher can be relieved so that he or she can attend to the development of an interdisciplinary unit, conferencing, team teaching, or visitations.

4. Total team activities (such as a guest speaker, field trip, assembly, field day, or intramurals) can be arranged.

5. An extra period once or twice a week can be created for extended advisory periods, silent sustained reading, study skills, etc.

6. An extra period can be created for a guest teacher.

7. The schedule can be rotated within the block so that each teacher sees each group at different times of the day.

8. The schedule can be shortened to provide time for mini-courses.

9. Home-base, mini-, or maxi-classes can be created to accommodate an interdisciplinary unit.

10. A maxi-class period can be created to accommodate an extended period for science labs, projects, research, presentations, etc.

10 MINUS 1

Ways To Flex A Block Schedule

The block schedule is at the heart of the middle school. It is designed to accommodate a program that meets the needs and characteristics of the middle grade youngster. It has three main parts: advisory, basic skills, and physical education/exploratory classes. The basic skills interdisciplinary team of teachers has a block of time for academic instruction which can be manipulated to meet the teachers' needs and the needs of their students.

The following ideas are based on a block of time consisting of five 45-minute "periods" for a total of 225 minutes.

1. Use one hour for a total team guest speaker experience which leaves 165 minutes for:
   a. Five 33-minute mini-periods
   b. Four 41-minute periods

2. Create seven 32-minute mini-periods.
   a. Each regular block teacher teaches his or her normal class while two guests teach additional classes.
   b. All regular block teachers plus two guests teach interest classes.

3. Create a 75-minute maxi-class.

75	SCIENCE	SOC. STUDIES	MATH	LANG. ARTS	READING
37	SOC. STUDIES	MATH	LANG. ARTS	READING	SCIENCE
37	MATH	LANG. ARTS	READING	SCIENCE	SOC. STUDIES
37	LANG. ARTS	READING	SCIENCE	SOC. STUDIES	MATH
37	READING	SCIENCE	SOC. STUDIES	MATH	LANG. ARTS

4. Use the entire block of time for a combination large group/small group experience.

   A. Team Meeting

   B. Guest Speakers

   C. Mini-Conference

   D. Drama Presentation

   E. Advisory Skit Presentations

   F. Team Awards Assembly

   G. Team Movie

   H. Trivia Bowl

   I. Jeopardy Bowl

   J. Field Trip

   K. Career Day

   L. Team Students Work at Elementary School

   M. Science Fair Project Displays and Presentations

   N. Interdisciplinary Unit Group Activity

   O. Team Intramurals

5. Create an extra period one day per week (six 37-minute "periods").

   A. Sustained Silent Reading

   B. Introduction of Skill of the Week

   C. Introduction of Vocabulary of the Week

   D. Team Meeting

   E. Current Events

   F. Teaching Skills for Standardized Testing

   G. Study and Organization Skills

   H. Mini-Interest Classes

   I. Any Team Unity/Identity Activity

6. Rotate schedule within the block.

Week One 1-2-3-4-5

Week Two 5-1-2-3-4

Week Three 4-5-1-2-3

       etc.

7. Implement a drop schedule within the block.

A.	Week 1	Week 2	Week 3	etc.
	##	1	1	
	2	##	2	
	3	3	##	
	4	4	4	
	5	5	5	

B. Periodically, run four classes instead of five to allow a team member to be engaged in one or more of the following activities:
   1) Team Teaching
   2) Student Remediation
   3) Student Enrichment
   4) Planning Future Team Activities
   5) Staff Development Activities
   6) Parent Conferences
   7) Planning an IDU (Interdisciplinary Unit)

8. Switch teachers within the block! Periodically, without telling the students beforehand, the team teachers should switch teaching assignments for a day.

9. Place half of the students and two teachers with a guest speaker for half of the block time (112 minutes) while the other three teachers are teaching the other half of the team in 37-minute periods. After the 112-minute time interval, switch the two groups.

Example: Upon completing a two-person IDU, the language arts teacher and the reading teacher may wish to culminate the activity with a speaker.

TEN (MINUS 1) SAMPLE SCHEDULES

SAMPLE SCHEDULE 1: FLEXING THE BLOCK
(Adjusting For Special Events)

	MONDAY	TUESDAY	WEDNESDAY	THURSDAY	FRIDAY
1.	Advisory	Advisory	Advisory	Advisory	Advisory
2.	Math	Math	Math / Science	Math	Total Team Science Test
3.	Science	Science	Social Studies / Language Arts	Science	Math
4.	Social Studies	Social Studies	Total Team Guest Speaker	Social Studies	Science
5.	Language Arts	Language Arts		Language Arts	Social Studies
					Language Arts

SAMPLE SCHEDULE 2: FLEXING THE BLOCK

(Each Teacher Meets With Each Group Every Other Day—On Friday, Meets With All Groups)

	MONDAY	TUESDAY	WEDNESDAY	THURSDAY	FRIDAY
1.	Advisory	Advisory	Advisory	Advisory	Advisory
2.	Teacher A Group 1	Teacher A Group 2	Teacher A Group 1	Teacher A Group 2	Teacher A Group 1
3.					Teacher A Group 2
4.	Teacher A Group 3	Teacher A Group 4	Teacher A Group 3	Teacher A Group 4	Teacher A Group 3
5.					Teacher A Group 4

A similar pattern is followed for all team teachers.

SAMPLE SCHEDULE 3: FLEXING THE BLOCK

(Rotating The Schedule Daily)

	MONDAY	TUESDAY	WEDNESDAY	THURSDAY	FRIDAY
1.	Advisory	Advisory	Advisory	Advisory	Advisory
2.	Math	Language Arts	Social Studies	Science	Math
3.	Science	Math	Language Arts	Social Studies	Science
4.	Social Studies	Science	Math	Language Arts	Social Studies
5.	Language Arts	Social Studies	Science	Math	Language Arts

SAMPLE SCHEDULE 4: FLEXING THE BLOCK

(A Special Week)

	MONDAY	TUESDAY	WEDNESDAY	THURSDAY	FRIDAY
1.	Advisory	Advisory	Advisory	Advisory	Advisory
2.	Math	Math	Math	Math	History (Four hours set aside to watch and discuss a historical movie)
3.	Science	Science (Time set aside for a 2-day experiment)		History	
4.	English	English	English	Extended English Reading	
5.	English	English			
6.	Exploratory	Exploratory	Exploratory	Exploratory	Exploratory
7.	P.E.	P.E.	P.E.	P.E.	P.E.

Note: Exploratory / P.E. teachers can also flex their blocks.

SAMPLE SCHEDULE 5: FLEXING THE BLOCK

(Focus On The Elective Team)

Grade 6	15 min. Advisory	96 min. ELECTIVE TEAM	96 min. INSTRUCTIONAL TEAM	48 min. LUNCH	144 min. INSTRUCTIONAL TEAM
Grade 7	15 min. Advisory	144 min. INSTRUCTIONAL TEAM	96 min. ELECTIVE TEAM	48 min. LUNCH	96 min. INSTRUCTIONAL TEAM
Grade 8	15 min. Advisory	144 min. INSTRUCTIONAL TEAM	48 min. LUNCH	96 min. INSTRUCTIONAL TEAM	96 min. ELECTIVE TEAM

SAMPLE SCHEDULE 6: FLEXING THE BLOCK
(Using Mini-Time Blocks)

	SIXTH GRADE			SEVENTH GRADE			EIGHTH GRADE	
	X	Y	Z	Q	R	S	M	N
9:00 9:10 9:20 9:30								
9:40	ADVISORY							
9:50 10:00 10:10 10:20 10:30 10:40 10:50								10:30
11:00 11:10 11:20	Lunch	Lunch					P.E. / EXPLORATORY	
11:30 11:40 11:50 12:00			Lunch	Lunch				12:00
12:10 12:20 12:30 12:40					Lunch	Lunch		
12:50 1:00 1:10 1:20				P.E. / EXPLORATORY			Lunch	Lunch
1:30 1:40 1:50 2:00 2:10								1:30
2:20 2:30 2:40 2:50 3:00 3:10 3:20 3:30 3:40	P.E. / EXPLORATORY							3:45
3:50 4:00								

59

SAMPLE SCHEDULE 7: FLEXING THE BLOCK
(When Each Grade Level Has Two Teams)

Time	6-1	6-2
8:15	HOMEBASE	HOMEBASE
8:25	ACADEMIC CLASSES	ACADEMIC CLASSES
10:00	SPECIAL INTEREST	SPECIAL INTEREST
10:45	LUNCH	LUNCH
11:11	ACADEMIC CLASSES	ACADEMIC CLASSES
12:45	ARTS	PHYSICAL EDUCATION
1:36	PHYSICAL EDUCATION	ARTS
2:23		

Time	7-1	7-2
8:15	HOMEBASE	HOMEBASE
8:25	LANGUAGE ARTS	SCIENCE
9:13	SOCIAL STUDIES	MATH
10:00	SPECIAL INTEREST	SPECIAL INTEREST
10:45	ARTS	PHYSICAL EDUCATION
11:32	LUNCH	LUNCH
11:58	PHYSICAL EDUCATION	ARTS
12:45	MATH	LANGUAGE ARTS
1:36	SCIENCE	SOCIAL STUDIES
2:23		

Time	8-1	8-2
8:15	HOMEBASE	HOMEBASE
8:25	ARTS	PHYSICAL EDUCATION
9:13	PHYSICAL EDUCATION	ARTS
10:00	SPECIAL INTEREST	SPECIAL INTEREST
10:45	LANGUAGE ARTS	MATH
11:32	SOCIAL STUDIES	SCIENCE
12:19	LUNCH	LUNCH
12:45	SCIENCE	LANGUAGE ARTS
1:36	MATH	SOCIAL STUDIES
2:23		

SAMPLE SCHEDULE 8: FLEXING THE BLOCK

(Team Rotation Schedule)

Opening Bell: 8:40 A.M.

	G Team & T Team	W Team & S Team	C Team & B Team
8:40 – 9:10	——————————— Advisor-Advisee Time ———————————		
9:10 – 9:55 9:57 – 10:42	SKILLS	EXPLORATORY	CORE & P.E.
10:44 – 11:29 11:31 – 12:16	CORE & P.E.	SKILLS	EXPLORATORY
12:16 – 1:10	——————————— LUNCH ———————————		
1:12 – 1:57 2:00 – 2:45	EXPLORATORY	CORE & P.E.	SKILLS
2:45	Dismissal Bell	On Dec. 1: G & T take W & S schedule. W & S take C & B schedule. C & B take G & T schedule. On March 15: Rotate ahead one block to complete cycle.	

61

SAMPLE SCHEDULE 9: FLEXING THE BLOCK
(Common Flexible Schedule For All Teams)

Grade 6
- 9:15–9:37 Advisory
- 9:40–10:20 P.E. or EXPLORATORY
- 10:23–11:03
- 11:03–11:33 Team A / Team B / Team C Lunch
- 11:35–12:05 Team D / Team E ½ Lunch
- 12:56–1:26 Team E ½ Lunch
- 3:30

Grade 7
- 9:15–9:37 Advisory
- 10:30–11:00 Team A / Team B / Team C Lunch
- 11:35–12:05 Team D / Team E
- 2:07–2:47 P.E. or EXPLORATORY
- 2:50–3:30

Grade 8
- 9:15–9:37 Advisory
- 11:33–12:13 EXPLORATORY | P.E.
- 12:16–12:53 Team A / Team B / Team C Lunch | EXPLORATORY
- 12:56–1:26 P.E. | Team D / Team E Lunch

Note option of splitting a team for separate lunch times if necessary (shown on Grade 6 schedule).

10 TIMES 3

Suggested Middle School Exploratory Offerings

Exploratory classes are an integral part of an effective middle school program. They are taught by specialists in their fields and are offered in 4½-, 6-, 9-, and/or 18-week blocks of time. It is important that middle level youngsters experience a wide range of exploratory offerings so that they can make informed choices about elective offerings when they become high school students.

1. Agriculture
2. Band
3. Business Education
4. Careers
5. Choir
6. Chorus
7. Computer Literacy
8. Crafts
9. Drama
10. Environmental Studies
11. Fine Arts
12. Foreign Cultures
13. Foreign Languages
14. Health and Safety
15. Home Economics
16. Horticulture
17. Industrial Technology
18. Industrial Arts
19. Junior Great Books
20. Keyboarding
21. Learning/Living Skills
22. Newspaper
23. Oral Communication
24. Orchestra
25. Reading Lab (developmental/remedial)
26. Street Law
27. Student Assistance
28. Study Skills
29. TAG or Talents Unlimited
30. Yearbook

In most instances, physical education is not considered part of the exploratory program. Because health and physical fitness are considered to be of such great importance for young people today, physical education is a part of the regular daily program for most middle level students.

10 Suggested Mini-Courses

Mini-courses are short-term, academic or non-academic, high-interest, in-depth instructional courses, usually scheduled once a week for four to six weeks. Each session lasts from 60 to 90 minutes. Students select the mini-courses they wish from a list they have helped to establish with staff input.

Suggested Mini-Courses:

1. *Babysitting Tips* . . . Learn how to earn extra money by becoming a skilled babysitter. This course will give you suggestions, tips, and creative ideas for taking care of children.

2. *Blast Off!* . . . Choose a model rocket or airplane, order from a catalog, and pay for your selection. After construction of the kits, models will be test-flown.

3. *Fancy That* . . . Learn the art of calligraphy through practice with pen nib and India ink. Final products will be on parchment paper, matted, and ready for framing.

4. *Let's Dance* . . . Have fun learning line dancing, group dancing, and square dancing. Create your own routine and produce your own music video.

5. *Cartoon Fun* . . . Instead of doodling, why not draw your own cartoons? In this class you will develop characters, express your ideas, and create your own comic strip.

6. *Tech-Talk* . . . Explore a variety of computer software including logic games, crossword magic, word search, print shop, micro-illustrator, CD ROM references, adventure/journeys, and more!

7. *Show Off* . . . Do you have a special talent? Develop alone or with others an aerobic jumprope dance or other routines for a command performance.

8. *Say "Cheese"* . . . Explore photography as you load, snap, and develop your own photographs.

9. *Chef's Special* . . . Create and enjoy tantalizing appetizers, desserts, candies, sandwiches, and more! Keep the recipes; enjoy the results!

10. *In Pursuit* . . . Join us in a trivia board game. Share your expertise and help your team to victory.

10 MINUS 6

Assumptions About Ability Grouping And What The Research Shows About Ability Grouping

1. Assumption One: Ability grouping promotes achievement as students can advance at their own rate with other students of similar ability.

Research Findings:
There is little evidence that ability grouping or tracking improves academic achievement, while there is overwhelming evidence that ability grouping retards the academic progress of students in low- and middle-ability groupings.

2. Assumption Two: Teachers can provide more appropriate materials and subject content to students of similar abilities. High-ability students receive more challenging instruction, low-ability students receive opportunities for success.

Research Findings:
(1) Ability grouping and tracking affect instructional pace, time, and quantity, as well as teacher expectations. High-ability groups receive more time on task, more complex curriculum, more effective instruction, and more homework than low-ability groups.

(2) Often instruction in low-ability grouped classes is in conflict with how students learn. Students are not expected to synthesize material or apply content to problem situations; rather, the curriculum content has a recipe approach that emphasizes component skills.

(3) Ability grouping and tracking tend to widen the achievement and knowledge gaps between groups of students. The net effect of ability grouping and tracking is to exaggerate initial differences between students, rather than to accommodate them.

3. Assumption Three: Less-capable students will suffer less emotional and educational damage from being in classrooms of peers with similar ability levels than they would from daily contact with higher achieving peers. Students are challenged to do their best in a more realistic range of competition.

Research Findings:

(1) Ability grouping can predetermine students' future opportunities and aspirations.

(2) The affective development of students suffers with ability grouping and tracking. High-achieving students have high self-concepts in both homogeneous and heterogeneous groupings. Low-achieving students in homogeneous classes tend to have lower self-concepts that low-achieving students in heterogeneous classes.

(3) Ability grouping and tracking have negative effects upon peer interactions within schools. Friendship choices among students are limited by their ability groups or curriculum track.

(4) Ability grouping serves as a form of segregation by race, socioeconomic background, gender, language, and special education status. All relevant studies have found that a disproportionate number of students from racial and language minority backgrounds, as well as low-income and disabled students, are placed in low-ability groups. This disparity in placement suggests that discriminatory procedures are used to determine ability levels and tracks.

4. Assumption Four: Ability grouping eases the task of teaching, and is the best way to cope with the broad spectrum of student diversity.

Research Findings:

(1) It is unclear whether ability grouping does in fact ease the task of teaching for all ability level classes. Segregating the most successful students often creates a climate in low-ability groups that discourages focused study, thereby creating a "critical mass of discouragement."

(2) Ability grouping is an ineffective means of addressing individual differences. Most teachers teach uniformly, rather than matching instruction to meet a diversity of learning styles. Too few teachers regularly utilize interactive and student-centered instructional approaches such as cooperative learning. The most common form of instruction tends to be competitive whole-group instruction, with common assignments, due dates, and tests, and uniform evaluation and grading practices.

Adapted from "Structuring Schools For Student Success: A Focus On Ability Grouping." The Massachusetts Department of Education, January, 1990. Used by permission.

10 Creative Approaches To A Positive Classroom Climate

1. Ask students to discuss how they have handled the tantrums or inappropriate behavior of younger siblings or of children who have been in their care.

2. If students are having a hard time "settling down," give them 5 minutes of writing time during which they are permitted to write anything they want. No one will see what they write, and when the designated time is over, papers will be torn up and thrown away. Then it's time for work!

3. If a student criticizes you, smile (even when you don't feel like smiling) and respond positively to the criticism. If you agree, say something like "In fact, I am probably more _____ than you realize." If you don't feel the criticism is warranted, you might say, "Do you think so? I wasn't aware of that." Either way, continue with the lesson.

4. Try to leave your "anger response" outside of the classroom. If students see they are unable to goad you into anger, this takes away some of their perceived power to disrupt.

5. Call on your sense of humor to defuse a tense situation or elicit group support for an unpopular cause. You will be amazed at how effective a good laugh or even a big grin can be.

6. The use of group approval or focusing on a child who is doing well may be effective when maintaining discipline with young children, but public approval or disapproval may backfire with your middle schoolers. Try speaking privately with a student who misbehaves or needs extra support, using a foundation of previously-developed rapport to guide the conference.

7. Inappropriate behavior may stem from boredom or frustration. If the entire class is exhibiting behavior problems, reconsider your instructional material or teaching strategy. More interestingly appropriate materials and presentations may automatically eliminate many behavior problems.

8. Provide choices. For example, if your class is working in cooperative groups and one group appears to be finding it difficult to stay on task, give that group the choice of continuing to work as a group, or of splitting up to complete the assignment individually.

9. Arrange for older students to work as tutors or group leaders with your students and to serve as role models.

10. Allow students 30 minutes every Friday to engage in a free-time activity of their choice (even if it involves being "loud and silly") as a privilege earned by behaving with decorum during the week.

10 Guidelines For Developing A Discipline Program

1. Let students know what is expected: establish specific guidelines, rules, and consequences.

2. Always implement a consequence for misbehavior; be consistent, clarify the infraction, and simply restate your expectations.

3. Treat students with dignity; do not embarrass students in front of their peers.

4. Practice the three F's: be firm, fair, and free of anger.

5. Utilize effective teaching practices; provide instruction at levels that match the students' abilities.

6. Pay attention to students; "listen" to what students are thinking and feeling and convey understanding and empathy.

7. Involve students in decision-making; use student input in planning class activities when appropriate.

8. Provide opportunities for realistic success for every student; use praise and appropriate reinforcement techniques.

9. Vary your presentation style; include alternative delivery systems and student involvement.

10. Infuse humor into situations; laugh with your students and at yourself.

10 PLUS 12

Planning Strategies

1. Buy and use the best lesson plan book available.
2. Make long-range plans (well in advance) that lend themselves to constant revision and transition to manageable short-range plans.
3. Divide large projects into classroom-relevant smaller sections.
4. Delegate tasks when appropriate and possible.
5. Consult other people for answers, help, or input.
6. Make use of "classroom-ready" commercial materials when they fit into learning goals and developmental objectives.
7. Upgrade and downgrade priorities as needed.
8. Set out daily goals in order of priority.
9. Make a list of "TO DOs" every day.
10. Unless absolutely necessary, refuse to make decisions under stress.
11. Carefully select a time and place free of interruptions for completing paperwork.
12. Allow a reasonable amount of time for interaction on a one-on-one basis with students and don't allow less important tasks to take precedent over this important time.
13. Keep a list/copy of classwork and homework in a notebook for reference for students who have been absent.
14. Have presentation materials ready and accessible beforehand. Organize in folders by topic or instructional objective.
15. Capitalize on the use of student "experts" in the classroom whenever possible.
16. Utilize color as a classroom organizer. Color-code instructional areas with materials and supplies for easy access and return.
17. Color-code subject area notebooks (i.e., green for math, red for science, etc.) for quick reference and easy identification.
18. Color-code your gradebook using different colors for daily, test, or failing grades so it is easy to spot problems and average grades.
19. Keep a small pad of paper and a pen in your school mailbox for instant replies and on-the-spot notes.
20. Show a scheduled video or film only once, to the entire team, at the same time, freeing the remaining class periods for instruction instead of viewing.
21. Utilize uniform team time-saving procedures: conference form, substitute form, and team meeting agenda form.
22. Share and exchange teaching ideas, lesson plans, and creative activities with peers.

10 Teacher Timesavers and Stress Reducers and Twelve Teacher Time Wasters

TIMESAVERS:

1. Get the toughest tasks out of the way first.

2. Schedule your workload to coincide with your periods of highest productivity.

3. Avoid perfectionism. Set time limits for tasks.

4. Never do anything (e.g., lunch count, bulletin boards, cleaning, collecting papers, etc.) a student can do just as well.

5. Team up with other teachers for special projects, events, etc.

6. Learn to say NO to things you don't have time for.

7. Consolidate tasks (e.g., make telephone calls in groups rather than one at a time).

8. Handle each piece of mail only once.

9. Don't succumb to procrastination.

10. Take time to do something nice for yourself.

TIME WASTERS:

1. Rigid, non-flexible long-range plans.

2. Overuse of pencil-and-paper worksheets and other seatwork tasks requiring grades.

3. Telephone and/or public address system interruptions.

4. Disorganization and disarray. (If you can't find something, you're wasting time.)

5. Meetings when memos will suffice.

6. Lack of personal focus and/or objectives.

7. The inability to say "no" and/or to request extra time.

8. Unexpected visitors or observers.

9. Information which is delayed, inaccurate, and/or inadequate.

10. Trying to grade papers in a busy, noisy teachers' lounge.

11. Attempting to do too much at once; trying to be "all things to all people."

12. Unscheduled meetings at which attendance is required.

10 PLUS 3 Ways To Inform Parents And Caregivers And Involve Them In Their Middle Grader's School Progress

1. Parent-teacher conferences on a regularly-scheduled basis as well as for special needs.

2. Notes home: often, informative, and always open-ended with provision for response.

3. Parents' Night with ample opportunity for group discussion and question-and-answer sessions.

4. A strong parent-teacher organization founded on meaningful goals and clear channels of communication, with regularly-scheduled meetings, including at least one opportunity early in the school year for a potluck meal or other social opportunity.

5. A standing invitation to join the class for lunch in the school cafeteria (if school rules permit).

6. Book lists for suggested family readings, with short response sheets for opinions or extensions to be returned to the teacher.

7. A meaningful grading and report system including provision for explanation of grades, anecdotal records, and explanatory notes.

8. School and/or class newspaper, journal, or newsletter.

9. Student work sent home regularly with teacher comments attached.

10. A clear, concise, and complete student handbook explaining school philosophy, calendar, rules of conduct, grading systems, administration and faculty responsibilities, and other pertinent information, delivered at the beginning of the school year.

11. Published schedules for the year, quarter, and month, including all extracurricular and before-and-after school activities, made available as far in advance as possible.

12. Intramurals and other extracurricular activities planned to allow parent participation without undue stress or interruption of normal work schedules.

13. Invitation to assist with classroom projects and special events such as science fairs, field days, plays, off-campus field trips, etc.

NUTS AND BOLTS OF MIDDLE GRADES EDUCATION— TEACHER'S WRAP-UP, À LA BLOOM

KNOWLEDGE
List three factors determining the philosophy of an effective middle school.

COMPREHENSION
Identify some strengths of the middle school organizational pattern.

APPLICATION
Develop a sample flexible block schedule for a typical middle school.

ANALYSIS
Compare and contrast the advantages and the disadvantages of the middle school organizational pattern and the traditional junior high school organizational pattern.

SYNTHESIS
Create three good questions to ask a middle grade student to find out how he or she would evaluate the enrichment or extracurricular program in his or her school.

EVALUATION
Summarize the advantages afforded student and/or teachers through the middle school organizational program.

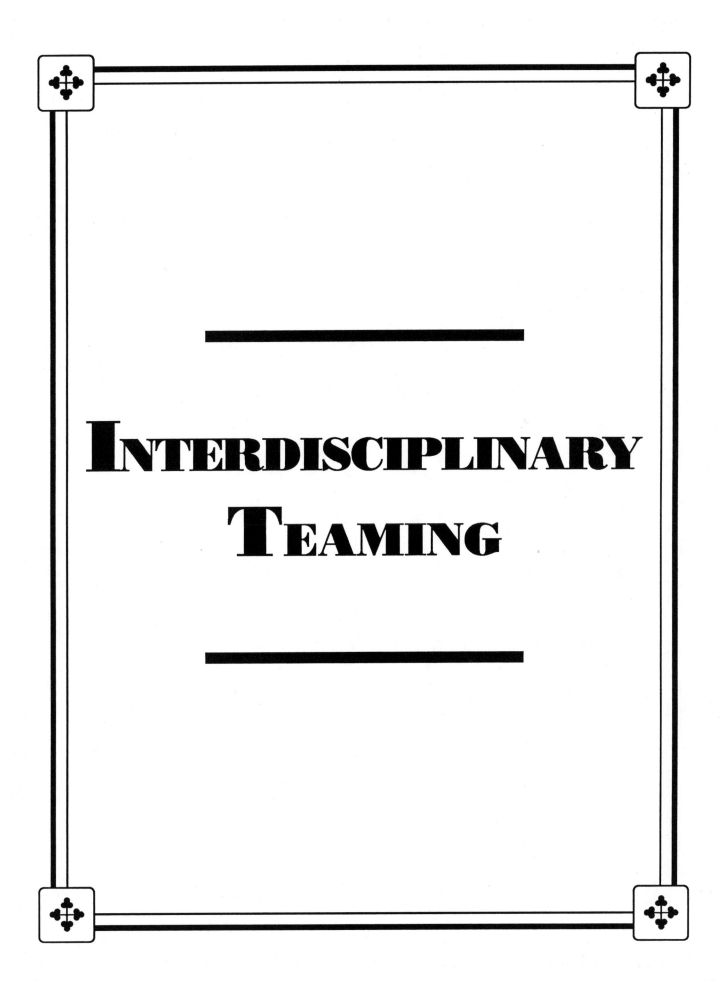

INTERDISCIPLINARY TEAMING

Interdisciplinary Teaming Overview

INTERDISCIPLINARY TEAMING ENCOURAGES:

- Conservation of time and space in an ever-expanding curriculum.
- Elimination of overlap in varied subject areas.
- Promotion of collaboration among students and teachers.
- Coordination of assignments.
- Reduction of fragmentation of learning from one discipline to another.
- Relevance of motivational and enrichment projects.
- Multiple use of resources, teaching tools, and instructional techniques.
- Recognition of interrelationships among different subjects.
- Promotion of critical and creative thinking through the application of skills and concepts across subject area lines.

ADVANTAGES FOR TEACHERS INCLUDE IMPROVED:

- Intellectual stimulation provided by closer association with colleagues.
- Discipline through use of varied teacher personalities, styles, and strategies.
- Delivery system provided through flexible schedules and group sizes.
- Colleague support through shared goals, esprit de corps, and communication.
- Evaluation through team input and assessment techniques.
- Time management through team meetings and common planning periods.
- Instruction through diversity in teacher talents, styles, and interests.
- Coordination of curriculum through interdisciplinary instruction and joint planning in areas such as homework, texts, grades, and field trips.

ADVANTAGES FOR STUDENTS INCLUDE IMPROVED:

- Student/teacher relationships through sense of belonging to established team or school family with special identity, customs, and rituals.
- Motivation and enthusiasm for learning through varied instructional materials, techniques, and personalities.
- Attendance and behavior because of consistent environment with common rules, guidelines, and procedures.
- Attitudes toward school through sharing of excellent teachers and not-so-excellent teachers.
- Opportunity for achievement through flexible grouping and scheduling options.
- Self-concept through team-initiated advisory groups.
- Chances for matching teaching styles with learning styles.

10 Important Interdisciplinary Teaming Questions To Find Answers For

How would you respond to each of these questions or tasks?

1. What are the advantages and potential disadvantages of the teaming process for teachers?

2. What are the advantages and potential disadvantages of the teaming process for students?

3. What are two different tools or techniques one might use to place teachers on a team?

4. What are some good reasons for a joint team planning period?

5. What are some things you might do to create a team identity for you and your students?

6. In your opinion, what is the single most important reason for teaming in the middle school? (Think of a reason that would be effective when "selling" middle school teaming to a parent or guardian.)

7. How does research support teaming in the school setting?

8. What do you think is the key role of the team leader?

9. What are two things that team members can do to support the team concept?

10. How can teachers determine their own readiness for teaming?

10 Definitions Essential To Teaming Success

1. Interdisciplinary Teaming: The interdisciplinary team is the "heart of the middle school" and requires that the *same* group of teachers share the *same* group of students housed in the *same* part of the facility for the *same* block of daily instructional time. Teams vary in size from two to six teachers representing core curriculum areas and serve students ranging from 70 to 150 in number.

2. Interdisciplinary Instruction: Teams of teachers combine their expertise and course content to integrate the disciplines and interface common areas of the curriculum.

3. Team Teaching: Team teaching is a practice that allows for two or more teachers as instructional leaders in the planning, teaching, and evaluating of a single lesson or a unit of study.

4. Flexible Block Schedule: A team of teachers shares a group of students for an uninterrupted block of instructional time ranging in length from 120 to 210 minutes each day. Teachers have flexibility during that period of time to group and regroup students for instruction as well as to vary the length of each instructional period.

5. Common Planning Time: Interdisciplinary teaming works best when teachers on the same team have a common planning period during which they can meet together on a daily basis to hold team meetings, student/parent conferences, and plan interdisciplinary instruction.

6. Team Identity: An interdisciplinary team works hard at "creating small-ness within bigness" for its group of assigned students. This is accomplished through the mutual development of a team name, colors, logos, slogans, cheers, handshakes, etc. It is also enhanced through team events such as team parties, traditions, celebrations, and contests.

7. Team Leader: Every interdisciplinary team has a team leader who facilitates the teaming process for its members by coordinating the team's meetings, activities, budget decisions, and communications with the school's administrative team.

8. Team Handbook: An effective interdisciplinary team develops a team handbook for the students and parents they serve. The purpose of this handbook is to share the team's philosophy, goals, policies, procedures, expectations, and plans for the school year.

9. Team Meeting: An interdisciplinary team holds daily team meetings during its common planning time in order to carry on the assigned duties and responsibilities of the team itself.

10. Team Rules and Discipline Plan: Interdisciplinary teams place a high priority on establishing a meaningful set of team rules and discipline procedures that are consistent throughout the school day regardless of the varied teacher personalities, styles, and disciplines.

10 Findings From The Published Literature About Teaming In The Middle School

1. FINDING

Sandra J. Golner and James H. Powell write:

Forming teams is the logical first step in the transition to a middle school configuration. Here we offer ten questions that middle level educators should ask as they embark upon this new venture of interdisciplinary teaming. The value of these questions lies not so much in pat answers but in the resulting discussion and clarification of purpose that is unique to each school. Each school, each faculty, each student body requires different solutions to different dilemmas. Your experiences with interdisciplinary teams may be enhanced by asking yourselves these questions:

1. How does teaming benefit students?
2. What are the benefits of teaming for teachers?
3. How are teams formed?
4. Who comprises the team?
5. What skills and attitudes should members have?
6. What does team organization look like?
7. What do effective teams do?
8. How are we doing?
9. How do you keep the momentum going?
10. Why will I love teaming?

Reference: Golner, S. and Powell, J. "Ready for Teaming? Ten Questions to Ask Before You Jump In." Middle School Journal, 24(1), 1992, 28–32.

2. FINDING

Elliot Merenbloom clarifies flexible scheduling:

Flexible scheduling suggests that the order of each day need not be the same. Group size, the order of the periods, and the length of each period can vary. Flexible scheduling is a way of responding to developmental needs of young adolescents. As students go through various physical and mental changes, attention span varies. Some lessons should be 30 to 35 minutes in length while others can go much longer. Flexible scheduling will allow teachers to work together to achieve a common goal—providing the best possible learning experience for pupils. In order to achieve flexibility, there must be a block-of-time schedule and teachers who are willing to utilize flexible or modular strategies.

Reference: Merenbloom, Elliot. The Team Process: A Handbook For Teachers. Columbus, Ohio: National Middle School Association, 1991.

3. FINDING
Thomas Erb and Nancy Doda conclude:

Of the many suggestions offered for reforming American public education in the 1990s, team organization is one of the most powerful. During the past decade, teaming has emerged as one of the few substantial reform concepts and practices with the capacity to transform the way schools operate for teachers and students. Because it facilitates communication and collaboration, teaming is an enabling reform that fosters collegiality and interpersonal affiliation. In this way, team organization is far more than an instructional innovation. It changes the professional and interpersonal dynamics of schools for everyone involved.

Reference: Erb, T. and Doda, N. Team Organization: Promise, Practices and Possibilities. Washington, D.C.: National Education Association, 1989.

4. FINDING
George concludes:

In schools where teaming is expected to occur, three factors usually determine whether or not such teaming actually occurs. One of these is common planning time. A second factor is interpersonal communication; a third factor is the level of team planning skills present among the members of the team.

Reference: George, P. and Lawrence, G. Handbook for Middle School Teaming. Glenview, Illinois: Scott, Foresman, and Company, 1982.

5. FINDING
Rima Miller points out:

It is generally agreed by those who study team efforts that there are four major reasons that teams fail.
1. Members do not understand the function, purpose, or goals of the team's effort.
2. Members do not know what roles to play or what tasks are their responsibility.
3. Members do not understand how to complete their tasks or how to work as part of a team.
4. Members do not "buy into" the function, purpose, or goals of the team's effort or they reject their roles or responsibilities.

Reference: Miller, Rima. Team Planning for Educational Leaders. Philadelphia, PA: Research for Better Schools, 1987.

6. FINDING

Joyce Epstein and Douglas MacIver state:

- About 42% of young adolescent students receive instruction from interdisciplinary teams of teachers at some time between grades 5 and 9.

- The bottom line is that at this time most schools do not use interdisciplinary teams, including about 60% of the middle schools and 75% of other grade organizations. Most students in the middle grades (58%) do not receive instruction from interdisciplinary teams.

- About 40% of the teams have no leader to coordinate and organize team activities. According to principals, teams with leaders spend more time on team activities and attain more benefits from teaming.

- Teachers spend almost half of their common planning time on individual work, not on team work.

- The researchers conclude: "If teaming is to be the keystone of middle grades education, schools have a long way to go to develop effective interdisciplinary teams of teachers."

Reference: Epstein, J. and MacIver, D. Education in the Middle Grades: National Practices and Trends. Columbus, Ohio: National Middle School Association, 1990.

7. FINDING

William Alexander and Paul George point out:

To achieve academic productivity, schools should be organized . . .

- so that decisions are made at the lowest possible level in the organization by teams of teachers working closely with students.

- so that the effects of size are minimized through teaching teams that plan for and work with a clearly identified group of students.

- with a class schedule that allows the greatest amount of uninterrupted learning time for teams of teachers working with the groups of students.

Reference: Alexander, W. and George, P. The Exemplary Middle School. New York, NY: Holt, Rinehart and Winston, 1981.

8. FINDING

John Lounsbury summarizes:

The creation of interdisciplinary teams is the right step to take for most middle level schools, but not the only or final step. Needed opportunities for integrating instruction and improving learning for kids are created immediately by teaming. Yet the full benefits of teaming come slowly and even have their limits. Establishing teams is only a stopover on the never-ending voyage to achieve truly lifelike integrated instruction.

Reference: Lounsbury, John, Ed. Connecting the Curriculum through Interdisciplinary Instruction. Columbus, Ohio: National Middle School Association, 1992.

9. FINDING

Paul George, Chris Stevenson, Julia Thomason, and James Beane write: Teaming optimizes the potential for all the team members to become acquainted with each other. The team constitutes an extended family of sorts within which students can form primary social affiliations. Team identities are usually enhanced by a team name, logo, motto, colors, mascot, rules, awards, rituals, traditions, and so on. Team meetings become forums for learning democratic processes. Awards, celebrations, plays, contests, and a host of one-of-a-kind projects further convey the team as a community that is worthwhile, represents positive ideals, and supports its members. At its best, the team serves as a positive answer for students' need to belong to a sanctioned and defined social group.

Reference: George, P., Stevenson, C., Thomason, J., and Beane, J. The Middle School—And Beyond. Alexandria, VA: Association for Supervision and Curriculum Development, 1992.

10. FINDING

Joanne Arhar summarizes: Does teaming make a difference in student outcomes? The answer is that it probably does, but not in direct, easily discernible ways. It appears as if teaming is a manifestation of a commitment on the part of teachers to engage in teacher-student relationships that facilitate growth and individual student development. That teaming causes the philosophical commitment is unlikely; that it gives teachers the ability to translate their commitment into action is almost certain. More important, teaming creates conditions that are directly related to student social bonding. It reduces isolation and anonymity; it allows teachers to know their students quite well; and it permits teachers to "gang up" on students in positive ways to enhance their learning.

Reference: Irvin, Judith L., Ed. Transforming Middle Level Education: Perspectives and Possibilities. Needham Heights, MA: Allyn and Bacon, 1992.

10 PLUS 4

Things To Remember When Developing Teams

1. Team development is evolutionary. It does not happen quickly.

2. Team members must be trained in the "art and science" of teaming so they share the same vision and understanding of what teaming is all about.

3. Team effectiveness and team activities will vary from site to site because implementation of interdisciplinary teams is unique to each location.

4. Not every team member will embrace the teaming concept and the empowerment that goes with it to the same degree.

5. All team members must be assured that the teaming concept will improve work life and the performance of students.

6. Team development will not follow a straight path but will encounter ups and downs in its evolution.

7. Team leaders and administrators must model the behavior they want their team members to display.

8. Teams are often highly motivated at the beginning of their teaming experience, but they require constant guidance, training, and support from leaders.

9. Team members should complement, not clone, one another's styles, temperament, skills, talents, and interests.

10. Team members who do not work well together should have procedures or provisions for changing work assignments.

11. Teams should begin making easy decisions before they are faced with difficult decisions.

12. As teams develop, operating policies, procedures, and systems will need to be changed to allow for continued growth and empowerment.

13. Teams should emphasize communication as the "soul" of their existence both within the team and outside the team.

14. Teams must be rewarded for their successes.

10 Pieces Of Data To Consider When Forming Teams

Each teacher should be asked the following:

1. What subjects are you certified to teach?

2. What subjects would you like to teach? Please list in priority order.

3. What grades would you like to teach? Please list in priority order.

4. What special interests/talents/hobbies do you have?

5. What special skills do you bring to the team?

6. How would you describe your basic teaching style?

7. Who are some staff members you would like to work with on a team?

8. Who are some staff members you would prefer not to work with on a team?

9. Where do you see yourself professionally in three to five years?

10. What else would you want your team members to know about you?

10 Decisions For Teachers To Make When Organizing Teams

1. What are the major responsibilities of the team leader and the team members?

2. What special skills/talents/interests/disciplines do you want represented by your team members?

3. How often will the team meet and what major purposes will these meetings serve?

4. What are the rules for attending, arriving late, or leaving early at the team meetings?

5. How will agendas and records of team meetings be managed?

6. How will we make decisions and solve problems as a team?

7. How will we handle differences, conflicts, and feedback in the functioning of our team?

8. How will we assess our effectiveness as a team?

9. What will be our primary goals and objectives for the year?

10. How will we involve other administrators and staff members in our teaming process?

10 Possible Team Member Traits To Consider

DIRECTIONS: Form a small group of three or four members. Pretend your group has been given the responsibility of selecting four persons to serve on an interdisciplinary team in a middle level school for the next year. First, read through the descriptions of potential team members. Next, decide which individuals would be your primary choices to work with and record the appropriate numbers in the spaces provided below. Finally, work with your group to reach a consensus on who should be on the team. Be prepared to defend your choices!

1. *Helen Humorous:* Helen is the funniest character in the group. She often makes everyone laugh with her keen sense of humor. When things get dull, you can count on Helen to liven things up. She always makes the best of a situation and helps others to do so as well.

2. *Tom Truthful:* Tom always tells what he feels. He never lies to the group or hides things from them. He will always tell team members the truth (and always with tact) when asked a direct question.

3. *Laura Leader:* Laura is a natural leader. She is well-respected and most people listen to her. She's careful to include other points of view when trying to make a group decision.

4. *Carl Creative:* Carl is the most creative teacher on the staff. He will stop at nothing to promote his innovative ideas and materials with the team. He tends to motivate both staff and students.

5. *Ida Informed:* Ida knows all about middle schools. She has a wealth of knowledge and experience in all areas of interdisciplinary teaming and instruction and will provide the group with information about every important middle school issue.

6. *Frank Favorite:* Frank knows the principal very well and can get special favors. He is very dedicated to the teaching profession and knows how to arrange his priorities when asking for budgetary support from the administration.

7. *Mary Motivation:* Mary knows the secret to inspiring both teacher and kids. She is constantly using original tools and techniques for keeping her colleagues on task and getting the tough jobs done.

8. *Wanda Worker:* Wanda is a workaholic and never minds going the extra mile to complete a project or an assignment. She truly enjoys doing "more than her share" and will often bail out a teammate when necessary.

9. *Ernie Energetic:* Ernie is a beginning teacher who has more energy than ten teachers put together. He did his student teaching in an exemplary middle school setting which serves as a training ground for some of the best middle school teachers in the country. What he lacks in experience, he makes up for with enthusiasm.

10. *Polly Professional:* Polly is a highly experienced elementary teacher with a desire to become the best middle school teacher in the district. She received the "Best Teacher of the Year Award" for her ability to develop interdisciplinary units. She has expert knowledge of ways to vary delivery systems and grouping of students for optimal learning conditions.

MY FOUR CHOICES FOR TEAM MEMBERS ARE:

Number	*Name*	*Because*
_____	_____	_____
		_____
_____	_____	_____
		_____
_____	_____	_____
		_____
_____	_____	_____
		_____

OUR GROUP'S FOUR CHOICES FOR TEAM MEMBERS ARE:

Number	*Name*	*Because*
_____	_____	_____
		_____
_____	_____	_____
		_____
_____	_____	_____
		_____
_____	_____	_____

10 MINUS 6

Teaming Dilemmas: What Would You Do?

All teams have interpersonal problems at one time or another. How would you and your team members deal with these teaming dilemmas?

1. Because he spends much time interacting with students, one teacher on your four-member team is often late to team meetings, and often leaves early. He is very cooperative in every other way, but his popularity with students interferes with his planning schedule.

2. One highly-structured and subject-matter-oriented teacher on your three-member team is a very poor advisor in your school's advisory program. Although her students thoroughly enjoy her science class, they detest her advisory period.

3. One teacher on your team is the seventh grade P.E. teacher at your 6–8 school. He has been assigned the role of facilitating the teaming process for your five-member seventh grade team with the hope that he will become more committed to and involved in the new middle school program. He resents this role because it interferes with his individual planning time and he doesn't feel he has anything to contribute to the core curricular areas.

4. Your teammate on your two-member team does not hold up her end of the bargain when it comes to teaming and interdisciplinary instruction. She is busy working a second job and has a tough personal situation at home. As a result, you are burning yourself out doing the work of two people so that integration of the subject matter areas can occur for your middle school students.

10 PLUS 15

Criteria To Determine How Well You Would Fit Into The Teaming Concept

DIRECTIONS: Use this self-check quiz to determine your potential as a middle school teacher working on an interdisciplinary team. Place a mark in the appropriate column on the left and remember to give yourself the benefit of the doubt!

YES   NO   DO YOU . . .

___ ___ **1.** Understand your own strengths and weaknesses as a person?

___ ___ **2.** Understand your own strengths and weaknesses as a teacher?

___ ___ **3.** Interact constructively with other adults?

___ ___ **4.** Interact constructively with young adolescents?

___ ___ **5.** Feel as a teacher you are approachable, responsive, and supportive to your peers and colleagues?

___ ___ **6.** Feel as a teacher you are approachable, responsive, and supportive to your students?

___ ___ **7.** Readily acknowledge the physical, intellectual, social, and emotional needs/characteristics of early adolescence?

___ ___ **8.** Regularly apply different and varied methods/activities in the teaching/learning process?

___ ___ **9.** Regularly use group processes and group learning techniques?

___ ___ **10.** Organize your curriculum in a way that facilitates the interdisciplinary approach to instruction?

___ ___ **11.** Willingly counsel an individual student with an identifiable need?

YES   NO   DO YOU...

___ ___ **12.** Design and conduct group activities that capitalize on individual differences and learning styles of students?

___ ___ **13.** Have the skills required to work in cooperative teaching situations—with other teachers, paraprofessionals, and resource persons?

___ ___ **14.** Accept the responsibility of multidisciplinary instruction in planning thematic and coordinated studies with other teachers?

___ ___ **15.** Seek out and enjoy teaching subjects outside of your own area of specialization?

___ ___ **16.** Readily acknowledge there are many ways—not just "my way"—of teaching students?

___ ___ **17.** Recognize that team members will have differences, disagreements, and conflicts, but also understand that these can and should be resolved?

___ ___ **18.** Believe in weekly team plans and meetings?

___ ___ **19.** Display a tactful honesty and willingness to work and plan together with team members?

___ ___ **20.** Demonstrate a willingness to utilize differences between, as well as similarities among, team members?

___ ___ **21.** Demonstrate a realization that your subject area is of no more or less importance than other subjects?

___ ___ **22.** Demonstrate a realization that ability grouping may not be compatible with interdisciplinary team teaching?

___ ___ **23.** Agree that team members ought to be flexible in individual scheduling to meet a particular student's needs?

___ ___ **24.** Display an interest in (not necessarily an understanding of) the other academic subjects?

___ ___ **25.** Show a sensitivity to the feelings of the other team members? (Can you eliminate petty and/or personal "gripes" that may interfere with the primary objectives of interdisciplinary team teaching?)

SCORING: Give yourself one point for every YES response.

20 – 25	You are definitely a middle school person.
15 – 19	You are definitely leaning towards a middle school commitment.
10 – 14	You are mildly interested in learning more about middle schools.
0 – 10	You are really an elementary or high school teacher at heart.

10 Ways To Rate Yourself As An Effective Team Builder

DIRECTIONS: On a scale of one to seven (1-7), how would you rate yourself as a team builder?

_____ **1.** I spend sufficient time selecting team members with the appropriate skills and attitudes required to make the teaming concept work.

_____ **2.** I encourage ownership among team members by allowing them considerable independence and autonomy in goal setting, problem solving, and delivery of instruction.

_____ **3.** I nurture and practice the spirit of teamwork throughout the school setting.

_____ **4.** I insist on open and honest communication at all times.

_____ **5.** I keep my word, my agreements, and my promises to people.

_____ **6.** I respect the personality differences and cultural diversities of others.

_____ **7.** I provide quality staff development opportunities for enhancing the teaming process.

_____ **8.** I value constructive criticism.

_____ **9.** I believe that teaming and collaboration will maximize the learning that takes place.

_____ **10.** I will coach and counsel team members who are not able to meet reasonable standards and expectations.

SCORING:
- A score of 60-70 means you are well aware of what it takes to be an effective team builder.
- A score of 40-59 is acceptable, although you need to sharpen your team-building skills and attitudes.
- A score below 40 means you aren't really a team player yet, but you may be willing to give it a try!

10 PLUS 4

Roles And Responsibilities Of A Team Leader

1. Functions as a liaison between the administration and team

2. Coordinates instructional programs within the team

3. Coordinates practices and procedures between own team and other teams

4. Serves on and/or appoints team members to various school or district committees

5. Schedules and coordinates administration of criterion-referenced and standardized tests

6. Prepares and submits the team budget for supplies, textbooks, audio-visuals, and equipment needs

7. Familiarizes new teachers and substitute teachers with the school program and the team practices and procedures

8. Disseminates trends, new approaches, and research findings to team members

9. Schedules and conducts team meetings

10. Assists in the selection of personnel that affects team activities including aides, volunteers, team members, substitute teachers, and support staff

11. Promotes public relations between team members and parent/school community

12. Facilitates communication among team members

13. Coordinates interdisciplinary instruction efforts

14. Maintains a high level of morale among team members

10 PLUS 1

Things On Which Team Members Should Agree

Team members should meet during the pre-school planning days. It is essential that the team members agree on . . .

1. Times for regular team meetings.

2. The ways to schedule students into classes.

3. The continual sharing of curriculum objectives leading to the development of interdisciplinary units.

4. Selecting and securing textbooks and other needed resources.

5. How and when to meet with parents and students.

6. A team classroom-management plan.

7. Ways to communicate in writing to parents.

8. A homework policy.

9. Field trip plans to extend classroom experiences.

10. Team assignments.

11. The importance of a professional approach to all team and school efforts to educate the children.

10 PLUS 20

Tools For Building A Team Identity

1. Team Name/Logo/Mascot/Colors/Slogan
2. Team Decorations for Door, Hallways, Rooms
3. Team Newspaper/Newsletter
4. Team Rules/Codes of Conduct
5. Team Rewards
6. Team Intramurals
7. Team Birthday Celebrations
8. Team Government
9. Team Recognition Days
10. Team Meals
11. Team Assemblies
12. Team Display of Student Work
13. Team T-Shirts
14. Team Bulletin Boards
15. Team Handbooks
16. Team Student Conference
17. Team Contests
18. Team Field Trips
19. Team Song
20. Team Parties
21. Team Scrapbook
22. Team Name Tags for Special Events
23. Team Honor Rolls
24. Team Calendar
25. Team Special Events and Activities
26. Talent Shows, Spirit Days, Dress-Up Days
27. Clean-Up Days, Community Projects
28. Academic Brain Bowls, Open House, Holiday Parties
29. Team Cheers/Songs/Choral Readings
30. Team Rituals

10 Things That Great Teams Do

1. Build a strong team identity, but be certain that the team's identity is compatible with and supportive of the school's overall identity.

2. Conduct regular team meetings with predetermined agendas and follow-up minutes. Appoint a team historian to maintain records of the team's progress throughout the year.

3. Hold regular parent and student conferences. Don't let a week go by without inviting some student(s) or parent(s) to become the focus of a productive discussion or action plan. Try to have conferences that "celebrate" an individual's success as well as those that are scheduled for solving problems.

4. Maintain a team calendar. Distribute this weekly or monthly calendar to both students and parents. Include as many important dates, events, and deadlines as you can to communicate all that is going on with your team members.

5. Maintain and use a flexible block schedule. Spend considerable time grouping and regrouping students for instruction and scheduling and rescheduling blocks of time for that instruction. Take full advantage of the opportunity to expand or reduce predetermined blocks of time for the academic subject areas in order to maximize the learning process.

6. Celebrate team successes. Don't let a day go by without taking time to review the high spots of the day or the high points of the week for yourselves, your students, or your parent community. Remember that a string of minor successes can lead to sensational ones!

7. Integrate subject matter. Look for ways to interface the different academic subjects every chance you get. Don't assume that students will automatically see the connections from class to class; you must help them understand the links between one content area and another.

8. Forget mistakes, but learn from them. All team members should feel comfortable in taking risks to tease their minds and stretch their imaginations. Some of your ideas or activities will falter, but develop the attitude that a group learns more from its failures than from its successes.

9. Plan "play" into the work week. It is all right to allow some free time or "wiggle room" into a weekly schedule for both teachers and students. Use this time for reflection and refocusing so that it becomes both enjoyable and productive.

10. Hold team "professional reading/learning" sessions. Try to build a professional library of resources for the team so that team members can continue to grow in their careers. Don't limit the materials to educational themes, but include as well books, pamphlets, tapes, journals in areas of business, economics, and politics.

10 More Things That Great Teams Do

1. Develop common discipline procedures. Be certain that all team members enforce the same rules in the same way so that students can't "play one teacher against another."

2. Establish common grading guidelines. Agree on a grading system that will be used by the team and develop a specific set of descriptors for each point on the grading scale to avoid discrepancies from one team member to another.

3. Coordinate homework. Communicate daily to determine types of homework to be required in the core content areas. Avoid overloading students with unrealistic homework tasks on any given day.

4. Coordinate the administration of quizzes and tests. Create a plan for assessing student achievement in the core subject areas so that no student is required to study for more than one major quiz or test at any one time.

5. Encourage a standard paper heading. Although this may seem like a minor point, the students do not find it so. It can minimize the frustration of a student who has to remember if the name and date go in the upper right hand corner for one class and in the lower left hand corner for another class.

6. Hold team detentions. Handling student discipline problems within the structure of the team is a major goal of the teaming process. Therefore, time and procedures for dealing with student detentions must be built into the team's schedule.

7. Conduct team "help sessions" for students. It is important that the team try to build into the weekly and monthly schedule of team activities time for helping, tutoring, or coaching students in the academic areas. These sessions could vary according to the schedule, with time blocks set aside before school, after school, and within the school day.

8. Provide students with opportunities for extra credit work. A written team policy should encourage any student to complete extra credit work for enrichment or remedial purposes, regardless of that student's ability level.

9. Give frequent student academic and personal progress reports. A bank of tools and techniques for recognizing cognitive and affective achievements in the classroom should become an integral part of the teaming process. Progress charts, awards assemblies, recognition banners, personal badges/buttons, and happy-grams to the home can all be parts of this celebration.

10. Monitor student academic and personal progress. Student folders, portfolios, notebooks, and anecdotal records should all be considered parts of the accountability process for keeping track of where students stand both academically and personally. Learning logs, journals, and projects can all be parts of this data-collecting effort.

10 Barriers For Effective Teams To Overcome

1. **PERSONALITY CONFLICTS**
Recognize and appreciate diversity and make allowances for different needs, characteristics, moods, and personalities within the team.

2. **INCONSISTENCY IN STUDENT EXPECTATIONS**
Recognize that team members all view the teaching and learning process differently and that it is the team's responsibility to synthesize these expectations when making decisions.

3. **INCONSISTENCY IN TEACHER EXPECTATIONS**
Recognize the individuality of team members when setting personal goals and objectives for the school year and work to reach consensus on goals and objectives, in keeping with teacher talents.

4. **POOR PLANNING, ORGANIZATION, AND PREPARATION**
Recognize that teams often take shortcuts in planning or goal-setting for the school year, organizing resources, and preparing students and parents for the teaming process. It is critical that an effort be made in the opening weeks of school to set the tone for the next nine months.

5. **LACK OF SUPPORT FOR ONE ANOTHER OR DISLOYALTY**
Recognize that there will be times when team members do not offer one another the degree of support or loyalty required for making interdisciplinary teams successful. This is often due to teacher stress and/or burnout. Remember that when team members begin to experience these difficulties, time must be set aside immediately to resolve the divisive issues and get back on track.

6. POOR COMMUNICATION

Recognize that two-way communication is the very heart and soul of effective teaming and should become the first priority when dealing with the various members of the teaming process.

7. REFUSAL TO SHARE IDEAS AND MATERIALS

Recognize that in the past many teachers have been programmed to hoard materials and hide ideas rather than share resources and exchange information. Teaming requires collaboration on a daily basis to maximize learning and growing for students *and* for teachers.

8. DIFFICULTY WITH INDIVIDUAL TEAM MEMBERS

Recognize that on some teams there will be teachers who don't want to be there for reasons ranging from individual feelings of inadequacy to ignorance of the teaming concept. For the good of the students, each team member must accept individual strengths and weaknesses within the team.

9. INABILITY TO VARY DELIVERY SYSTEMS

Recognize that it is not enough to recognize the grouping of teachers and students into teams, but that the restructuring of instructional time and techniques is also critical to the redesign of middle-level classrooms.

10. POOR PUBLIC RELATIONS

Recognize that teachers must do a better job of "tooting their own horns" and letting the public know the advantages that teaming brings to the schooling process. Teaming is compatible with today's workplace with its emphasis on quality teams, shared decision-making, and empowerment of workers. Let the world know that today's middle school classrooms now represent a more realistic training ground for tomorrow's business settings.

10 Ideas For Developing A Team Handbook

It is suggested that each interdisciplinary team develop a team handbook for use by both students and parents. The purpose of the handbook is to provide relevant information about the team to which a given student is assigned. Possible contents of a teaming handbook are given below.

1. PROFILE OF TEAM MEMBERS
A short biographical sketch of each teacher on the team is a good way to begin the teaming handbook. This information can be written in an essay, outline, or short paragraph format. Teachers might want to tell something about their childhoods, families, hobbies, special interests, travels, pet peeves, previous teaching experiences, and future goals.

2. TEAM IDENTITY SHEET
An outline of the team's unique characteristics and plans for the year should be included. Briefly describe the team's name, color, logo, slogan, cheers, secret handshake, traditions, rituals, and celebrations.

3. TEAM GUIDELINES AND PROCEDURES
An overview of the team's rules for student discipline, for absences, for homework, for make-up work, and for grades should also be a part of the teaming handbook.

4. TEAM SCHEDULE OF CLASSES
A brief explanation of how the students spend their time in school is appropriate for the teaming handbook. A block schedule might also be part of this section.

5. **STUDENT/PARENT CONFERENCE PLANNING SHEET**
A sample of the student/parent conference planning sheet should be part of the handbook so that students know what to expect when they attend a teacher/student conference. It should be noted that all teachers on the team should be present for a student/parent conference, which is generally held during the team's common planning period.

6. **PARENT CONFERENCE PLANNING SHEET**
A sample telephone report form should be part of the handbook so that parents can see that team teachers keep records of telephone contacts with the home.

7. **TEAM MEETING AGENDA**
It is useful to include a sample team meeting agenda in the handbook as a reminder to both students and parents that much school-day time is spent planning and evaluating the team's instructional program.

8. **TEAM MEETING MINUTES**
A sample of minutes from a typical team meeting can be a useful tool in showing students and parents the kinds of tasks completed during the team's common planning periods.

9. **TEAM CALENDAR OF SPECIAL DATES AND EVENTS**
Students and parents will appreciate a list of the planned rituals, celebrations, traditions, events, and special dates which will have an impact on their time and energies during the school year. This calendar can be used as a vehicle for planning both short-term and long-term activities.

10. **STUDY HINTS**
The teaming handbook is a good place in which to remind students and parents of the importance of cultivating good study habits while in school. This section might include everything from hints on how to study for a test to suggestions for writing an effective research or book report.

10 PLUS 2 Ways To Use Common Planning Time

1. Hold formal and informal team meetings to discuss students, parents, schedules, curriculum issues, school business, and team policies and procedures.

2. Plan grade level/departmental meetings or sessions with administrators and/or colleagues to foster communication and an appropriate level of shared decision-making.

3. Offer special staff development activities or a mini-workshop for self-improvement, including short audio/visual training tapes, lectures by district personnel, or programmed texts/workbooks.

4. Develop interdisciplinary approaches or units. This could be a high priority for common planning time get-togethers. Try integrating a concept, skill, or topic on a daily basis in at least some small way to help students understand the correlation between their teachers, subject areas, and skills development.

5. Reward students. Celebrating student success should be a regular occurrence and should vary from appreciation roles and verbal praise to student work displays.

6. Conduct student and parent conferences. It is important to build "talking" time into the weekly schedule for dealing with both student and parent problems as they arise. Remember, "an ounce of prevention is worth a pound of cure."

7. Share teacher ideas, concerns, worries, failures, and successes. Fostering morale, emotional health, and well-being and providing outlets for sharing "war stories" or brainstorming creative ideas are musts.

8. Update team records. Documenting team events, discussions, and decisions is important to team success. This includes everything from student records to team minutes so that paperwork does not become a burden at any given time.

9. Organize team events, celebrations, or field trips. Building a strong team identity depends upon a team's ability to plan and implement a wide variety of special happenings for all teachers and student members of the team.

10. Update team calendar to coordinate course requirements, test dates, class excursions, and special lesson plans. Avoiding duplicate or conflicting class requirements or regulations can pave the way for considerable academic achievement.

11. Brainstorm solutions to problems or alternatives for decisions. Holding short stand-up team meetings during the day can help solve short-term problems or aid in making short-term decisions as they come up.

12. Enjoy a social time with special treats or a potluck lunch. Take time for fun and socializing among yourselves.

10 MINUS 3

Guidelines For Setting Team Discipline Rules

Classroom rules, regulations, rewards, and penalties should be established early in the school year. It is also important to involve students in the rule-setting process. Some factors to consider in developing a set of team rules for consistent classroom follow.

1. Rules should be limited to four or five simple reminders or behaviors.

2. Rules should be written in clearly stated sentences.

3. Penalties should be specific, fair, and consistently enforced by all team members.

4. Rules and penalties should be posted in each team and classroom area.

5. The administration should approve the "last resort" or "bottom line" clause in the list of penalties.

6. A longer list of rewards to reinforce acceptable behavior should also be developed and posted in each team and classroom area.

7. Parents should have copies of the team classroom management system of rules.

10 Steps For An Effective Parent Conference

1. Document academic or behavior problems through use of observation checklists, anecdotal records, test scores, work samples, and teacher reports. Try to include positive as well as negative evidence in your portfolio.

2. Arrange the conference time and place so that both are convenient for parents and team members. Encourage parents/guardians *and* student to attend.

3. Approach the conference with a positive "can do" attitude. Discuss the student's strengths and successes before discussing problem areas.

4. Encourage the parents/guardians to talk and share their perceptions while you listen carefully to what is being said. Take notes and ask clarifying questions.

5. Allow ample time for parents/guardians to air their frustrations and concerns without getting defensive or interrupting a train of thought. Try to use body language and verbal comments that are reassuring, such as: "I can see why you feel as you do" or "That makes sense to me."

6. Make certain that all team members provide input at all stages of the conference including its preparation, implementation, and follow-up.

7. Develop an action plan that focuses on specific strategies and responsibilities for improving the problem areas. Record who is to do what, when, and how.

8. Keep all team members and parents/guardians focused on the problem areas identified for resolving at this conference. Try to discourage digression from the task at hand.

9. Dismiss parents/guardians in a positive way so that they feel their time and energy have been well spent and so that they know exactly what has to be done to help the student.

10. Above all else, make certain to follow the established plan of action in a timely fashion and arrange for a follow-up conference or discussion. Monitor the plan of action strategies in a consistent manner.

10 PLUS 10

Techniques For Effective Team Meetings

1. Plan the meeting cooperatively.

2. Acknowledge the schedules of others.

3. Provide ample lead time.

4. Keep a portion of the agenda open.

5. Stay on task.

6. Keep presentations/discussions short and to the point.

7. Make space ready and presentable for the meeting.

8. Eliminate distractions.

9. Schedule time to socialize if possible.

10. Feed the troops.

11. Value humor.

12. Learn to read silence.

13. Manage hostility.

14. Respect differences.

15. Protect confidentiality.

16. Stretch for closure.

17. Invite participant feedback.

18. Retire useless practices.

19. Establish priorities.

20. Evaluate results.

10 PLUS 2

Characteristics Of Effective Teaming

1. Teams should be balanced and include team members who have varied teaching and learning styles. Learning styles inventories can be used to identify modalities, right/left brain tendencies, and preferred instructional modes.

2. Teams should include team members with the appropriate subject matter competencies. A four-member team should include the specialties of math, science, social studies, and language arts/English/reading. A three-member team should include any three of these areas with a strong backup in the fourth area. A two-member team should include experiences/training/degrees in a science/math combination and a language arts/social studies combination.

3. Teams should be assigned or housed in specific team areas with adjacent classrooms. School floor plans can be adapted to the teaming process by designating sections of the building for trade/team assignments and reassigning space to accommodate those teachers working together.

4. Teams should have a common planning space so that team members can meet daily for team meetings, house shared materials for mutual accessibility, hold student or parent conferences in close proximity to one another, and store team records or files.

5. Teams should have a common planning time to facilitate daily meetings which are needed to: (a) determine schedules; (b) discuss students; (c) develop interdisciplinary units; (d) plan goals and objectives; (e) design special team events/activities; and (f) evaluate programs.

6. Teams should designate a team leader as well as key roles and responsibilities for both the team leader and team members.

7. Teams should hold regular team meetings with predetermined agendas and concise minutes.

8. Teams should strive to preserve team autonomy and flexibility in planning, implementing, and evaluating instructional practices for team members and their students.

9. Teams should share decision-making tasks with the administration whenever and wherever possible to do so. This requires both a mutual commitment and respect among all parties involved.

10. A team should be accountable for its own budget and supplies whenever possible. This encourages both wise spending and maximum use of resources by the team.

11. Teams should include specialists and other support staff members in team decisions and activities. Exploratory teachers and guidance counselors, for example, can add a great deal of valuable input when dealing with issues ranging from student behavior to interdisciplinary units.

12. Teams should respect the similarities and differences which exist among team members and practice the art of compromise or negotiation to accomplish team goals and objectives.

A List Of Advantages And Disadvantages Of Varying Team Sizes

An important decision one must make in setting up an interdisciplinary team organization for a given school setting is the size or sizes of teams servicing the students and teachers in the school. There are both distinct advantages and disadvantages for teams ranging from two-person teams to five-person teams.

TWO-PERSON TEAM

ADVANTAGES

1. Fewer students—teachers know each student better
2. Variety of subjects may be taught
3. Ease of integrating the disciplines
4. Ease of getting together for meetings
5. Fewer personality conflicts
6. No "odd man" out
7. More secure environment
8. Good transition from single teacher at 5th grade level to two-person team at 6th grade level

DISADVANTAGES

1. Students deal with a limited number of teaching personalities
2. May burden teachers with too much preparation
3. Not as much back-up for absenteeism
4. Limited diversity in teaching styles

THREE-PERSON TEAM

ADVANTAGES

1. Diversity of instructional materials and methods (three heads are better than one)
2. Group will usually teach one subject in common and may integrate subject areas easily
3. Diversity in teaching styles
4. More opportunity to group students according to ability

DISADVANTAGES

1. Sometimes difficult to find a common subject to teach
2. Increased likelihood of "two against one"

FOUR-PERSON TEAM

ADVANTAGES

1. Usually one major subject per teacher (requiring one preparation)

2. Good transition to high school

3. Teacher may specialize if so desired

4. More opportunity to ability-group students within a team

5. Greater diversity of instructional materials and methods (four heads are better than one)

6. Greater diversity in teaching styles

DISADVANTAGES

1. Sometimes more difficult for members to meet

2. Greater potential for personality conflicts

3. May be more difficult to gain and maintain consistency in program

4. Teachers may specialize too much and become departmentalized

FIVE-PERSON TEAM

ADVANTAGES

1. Usually one major subject per teacher (requiring one preparation)

2. Good transition to high school

3. Teacher may specialize if so desired

4. More opportunity to ability-group students within a team

5. Greater diversity of instructional materials and methods (five heads are better than one)

6. Greater diversity in teaching styles

7. Possibility of using one individual as remedial teacher with smaller groups of students

DISADVANTAGES

1. Sometimes more difficult for members to meet

2. Greater potential for personality conflicts

3. May be more difficult to gain and maintain consistency in program

4. Teachers may specialize too much and become departmentalized

A Working Definition Of A Flexible Block Master Schedule

A flexible block schedule is a "chunk" of uninterrupted teaching time allocated to a given group of students and teachers on an interdisciplinary team. It allows the team to do one of several things:

1. Vary size of instructional groups of classes

2. Vary frequency or number of times a group or class meets

3. Vary length of instructional time for a group or class

4. Vary order or sequence of meeting times

5. Vary number of groups or classes that meet within an established block of time

In short, flexible block scheduling is a way of better responding to the needs of young adolescents. It allows the students and teachers to master the master schedule.

Note: For examples of flexible block schedules, see pages 54-62 in the Nuts And Bolts module.

Sample Interdisciplinary Team Assignment Data Sheet

Directions: Complete this information for the administrator to consider in assigning you to a team.

1. Name _____

2. Current Assignment

   A. Building _____

   B. Subject or Position_____

   C. Grade Level_____

   D. Certification Area(s) _____

3. Learning Modalities (rank order from 1–3 with 1 being your dominant learning style).

   _____ Visual   _____ Auditory   _____ Kinesthetic

4. Right Brain/Left Brain Dominance
   Score _____

5. Results of Gregoric _____
   _____
   _____

6. Results of LSI Inventory _____
   _____
   _____

7. Other information you feel is relevant _____
   _____
   _____
   _____
   _____

Sample Interdisciplinary Team Evaluation Report

NAME _____ TIME _____

DAY _____ DATE _____

This form is designed to inform you of your child's performance in his academic work and/or his citizenship for _____ marking period.

Circled areas apply at this time. The evaluation scale is as follows:

1 – Excellent   2 – Satisfactory   3 – Needs Improvement   4 – Unsatisfactory

	MATH	ENGLISH	SOCIAL STUDIES	SCIENCE
1. Preparation for class	1 2 3 4	1 2 3 4	1 2 3 4	1 2 3 4
2. Completion of required work	1 2 3 4	1 2 3 4	1 2 3 4	1 2 3 4
3. Attentiveness in class	1 2 3 4	1 2 3 4	1 2 3 4	1 2 3 4
4. Study habits	1 2 3 4	1 2 3 4	1 2 3 4	1 2 3 4
5. Class Participation	1 2 3 4	1 2 3 4	1 2 3 4	1 2 3 4
6. Test results	1 2 3 4	1 2 3 4	1 2 3 4	1 2 3 4
7. Punctuality	1 2 3 4	1 2 3 4	1 2 3 4	1 2 3 4
8. Self-discipline	1 2 3 4	1 2 3 4	1 2 3 4	1 2 3 4
9. Cooperation	1 2 3 4	1 2 3 4	1 2 3 4	1 2 3 4
10. Courtesy	1 2 3 4	1 2 3 4	1 2 3 4	1 2 3 4
11. Respect for rights of others	1 2 3 4	1 2 3 4	1 2 3 4	1 2 3 4
12. Respect for school property	1 2 3 4	1 2 3 4	1 2 3 4	1 2 3 4
13. Attitude	1 2 3 4	1 2 3 4	1 2 3 4	1 2 3 4
14. Organization	1 2 3 4	1 2 3 4	1 2 3 4	1 2 3 4
15. Classroom behavior	1 2 3 4	1 2 3 4	1 2 3 4	1 2 3 4
16. Grade to Date				

COMMENTS

_____

Team Teacher, Math

_____

Team Teacher, English

_____

Team Teacher, Social Studies

_____

Team Teacher, Science

If necessary, your child's advisory teacher, elective area teacher, and physical education teacher have made comments.

_____

Parent Signature

109

10 PLUS 1

Questions To Use During A Team Interview

School_____ Team Number _____

Name _____ Grade Level _____

These questions are to be used when a person who is not a member of a given team is called in to interview selected team members regarding the effectiveness of the team duty time and member's feelings about interdisciplinary team organization. Responses should be recorded on a separate piece of paper.

1. How do you generally feel about being a member of an interdisciplinary team?

2. What is the best thing about being a member of your team?

3. What is the most difficult thing about being a member of your team?

4. How do you feel about the effectiveness of your team meetings?

5. Tell me something about the face-to-face parent conferences conducted by your team.

6. Tell me something about the student conferences conducted by your team.

7. Tell me about how your team used the services of resource personnel in your building, such as counselors, house leaders, psychologists, and special education teachers.

8. Tell me about the coordination of instruction and scheduling in your team.

9. State three things that your team is doing to help meet the needs of your students.

10. State three things that your team is doing to help meet the needs of the adult team members.

11. State three things that your team has done to help build team identity with your students.

From *How To Evaluate Your Middle School* by Sandra Schurr. Columbus, OH: National Middle School Association, ©1992. Used by permission.

A Sample Team Self-Evaluation Checklist

School_____   Team Number _____

Name _____   Grade Level _____

This checklist should be completed individually by all members of an interdisciplinary team. Afterwards the team leader should facilitate a meeting where responses are shared and consensus is reached. The agreed-upon answers should be recorded on a master sheet, kept in the team master notebook, and reviewed on a regular basis.

	Always	Frequently	Infrequently	Never	Comments
1. Our team meets on a regular basis.					
2. All team members are present at our team meetings.					
3. All team members come to our meetings on time.					
4. All team members stay for the duration of our meetings.					
5. Our team talks about ways to best meet the needs of students.					
6. Our team works effectively with resource personnel, such as our counselor and our house leader.					
7. The members of our team support the efforts of our team leader.					

Self-Evaluation Checklist

	Always	Frequently	Infrequently	Never	Comments
8. Every member of our team participates in the decision-making process.					
9. The team's decisions are implemented.					
10. Our team keeps a team notebook which includes agenda, minutes, parent conference forms, student conference forms, and other information pertaining to our team.					
11. Our team has goals and objectives for the school year.					
12. Our team periodically evaluates its goals and objectives.					
13. Our team members use team duty time to correlate subject matter and to plan for interdisciplinary instruction.					
14. Our team members conduct face-to-face parent conferences during team duty time.					
15. Our team members use team duty time to conduct student conferences.					
16. Our team discusses ways to use our block time effectively.					
17. Our team groups and regroups students for instruction within our team.					
18. Our team changes our "regular" schedule to accommodate teacher and student needs.					
19. Our team has an agenda for all team meetings.					

Self-Evaluation Checklist

		Always	Frequently	Infrequently	Never	Comments
20.	Our team follows the agenda at our meetings.					
21.	Our team planning time is kept strictly for team business.					
22.	The team paces itself and allows for "ups" and "downs," cycles of hard work and relaxation.					
23.	The team regularly takes time to provide outlets for members to share ideas and frustrations.					
24.	Our team members inform the exploratory teachers about decisions reached at our team meetings.					
25.	Our team coordinates the amount of homework given to students so that it is spread out over the week.					
26.	Our team coordinates test days so that students do not have more than one test on a given day.					
27.	Our team has established team procedures and policies for our students.					
28.	Our team has established a team identity through the use of a team name, team logo, team assemblies, etc.					
29.	Our team plans, implements, and evaluates at least two interdisciplinary units a year.					

TEACHER'S INTERDISCIPLINARY TEAMING WRAP-UP, À LA BLOOM

KNOWLEDGE
In your own words, define Interdisciplinary Teaming.

COMPREHENSION
Explain how Interdisciplinary Teaming could be used in your classroom to help students reach learning goals and develop social skills.

APPLICATION
Review your notes on Interdisciplinary Teaming and write a summary statement of the characteristics of an effective interdisciplinary team.

ANALYSIS
Infer ways that Interdisciplinary Teaming in the schools is compatible with teaming in the workplace.

SYNTHESIS
Design a marketing plan to promote the teaming concept with your students, parents, and school administrators.

EVALUATION
Determine three reasons an interdisciplinary team might be successful and three reasons the same team might be unsuccessful.

ADVISORY

Advisory Concept Overview

AN ADVISOR/ADVISEE PROGRAM IS:

- An affective educational program designed to focus on the social, emotional, physical, intellectual, psychological, and ethical development of students.

- A program providing a structured time during which special activities are designed and implemented to help adolescents find ways to fulfill their identified needs.

- Intended to provide consistent, caring, and continuous adult guidance at school through the organization of a supportive and stable peer group that meets regularly under the guidance of a teacher serving as advisor.

ADVISORY HELPS TO MEET THE NEEDS OF THE FOURTH R.

Traditionally, the schooling process has emphasized the three R's—reading, writing, and arithmetic—as the key curricular areas for middle level programs. In the complex and technological world of the Information Age, however, a fourth R, referred to as "relationships," has taken on new meaning and new responsibility. School advisory programs must play a major role in helping our young people through the turbulence and hurdles of early adolescence.

ADVISORY HELPS TO BRIDGE THE GAP BETWEEN ELEMENTARY SCHOOL AND HIGH SCHOOL.

The advisory program helps bridge the gap between the self-contained elementary school and the independent world of high school. It offers middle school students the best of both worlds because it provides every student with an advisor who has a special concern for the student as an individual and encourages independence and personal growth needed for high school success.

ADVISORY HELPS BUILD SELF-AWARENESS AND PERSONAL ESTEEM.

Finally, an advisory program is needed to help students feel good about themselves and the contributions they can make to their school, community, and society. It can serve as a prescriptive antidote for the unmotivated learner or the at-risk student who can be coerced into negative behaviors. In the years ahead, society will be dependent on the middle level students of today. An effective advisory program will help young adolescents become happy, fully-functioning citizens of our world.

10 Important Advisory Questions To Find Answers For

1. Why is affective education critical in today's complex and technological world?

2. Is it possible for attitudes to be taught?

3. How can advisory ease the transition between elementary and middle school, and between middle and high school?

4. What are some things advisors can do to become better prepared to meet individual needs in a group setting?

5. How can an advisory program that has gotten off to a bad start be redirected and revitalized to become a positive influence in students' lives?

6. What steps can administrators take to positively influence a schoolwide advisory program?

7. How can parents be effectively involved in advisory activities?

8. How can after-school and community enrichment activities be incorporated into an advisory program?

9. What are some pitfalls new advisors should be alert for and how can experienced advisors help them avoid these pitfalls?

10. How can advisors support and reinforce one another's efforts in order to build a strong and effective schoolwide advisory program?

10 PLUS 1

Definitions Essential To Advisory Success

1. **Academic:** In the context of this program, academic education means the regular curriculum of a school, including Math, Language Arts, Science, and Social Studies. This type of educational focus is sometimes placed in opposition to affective education, but the two are intertwined and both should be included in the school's curriculum.

2. **Adolescence:** Adolescence is a transitional time that begins with puberty and ends with adulthood. It is the time when the human body and mind mature. The young adolescent's body is changing, thinking is growing more complex, and the future as an adult looms. Combine these internal changes with a world that is often scary and challenging, and it is understandable that adolescent behavior is sometimes erratic.

3. **Affective:** A dictionary definition of affective is "relating to, arising from, or influencing feelings or emotions." Affective education addresses the issues that affect student emotional health, self-esteem, confidence, and maturity, and it is important that we not diminish its value. When emotional health is threatened, all learning is difficult.

4. **Cognitive:** Cognitive learning has to do with conscious intellectual activity, as in thinking, reasoning, remembering, or imagining. Though we know that thinking can never be completely separated from emotion, the word cognitive is sometimes used to mean pure conscious thinking unattached to emotion.

5. **Consistency:** In an advisory program, consistency is important in two ways. It is important that meeting times are scheduled with some consistency so that the student will have a home base he or she can count on. Consistency is also important in the way the advisor relates to students. Aiming for consistency doesn't mean that an advisor cannot change his or her mind. It does mean that an advisor will establish an atmosphere of trust by avoiding unpredictable behavior such as establishing rules one day and dispensing with them the next.

6. **Communication:** The ability to make one's thoughts and feelings known is a valuable component of self-esteem. One goal of the advisory program is that students will learn the skills to communicate their feelings, needs, wants, and ideas to others, and will be receptive to others' efforts to communicate.

7. **Egocentric:** Being egocentric means to be limited in outlook or concern to one's own activities or needs (or to those of one's own group). It is important to understand that it is normal for an adolescent to be "wrapped up in oneself." It does not mean a youngster is doomed to be bad or selfish. The egocentricity of adolescence is a natural stage of growth, and the fortunate child will grow to broaden his or her outlook and develop a wider concern for others.

8. **Negative:** Something negative is that which tends to diminish a child's sense of self-worth, that inhibits personal growth, or that opposes constructive development or maturation. An influence, an attitude, and a response can all be negative.

9. **Positive:** This is the type of attitude that a caring advisor strives to cultivate. A positive influence is that which helps a child grow toward independence and maturity.

10. **Relationship:** Many are beginning to understand that relationship is the key to a healthy personality, which in turn is the foundation for achievement, learning, and growth. The advisory program provides a caring adult who will offer a positive relationship that will help a child mature. The program also fosters positive relationships with the child's peers by setting up a non-critical environment in a group setting.

11. **Self-esteem:** A strong sense of self-worth, or self-esteem, is the foundation that enables a person to overcome adversity, to achieve independence, and to meet difficult challenges. Self-esteem is sometimes called self-confidence or self-respect. Those who respect themselves tend to respect others; those who care for themselves tend to care for others. Self-esteem is related to, among other things, personal accomplishments, the ability to relate to others, the ability to communicate, and the good fortune to know someone who listens and tries to understand.

10 PLUS 2

Findings From The Published Literature To Document The Need For An Advisor/Advisee Program

1. FINDING
William M. Alexander and Paul S. George stress:

The fundamental purpose of the advisor/advisee program, regardless of its design in any particular school, is to promote involvement between a teacher and the students involved in the advisory group. Every student needs to have a relationship with at least one adult in the school which is characterized by warmth, concern, openness, and understanding. Such a program focuses on what has been called the "fourth R," relationships: interpersonal relationships which produce growth for both people involved. Good middle schools cannot be places where teachers and students pass by each other without recognition or attachment, like the stereotypical ships in the night.

Reference: Alexander, William M. and George, Paul S. The Exemplary Middle School. New York: Holt, Rinehart and Winston, 1981, p. 90.

2. FINDING
ASCD Panel On Moral Education writes:

In recent years, the educational community has given substantial attention to excellence in our schools. An emphasis on moral education, we believe, is essential to that end. Moral education is not just another educational fad; it is an old and revered school mission. And with good reason. At the heart of democracy is the morally mature citizen. A society whose citizens are not morally mature and cannot trust one another resorts to external force and can even evolve into a police state. Similarly, a school whose students are not morally mature is tempted to create an environment of repression. Schools must contribute to the development of morally mature individuals who, in turn, will help to ensure the existence of a just and caring society.

Reference: ASCD Panel On Moral Education, "Moral Education in the Life of the School," Educational Leadership. Association for Supervision and Curriculum Development, Alexandria, Virginia, Volume 45, Number 8, May, 1988.

3. FINDING
Larry Cuban concludes:

There are instructional approaches that build on the strengths that students bring to school, instructional strategies that make linkages with life experiences of students and exploit a growing knowledge about active learning and the importance of student involvement in developing higher-order thinking skills. Such ways of teaching at-risk students further develop their store of language, connect abstract ideas with student background, and move back and forth between student experiences and school concepts.

Reference: Cuban, Larry. "At-Risk Students: What Teachers and Principals Can Do," Educational Leadership. Association for Supervision and Curriculum Development, Alexandria, Virginia, Volume 46, Number 5, February 1989, p. 31.

4. FINDING
Robert DeBlois shows that:

The myths and realities about dropouts are hard to sort out, but the bulk of information suggests that most dropouts do not have low I.Q.'s. The characteristic that dropouts most often share is that they are two years behind their peers in reading and math skills (by the time they reach the seventh grade, they have been kept back a grade for one or more years). Many dropouts also possess a very low sense of self-esteem. Students drop out because they feel they cannot get along in their specific school. This is evidenced by their high level of absenteeism and lack of participation in school activities. They feel alienated from the school, and see themselves as being on the other side of the fence from their teachers. Most of them do not consult with an adult at the school before leaving. It may be for this reason that psychologist Urie Bronfenbrenner called schools "one of the most potent breeding grounds of alienation in American society."

Reference: DeBlois, Robert. "Keep At-Risk Students In School: Toward A Curriculum For Potential Dropouts." NASSP Bulletin, Volume 73, Number 516, April 1989, pp. 6–7.

5. FINDING
David Elkind reports:

We hurry young people as children and then unplace them as teenagers. We cannot, dare not, persist on this dangerous course of denying young people the time, the support, and the guidance they need to arrive at an integrated definition of self. Teenagers are the next generation and the future leaders of this country. Their need is real and pressing. We harm them and endanger the future of our society if we leave them, as our legacy, a patchwork sense of personal identity.

Reference: Elkind, David. All Grown Up & No Place To Go. New York: Addison-Wesley Publishing Co., 1984, p. 21.

6. **F**INDING
Thomas L. Good and Rhona S. Weinstein summarize:
Research based on the Brophy and Good 1974 model shows that many teachers vary sharply in their interaction with high- and low-achieving students. Good and Brophy (1984) summarize some of the common ways in which teachers have been found to differ in their behavior toward students believed to be more and less capable:

1. waiting less time for lows to answer

2. giving lows answers or calling on someone else rather than trying to improve their responses by giving clues or additional opportunities to respond

3. inappropriate reinforcement . . . rewarding inappropriate behavior or incorrect answers by lows

4. criticizing lows more often for failure

5. praising lows less frequently than highs for success

6. failing to give feedback to the public responses of lows

7. generally paying less attention to lows or interacting with them less frequently

8. calling on lows less often to respond to questions

9. seating lows further from the teacher

10. demanding less from lows

11. interacting with lows more privately than publicly and monitoring and structuring their activities more closely

12. differential administration or grading of tests and assignments in which highs but not lows are given the benefit of the doubt in borderline cases

13. less friendly interactions with lows, including less smiling and fewer other nonverbal indicators of support

14. briefer and less informative feedback to the questions of lows

15. less eye contact and other nonverbal communication of attention and responsiveness

16. less use of effective but time-consuming methods with lows when time is limited

17. giving longer reading assignments, providing more time for discussion, and generally demanding more from high than low groups

18. interrupting lows more often when they make reading mistakes

19. less often asking high-level comprehension questions of low groups

Reference: Good, Thomas L. and Weinstein, Rhona S. "Teacher Expectations: A Framework for Exploring Classrooms," Improving Teaching. Association for Supervision and Curriculum Development, Alexandria, Virginia, 1986, pp. 65–66.

7. FINDING

Howard J. Johnston and Glenn C. Markle summarize:

Attitude formation and change is possible in schools because attitudes are learned. Children are not born liking or disliking specific school subjects, nor do they enter the world with positive or negative self-concepts. Such attitudes are the result of learning experiences in the home, community, and school. While some attitudes are firmly established by the time students enter the middle school, it is nevertheless true that middle school teachers can have a profound effect on students' attitudes. Systematically or unwittingly, teachers influence student attitudes through classical conditioning, operant conditioning, and modeling.

Reference: Johnston, J. Howard and Markle, Glenn C. *What Research Says to the Middle Level Practitioner*. Columbus, OH: National Middle School Association, 1986, p. 79.

8. FINDING

A. Mikalachki concludes:

It appears that cognitive learning does not take into account either the feelings and concerns of the student or the social environment that affects those feelings and concerns. But . . . they have inevitable consequences. Cognitive learning cannot take place in a state of affective disorder, and we can no longer assume that the family or some other agency will take responsibility for the student's (total) affective development. It is imperative that school systems devote both their wits and their financial resources to the production of programs of affective learning. In them lies a response not only to youth alienation but also to many other human problems that challenge the educational system.

Reference: James, Michael. *Advisor/Advisee Programs: Why, What, and How*. Columbus, OH: National Middle School Association, 1986, p. 2.

9. FINDING
E. Friedenberg writes:

Adolescence is the period during which a young person learns who he (or she) is and what he (or she) really feels. It is the time during which he differentiates himself from his culture, though on the culture's terms. It is the age at which, by becoming a person in (her) own right, (she) becomes capable of establishing deeply felt relationships with other individuals perceived clearly as such.

Reference: Noar, Gertrude A. Junior High School: Today and Tomorrow. Englewood Cliffs, NJ: Prentice-Hall, 1961, p. 29.

10. FINDING
Gertrude A. Noar states:

The responsibility of the school instructional program was to meet four needs which related to youngster's emotions:

1. The need for security and affection, which creates a feeling of being wanted and a sense of belonging.
2. The need for recognition and reward.
3. The need for achievement and success.
4. The need for fun and adventure—new experiences, both educational and recreational.

Reference: Noar, Gertrude A. Junior High School: Today and Tomorrow. Englewood Cliffs, NJ: Prentice-Hall, 1961, p. 32.

11. FINDING
Gregory P. Stefanish points out:

If one reflects on current statistics concerning adolescents and the conditions under which they live, a need for substantive changes in the way we work with adolescents is apparent.

- The divorce rate is approaching 50 percent.

- Forty-three percent of those arrested for serious crimes in the U.S. in 1980 were juveniles, and youth crime is increasing by more than 10 percent a year.

- Alcoholism among teenagers increased 800 percent between 1970 and 1980.

- In the 1970s the number of students having intercourse increased by two-thirds.

- Four out of ten girls will become pregnant during the teenage yearstwo of ten will have a child and 96 percent of teenage mothers keep the child.

- One-third of all abortions are given to teens.

- The second leading cause of death among teenagers, after accidents, is suicide.

Reference: Stefanish, Gregory P. "If I Knew It Would Be This Easy I Wouldn't Have Worried So Much!" Middle School Journal, February 1986, p. 7.

12. FINDING
Paul S. George and Lynn L. Oldaker cite:

Among the recommendations that emerged from a Phi Delta Kappa outlier study of the characteristics of schools that had what that association called good discipline were several that middle school advocates would claim as central to the middle-school approach to the education of young adolescents.

1. A school should develop ways of improving the ways that people in the school work together to solve problems.

2. A school should develop the means to reduce authority and status differences among all persons in the school.

3. A school should increase and widen each student's sense of belonging in the school.

4. A school should find a way to deal with the personal problems that affect life within the school. Programs called "advisor-advisee" are advocated.

5. A school should improve physical and organizational arrangements so that these factors reinforce other efforts.

Reference: Wayson, W.W., DeVoss, G.G., Kaeser, S.C., Lasley, T., Pinnell, S.S., and the Phi Delta Kappa Commission on Discipline. Handbook for Developing Schools With Good Discipline. Bloomington, IN: Phi Delta Kappa, 1982, p. 39.

10 Characteristics Of A Quality Advisory Program

1. Advisory meets a minimum of three times a week for 20–30 minutes a day.

2. Advisory groups are manageable in size.

3. Advisory teachers support the advisory concept and work to increase their knowledge and understanding of it.

4. Advisory activities are varied and student-centered.

5. An advisory program has its own name, logo, and identity.

6. Advisory teachers are highly informed about the unique needs and characteristics of their advisory students (advisees).

7. Advisees look forward to advisory time and tasks.

8. Advisory sessions have a common core curriculum with flexibility in its implementation.

9. Advisory periods are held the first part of the school day.

10. An advisory teacher becomes the single most important adult in the school for his or her advisory students.

10 PLUS 2

Decisions To Be Made Regarding An Advisory Program

1. Who will serve on the advisory committee for developing, implementing, and evaluating the advisory program?

The committee should include a combination of administrators, counselors, parents, students, and teachers at all grade levels and/or department areas.

2. What will be the advisory program's name, logo, or slogan?

Every advisory program should have a special identity that separates it from the academic program.

3. Who will be the advisors, and who will be exempt from being an advisory teacher?

All teachers and administrators should be advisors except for the principal and the guidance counselor. It is the job of these two people to coordinate and monitor the entire advisory program.

4. If there are one or two teachers who adamantly oppose their involvement in the advisory program or who might even cause harm to the advisory program, should they be required to participate?

Any teacher who would not benefit the advisory program should be given alternative responsibilities during the school day which could range from supervisory tasks to clerical tasks.

5. How big should advisory groups be?

Advisory groups should have no more than 20–22 students.

6. How should advisees be assigned to advisors?

Students should be allowed to choose their advisory teachers when possible through a formal selection process. However, assigning students to advisors also works out well as long as there is a process for moving students when a situation is not working out for either student or teacher.

7. Should advisors keep their students all three years or should they change each year?

Advisors should keep their students all three years if possible. However, moving students to different advisors each year can be successful if the structure of the school mandates such an arrangement.

8. Which grades should be included in a formal advisory program?

All grades within a given school setting should be involved in the advisory program.

9. How often should advisory groups meet?

Advisory groups should meet on a daily basis for 20–30 minutes. If this is not possible, advisory groups should meet a minimum of two to three times a week.

10. When should advisory groups meet during the day?

Advisory groups should meet first thing in the morning to get the school day off on the right foot and to establish the climate for the day's activities.

11. How should advisory time be used most effectively?

The advisory program should have an established curriculum that must be followed by all advisors with optional materials and experiences available for variety and change of pace.

12. Is training required for teachers who will be advisors?

Training in the advisory concept and the curriculum should be given to all staff members prior to implementation of the program.

10 Responsibilities Of An Advisor

1. The advisor more than any other person in the school should be the advocate for his or her advisees.

2. The advisor should become informed of all activities regarding his or her advisees and should act on the information accordingly.

3. The advisor should be the group leader and should implement the established building or district advisory program.

4. The advisor should carry out "housekeeping" responsibilities for the school day such as attendance and lunch count.

5. The advisor should strive to develop a feeling of trust and caring within his or her advisory group.

6. The advisor should at all times regard conversations and interaction between advisor and advisee as confidential.

7. When appropriate the advisor should be willing to share his or her own feelings and personal experiences to serve as a positive role model for advisees.

8. The advisor should take advantage of training and professional growth opportunities related to advisory effectiveness.

9. The advisor must work cooperatively with faculty and administration to develop and maintain a harmonious schoolwide advisory program.

10. The advisor should foster quality communication and relationships among parents or guardians of advisees.

10 Ways Teachers Can Prepare Themselves For The Role Of Advisor

1. To be an affirming advisor, it is more important to listen than to give advice. Don't feel frustrated if you can't instantly solve a student's problems. Realize that you *are* helping—by listening, and by responding positively to the student.

2. It takes time for an atmosphere of trust to evolve within a group. Don't expect too much too soon. Allow time for trust to develop.

3. An atmosphere of trust can be established only when the adolescent believes that confidences will not be betrayed. It is important to respect the privacy of your students. Discuss also with your colleagues those circumstances under which it might be in the child's best interests to reveal a confidence, as when the child or another is in real danger.

4. Develop and practice good observation skills. Be sensitive to student attention spans, health and social habits, mood swings, and body language. Use anecdotal records, checklists, and other quick-and-easy recording devices to gather data that will help you know students better.

5. Teach yourself to facilitate discussions that are not simply question-and-answer sessions. Learn to ask the kind of open-ended question that stimulates thinking.

6. A sense of humor will get you through the year. You may not be a comedian, and that is perfectly all right. A fine and useful sense of humor simply means that you don't take yourself too seriously, and that you choose to see humor in a situation.

7. When working with young people, it is much more effective to *model* good coping skills than it is to give lectures. Attention to your own personal growth may be the best gift you can give your students.

8. Give students *time* to think. There is nothing wrong with a little silence as a child is groping for a way to express a feeling or idea.

9. Learn to be tolerant of the values of your students if they differ from your own.

10. If you can make a special attempt to understand the uncertain, often bewildering, position of an adolescent, you will become more accepting and non-judgmental—two traits that truly might make a difference in a young life.

10 PLUS 10

Dos And Ten Don'ts For Advisors

DO

1. Do agree to take an advisory group and give it your best effort.

2. Do serve as the key adult advocate in the school for each of your advisory students.

3. Do compile a detailed profile or portfolio of important information about each of your advisory students.

4. Plan and carry out regularly-scheduled programs comprised of an abundance of hands-on and interactive activities.

5. Plan lessons and projects to enhance advisees' self-esteem and sense of self-worth.

6. Give advisees ownership in the program through opportunities for decision-making and activity selection.

7. Honor your advisees and respect their individuality.

8. Hold all confidences sacred and secret.

9. Do be tolerant.

10. Be quick to listen and slow to criticize.

11. Be open-minded and attentive to values and beliefs differing from your own.

12. Do foster quality communication and interaction with the parents of your advisory students.

13. Do promote the advisory concept throughout the school community every chance you get.

14. Do implement the established advisory curriculum and take advantage of the optional ways to use advisory time.

15. Do share "part of yourself" with advisory students when appropriate to do so.

16. Do place a high value on the advisory program as an integral part of the school day and the school curriculum.

17. Do seek support and training for your advisory role from colleagues and administrators.

18. Maintain your faith in the advisory program regardless of the program's shortcomings or limitations.

19. Do strive to grow each year in your role as an advisory teacher.

20. Cultivate and maintain a sense of humor at all times even when it hurts.

DON'T

1. Don't have unrealistic program expectations—too much, too fast, too soon.

2. Don't put barriers between yourself and the students.

3. Don't copy another school or district program without personalizing or customizing it to meet your students' needs.

4. Don't expect all students in your advisory group to like each other or you, especially in the beginning.

5. Don't tolerate student put-downs of any type.

6. Don't forget to help one another to be successful in the program.

7. Don't be unwilling to seek outside resources.

8. Don't forget to have fun with your kids.

9. Don't be unprepared.

10. Don't doom the program to failure by complaining about it or discussing it in a negative manner.

ADVISORY PROGRAM SCHEDULING

OPTION ONE:

Student begins each day with advisory teacher for a designated 20–30 minute period of time.

Advantages:

1. Student starts the day on a positive note with small advisory group and teacher advocate.
2. Academic school day is not broken up by affective advisory program.
3. Schedule is consistent and easy to follow.

Disadvantages:

1. Advisory time can too easily be used up for housekeeping and administrative tasks with little time left for advisory activities.
2. Student has no time to report or reflect on how school day is going.
3. Advisory preparation time adds to burden of school-day preparation.

OPTION TWO:

Student begins each day with advisor. They spend 10 minutes on housekeeping or administrative tasks. On two designated days each week, 5–10 minutes are deducted from each class period so that an additional or longer advisory period is created and inserted between two other periods. It is during this time that the organized curriculum is implemented.

Advantages:

1. Two advisory periods are available on selected days, one for advisory tasks and one for administrative tasks.

2. Student begins each day on a positive note with advisory group and teacher advocate.
3. Administrative or housekeeping tasks are not taken away from academic time.
4. Advisory is easy to schedule as advisory time can be scheduled between any two periods.

Disadvantages:

1. Advisory tasks possible only two days a week, so advisory becomes more administrative than affective in nature.
2. Advisory adds to school-day preparation time.
3. Teacher must teach an additional period two days per week.

OPTION THREE:

A school can institute a "drop period" schedule to accommodate the advisory program. For this option, a period is eliminated from the daily schedule on a rotating basis (either two, three, four, or, ideally, five days a week), and the advisory class is put in its place.

Advantages:

1. The planner has a fair amount of scheduling freedom. When advisory time is scheduled daily, two days can be devoted to formal advisory curriculum activities, one is set aside for administrative tasks, and the remaining two days may be used for alternative advisory activities. When fewer days are allotted for advisory classes, the scheduler will, of course, plan other combinations of advisory activities.
2. The burden of giving up academic time to make room for advisory time is shared among the teachers.
3. Scheduling is easy as a period is eliminated from the daily schedule on a rotating basis.
4. Advisory time is scheduled in place of something else and not in addition to everything else.

Disadvantages:

1. Some effort required to plan rotating schedule.
2. May be difficult to meet state guidelines for prescribed academic day.

Adapted from *Advisory Middle Grades Advisee/Advisor Program* by Imogene Forte and Sandra Schurr. Nashville, TN: Incentive Publications, 1991. Used by permission.

OVERVIEW OF ONE MODEL FOR A COMPLETE MIDDLE GRADES ADVISORY PROGRAM

One model for a complete middle grades advisory program for three grade levels incorporates four major themes.

1. **School Culture & Academic Survival**
2. **Communication**
3. **Self-Concept & Relationships**
4. **Problem-Solving & Decision-Making**

In this program each theme contains a total of nine separate lesson plans that have a standard format and optional set of advisory tasks for extension or follow-up activities. It is recommended that the School Culture & Academic Survival and Communication themes be presented during the first semester and that the second semester's focus be on Self-Concept & Relationships and Problem-Solving & Decision-Making. Because advisory programs vary from school to school with regard to scheduling and time allocations, this curriculum is planned to afford flexibility in presentation to meet widely-varying individual school needs. The core set of required activities is supported by a collection of optional projects to accommodate advisory groups that meet daily or groups that meet fewer times each week. This program is designed to be flexible, manageable, and interactive.

The outline for each of the nine core curricular lesson plans is concise and uniform. Each activity has a title, purpose, points to ponder, and projects to pursue. The purpose is the objective of the lesson; points to ponder are discussion questions for the lesson; and the projects to pursue are extension ideas for the lesson. In addition, each of the four themes features a set of investigation topics on relevant subjects organized around Bloom's Taxonomy. It is suggested that advisory programs which meet all year long supplement this established curriculum with a variety of other school-based events such as silent sustained reading times, community speakers or projects, study periods, intramural competitions, and pencil-and-paper activities from supporting materials.

The following six pages present the scope and sequence charts for each of the four themes at three grade levels, the table of contents of activities for each level, program overview for each level, and a sample lesson plan for each level.

Adapted from *Advisory Middle Grades Advisee/Advisor Program* by Imogene Forte and Sandra Schurr. Nashville, TN: Incentive Publications, 1991. Used by permission.

Scope & Sequence Charts For Three Levels

SCHOOL CULTURE & ACADEMIC SURVIVAL

	SCHOOL CLIMATE	SOCIETY	CODE OF CONDUCT	*X-CUR. ACT. & CELEB.	TRADITIONS & HEROES	LEARNING STYLES	STUDY HABITS	TEST-TAKING	HOME/SCHOOL CONNECTIONS
Level I	Transition	Fire & Tornado Drills	Dress Code	Clubs & Teams	School History	Determining Your Style	Planning	Types of Tests	Homework
Level II	Spirit	Public Address System	Behavior Expectations	Assemblies & Performances	Newspapers & Yearbooks	Learning Process	Organizing	Test-Taking Tips	Report Cards
Level III	Pride	Visitor Procedures	Attendance Policies	Community Involvement	Heroes	Right & Left Brain Learning	Using Technology	Using Test Results	Parent Conferences

* EXTRACURRICULAR ACTIVITIES & CELEBRATIONS

COMMUNICATION

	BODY LANGUAGE	SPEAKING	LISTENING	READING	WRITING	CONVERSATIONS	MEDIA	ENRICHMENT ARTS	HOME/SCHOOL
Level I	Nonverbal Communication	Discussion	General Listening	Reading for Survival	Social Writing	Gossip	Telephone	Art	Communication Boosters
Level II	Mood Portrayal	Argumentation	Personal Listening	Reading for Information	Organizational Writing	Slang	Radio & Television	Music	Communication Barriers
Level III	Facial Expressions	Debate	Interpersonal Listening	Reading for Pleasure	Personal Writing	Profanity	Newspaper	Drama	Communication Boundaries

SELF-CONCEPT & RELATIONSHIPS

	AWARENESS	NEEDS	VALUES	EXPECTATIONS	SPECIAL INTERESTS	GROUP DYNAMICS	PEERS	AUTHORITY	CONFLICTS
Level I	Physical Self	Personal Needs	Values	Personal Goals (Long & Short-Term Goals)	Hobbies	Groups	Cliques	Parents	Prejudice
Level II	Social Self	Emotional Needs	Beliefs	Career Goals (Long & Short-Term Goals)	Talents	Teamwork	Peer Pressure	School	Stereotypes
Level III	Sexual Self	Social Needs	Ethics	Lifetime Goals (Long & Short-Term)	Avocations	Organizations	Boy/Girl Relationships	Community	Resolution Strategies

PROBLEM-SOLVING & DECISION-MAKING

	IDENTIFY PROBLEMS	PERSONAL HABITS	HEALTH & FITNESS	ROLE DECISIONS	RESPONSIBILITY	WORK ETHICS	TEENAGE PROBLEMS	RISK-TAKING	CHOICES
Level I	At Home	Rest & Relaxation	Nutrition	Membership	Responsibility for Time	Work as a Necessity	Stress & Runaways	Nature of Risk-Taking	Individual Choices
Level II	At School	Hygiene & Grooming	Exercise	Citizenship	Responsibility for Money	Work as a Responsibility	Depression & School Dropout	Dangers of Risk-Taking	Group Choices
Level III	In the Community	Courtesy and Consideration	Substance Abuse	Leadership	Responsibility for Natural Resources	Work as a Privilege	Pregnancies & Suicides	Growth of Risk-Taking	Impact Choices

Table Of Contents For Three Levels

PROBLEM-SOLVING & DECISION-MAKING
LEVEL I

TABLE OF CONTENTS

PROBLEM-SOLVING & DECISION-MAKING

INVESTIGATION TOPICS 76
HOME SWEET HOME 77
    Identifying Problems / At Home
R & R REVIEW 79
    Personal Habits / Rest & Relaxation
NUTRITION KNOW-HOW 81
    Health & Fitness / Nutrition
MEMBERS ONLY 83
    Role Decisions / Membership
TIME LINE 85
    Responsibility / Responsibility For Time
OFF TO WORK WE GO 87
    Work Ethics / Work As A Necessity
YOU CAN'T RUN AWAY FROM YOUR PROBLEMS 89
    Teenage Problems / Stress & Runaways
I'LL TRY MOST ANYTHING ONCE 91
    Risk-Taking / Nature of Risk-Taking
LET'S PULL TOGETHER ON THIS 93
    Choices / Group Choices
A PENNY FOR YOUR THOUGHTS 95
SUPPLEMENTARY ACTIVITIES & PROJECTS FROM
SUPPORTING MATERIALS 96

PROBLEM-SOLVING & DECISION-MAKING
LEVEL II

TABLE OF CONTENTS

PROBLEM-SOLVING & DECISION-MAKING

INVESTIGATION TOPICS 76
SCHOOL COOL 77
    Identifying Problems / Problems At School
TIME TO SPRUCE UP 79
    Personal Habits / Hygiene & Grooming
LIVING THE PLEDGE OF ALLEGIANCE 81
    Role Decisions / Citizenship
ACTION AUCTION 83
    Health & Fitness / Exercises
MONEY MATTERS 85
    Responsibility / Responsibility For Money
WHO'S RESPONSIBLE HERE? 87
    Work Ethics / Work As A Responsibility
EDUCATION IS THE ANSWER 89
    Teenage Problems / Depression & School Dropouts
LOOK BEFORE YOU LEAP! 91
    Risk-Taking / Dangers Of Risk-Taking
IS THIS RIGHT FOR ME? 93
    Choices / Individual Choices
A PENNY FOR YOUR THOUGHTS 95
SUPPLEMENTARY ACTIVITIES & PROJECTS FROM
SUPPORTING MATERIALS 96

PROBLEM-SOLVING & DECISION-MAKING
LEVEL III

TABLE OF CONTENTS

PROBLEM-SOLVING & DECISION-MAKING 76

INVESTIGATION TOPICS 77
COMMUNITY CONSCIOUS 79
    Identifying Problems / In The Community
IF YOU PLEASE 81
    Personal Habits / Courtesy & Consideration
SAY "NO!" 83
    Health & Fitness / Substance Abuse
TAKE ME TO YOUR LEADER! 85
    Role Decisions / Leadership
IT'S YOUR WORLD 87
    Responsibility / Responsibility For Natural Resources
PRIVILEGED TO WORK 89
    Work Ethics / Work As A Privilege
DON'T BECOME A STATISTIC! 91
    Teenage Problems / Pregnancies & Suicides
NOTHING VENTURED, NOTHING GAINED! 93
    Risk-Taking / Growth of Risk-Taking
I DIDN'T THINK IT WOULD TURN OUT THIS WAY! 95
    Choices / Impact Choices
A PENNY FOR YOUR THOUGHTS ....
SUPPLEMENTARY ACTIVITIES & PROJECTS FROM
SUPPORTING MATERIALS 96

Investigation Tasks For Three Levels

INVESTIGATION TOPICS

KNOWLEDGE

List the types of information found in your student handbook. Record five key points you do not want to forget.

COMPREHENSION

Paraphrase each of the following sets of guidelines found in your student handbook:
   a. Attendance Policy
   b. Dress Code
   c. Causes and Procedures for Suspension or Expulsion
   d. Access to School Clinic
   e. Use of School Library

APPLICATION

Prepare a true/false quiz to test your peers on the information in the student handbook.

ANALYSIS

Diagram a flow chart to illustrate the steps in following an important procedure found in the student handbook.

SYNTHESIS

Formulate a clever plan to ensure that every student in your class shares the student handbook with his/her parent(s) or guardian(s) at home.

EVALUATION

Defend this statement: Students, parents/guardians, and teachers should all have a role in developing the contents of a student handbook.

INVESTIGATION TOPICS

KNOWLEDGE

Record your responses to each of these starter statements:
   a. The main purpose of the school calendar is...
   b. The most important dates on the school calendar for me this year are...because...
   c. I refer to the school calendar most often when...
   d. One way to improve the usefulness of the school calendar for students is...

COMPREHENSION

Conclude what a visitor might be able to tell about your school culture by examining the school calendar.

APPLICATION

Develop a more extensive format for your school calendar that would improve its overall appearance and utility.

ANALYSIS

Debate this idea: "People who use calendars are more organized than people who do not."

SYNTHESIS

Plan a "thought a day" calendar for your advisory classroom for one month. List something for each day. Be sure to include a variety of ideas such as a famous person's birthday, riddles and jokes, important historical events, information trivia, quotations, or rhetorical questions.

EVALUATION

Determine all the reasons why you think school calendars are an important tool for students, parents, and teachers. Rank-order them from the most popular to the least popular. Now interview several people to find out their reasons for using the school calendar. Record your findings on a graph.

INVESTIGATION TOPICS

KNOWLEDGE

On your school campus map, label the rooms where you have classes, and trace the shortest route from one place to another.

COMPREHENSION

Study the school map, then summarize some ways you could improve your school's traffic patterns.

APPLICATION

Redesign the floor plan of your school to make it a perfect facility from a student's point of view.

ANALYSIS

Inspect the school map and show a spot that:

   a. Is popular with students.
   b. Is popular with teachers.
   c. Is the site of the greatest growth for most students.
   d. Has the most pleasant sounds, sights, or smells.
   e. Is a constant source of inspiration for its learners.
   f. Has the most potential for you.

SYNTHESIS

On the school map, uncover a location that has a real problem associated with it. Outline the problem and come up with a creative, unique solution to the problem.

EVALUATION

If your school could have just five rooms, what five would you choose and why?

Sample Lesson Plan—Level One

LET'S PULL TOGETHER ON THIS

PURPOSE

To examine the process and outcomes of group choices.

POINTS TO PONDER

1. What school or community groups do you belong to and why did you choose to get involved with them?

2. How do groups tend to make decisions or choices? How does *Robert's Rules of Order* help with this process?

3. What does it mean to reach consensus in making group choices? How does this differ from voting or the notion of "majority rules"?

4. When you are working with a group, what influences your decision-making ability or choices the most?

5. What do we mean by "lobbying" and how can it influence a group's decision-making process?

PROJECTS TO PURSUE

1. Obtain one or more examples of a group's constitution or bylaws to determine how they help the group make fair choices or decisions.

2. Design a consensus-building activity for your advisory class. Outline the task(s) and guidelines to be followed in making a choice or decision.

3. William Jennings Bryan said, "Destiny is not a matter of chance; it is a matter of choice." Write one paragraph reflecting your reaction to this statement. Then divide into small groups to discuss the various reactions, and think of specific examples of individuals or groups whose choices helped determine their destiny.

IS THIS RIGHT FOR ME?

PROBLEM-SOLVING & DECISION-MAKING
Choices
Individual Choices - Level II

PURPOSE

To explore choices and their consequences.

POINTS TO PONDER

1. What choices are you able to make about the schooling process? Consider choice of subjects to take, teachers, school hours, time and place to study, assignments to complete, and people to interact with.

2. What choices are you able to make about your life outside of school? Consider what you eat and wear, when you go to bed and get up, how you use your leisure time, who you choose as friends, and how you earn or spend your money.

3. It has been said that we live in a multiple option society. Do you agree or disagree with this statement and why?

4. What are some wise and unwise choices you have made recently? What influenced your decisions?

5. How could the schools offer students more choices in their learning process?

PROJECTS TO PURSUE

1. Create an advisory advice board or a "Dear ..." advisory column for your class. Practice giving and receiving advice that involves making decisions and choices.

2. Write a true story about a time when you had to make an individual choice. Divide the story into ten parts. Put each part on a separate card or piece of paper. Scramble these and let another student see if he/she can put them in the correct order.

3. Find a picture of someone making an individual choice. Write a story which includes the picture but leaves out the ending. Have several other people write an ending to the story. How and why do the endings differ?

Sample Lesson Plan—Level Three

I Didn't Think It Would Turn Out This Way!

PURPOSE

To evaluate influences and outcomes related to impact choice-making.

POINTS TO PONDER

1. It has been said that we are our choices. What does this mean to you?

2. How do the educational choices you make today influence your career choices of tomorrow?

3. Can you think of an experience you had where a choice you made was a good one short term but a poor one long term? Tell about it and what you might do differently now.

4. What might be the long-range impact of each of these immediate choices?

    a. A student decides to skip school.
    b. A friend decides to spread a malicious story.
    c. A teenager decides to run away from home.
    d. An athlete decides to smoke and drink at a party.
    e. A young consumer decides to shoplift at his/her favorite store.

5. What are some choices you can make to help you plan for the future?

PROJECTS TO PURSUE

1. Develop an ideal timeline that shows the important choices you hope to make for the future. Include important dates and events that project the next fifty years.

2. Go on an imaginary shopping spree and create a banner or mural to show how you would spend $1 million that you have just won at the state lottery. Be sure it reflects your personal choices for today and the future.

3. Draw a pictorial representation of an environmental issue that has created serious problems for today's generation because of poor choices from past generations.

10 PLUS 2

Children's Picture Books To Use To Help Students In Transition Express And Understand Feelings And Emotions

TITLE: *Alexander and the Terrible, Horrible, No Good, Very Bad Day*
AUTHOR: Judith Viorst
ILLUSTRATOR: Ray Cruz
PUBLISHER: Macmillan Publishing Company
SYNOPSIS: Join Alexander as he experiences a terrible day and decides that it probably wouldn't get any better—even in Australia.

TITLE: *The Fall of Freddie the Leaf: A Story of Life for All Ages*
AUTHOR: Leo Buscaglia, Ph.D.
ILLUSTRATOR: None
PUBLISHER: Charles B. Slack, Inc.
SYNOPSIS: In this allegory of life and death, Freddie the Leaf experiences friendship, growth, change, and death.

TITLE: *The First Forest*
AUTHOR: John Gile
ILLUSTRATOR: Tom Heflin
PUBLISHER: Worzalla
SYNOPSIS: In this moving story, we see greed and selfishness as harmful and tenderness and kindness as gifts which heal.

TITLE: *The Hating Book*
AUTHOR: Charlotte Zolotow
ILLUSTRATOR: Ben Schecter
PUBLISHER: Harper & Row
SYNOPSIS: This story reinforces the importance of communication, honesty, and understanding the reasons for our own and our friends' behaviors.

TITLE: *Hey, Al*
AUTHOR: Arthur Yorinks
ILLUSTRATOR: Richard Egielski
PUBLISHER: Sunburst Books
SYNOPSIS: In this story, Al the janitor and his dog Eddie find that the grass isn't "always greener" on the other side.

TITLE: *Love You Forever*
AUTHOR: Robert Munsch
ILLUSTRATOR: Sheila McGraw
PUBLISHER: Firefly Books
SYNOPSIS: This beautiful "lullaby" shows the enduring nature of parents' love for their children, no matter their age.

TITLE: *Oh, the Places You'll Go!*
AUTHOR: Dr. Seuss
ILLUSTRATOR: Dr. Seuss
PUBLISHER: Random House
SYNOPSIS: This is a wise and honest look at life and success, a challenge to us to be all that we can, no matter our age.

TITLE: *People*
AUTHOR: Peter Spier
ILLUSTRATOR: Peter Spier
PUBLISHER: Doubleday
SYNOPSIS: The beautifully-detailed illustrations in this book celebrate differences in people and the acceptance of the unique qualities which make us human.

TITLE: *The Runaway Bunny*
AUTHOR: Margaret Wise Brown
ILLUSTRATOR: Clement Hurd
PUBLISHER: Harper & Row
SYNOPSIS: In this story a bunny insists on running away. His mother constantly assures him that she will be there wherever he goes.

TITLE: *There's a Nightmare in My Closet*
AUTHOR: Mercer Mayer
ILLUSTRATOR: Mercer Mayer
PUBLISHER: The Dial Press
SYNOPSIS: This story shows us how a youngster faces his fears, especially the nightmare hiding in his closet.

TITLE: *The True Story of the Three Little Pigs (by A. Wolf)*
AUTHOR: Jon Scieszka
ILLUSTRATOR: Lane Smith
PUBLISHER: Viking Kestrel
SYNOPSIS: Here is the "real" story as told from the wolf's point of view. He feels that he was mistreated and misunderstood!

TITLE: *The Velveteen Rabbit*
AUTHOR: Margery Williams
ILLUSTRATOR: Florence Graham
PUBLISHER: Platt & Munk, Publishers
SYNOPSIS: Find out "How Toys Become Real" in this appealing story about a boy and his love for his toy bunny.

SAMPLE LESSON PLAN FOR USING A PICTURE BOOK TO EXPLORE BEHAVIORS

TITLE: *The Hating Book*
AUTHOR: Charlotte Zolotow
ILLUSTRATOR: Ben Schecter
PUBLISHER: Harper & Row
SYNOPSIS: This story reinforces how important it is to communicate, be honest, and try to understand the reasons for our own and our friends' behaviors.

POINTS TO PONDER AND DISCUSS

1. What was the basic conflict in the story?

2. Do you think there is a fine line between love and hate? Why do you feel as you do?

3. How can you tell when someone is mad at you?

4. How do you show your feelings when you are really angry with someone?

5. Do most people fight over important things or trivial things? Why?

6. Why is it so hard to say "I'm sorry"?

7. What are the things you don't like in other people?

PROJECTS TO PLAN AND DO

A. Prepare and present a skit showing an incident where a person is mad at someone else. What caused the problem? How did both parties act during the conflict? How was it resolved?

B. For a cooperative group of four: Cut the letters of the word FRIENDSHIP out of light-colored sheets of 9" x 12" construction paper (one letter from each sheet of paper). Using colored pens or pencils, on each letter write the names of friends and descriptive adjectives, all words whose initial letters are the same as the construction paper letter. Post in your classroom.

SAMPLE LESSON PLAN FOR USING A PICTURE BOOK TO DEVELOP APPRECIATION OF DIFFERENCES IN PEOPLE

TITLE: *People*
AUTHOR: Peter Spier
ILLUSTRATOR: Peter Spier
PUBLISHER: Doubleday
SYNOPSIS: The beautifully-detailed illustrations in this book celebrate differences in people. We are all "PEOPLE" on one planet and we have many similarities, but it is accepting one another's unique qualities which makes us human.

POINTS TO PONDER AND DISCUSS

1. What is the special idea that Peter Spier conveys in this book?

2. How does he highlight or celebrate the differences in people?

3. What if each person was a clone of everyone else? How would things be different?

4. What do you think makes you unique or different from your friends? other members of your family? kids living in other parts of the world?

5. What ten key words best describe the illustrations in this book?

6. What ten things would you do to change the world?

PROJECTS TO PLAN AND DO

A. Fill a bag with artifacts that represent who you are and bring it to school. Share them with a buddy, or with your classmates.

B. Choose a culture whose people are very different from you and research it. Select and share at least ten facts you learned from your study.

10 PLUS 10 Springboards For Discussion Starters And Journal Writing In Advisory

1. A reaction to a particular point with which you strongly agree or disagree.

2. A question about a concept that confuses you.

3. A description about a situation that frustrates you.

4. A paraphrase of a difficult or complex idea that interests you.

5. A summary of a special time or feeling.

6. A comment on what you think about a given person, place, or thing.

7. A reaction to an idea that confirms or questions a particular belief you hold.

8. A discussion of the pros and cons of an issue important to your well-being.

9. A comparison and contrast of two opposing ideas that intrigue you.

10. A history of a significant emotional event you experienced.

11. Which is the stronger sex—male or female?

12. Is it easier in today's world to be a kid or an adult?

13. Would you rather have good looks or good grades?

14. If you could see into your future, would you want to?

15. Which is better for you—cooperation or competition?

16. How would you define maturity?

17. What makes an ideal hero?

18. How would you recognize a perfect day?

19. Do people learn more from their mistakes or from their successes?

20. What would be the best thing that could happen to you?

10 PLUS 10

Possible Advisory Activities In Addition To Regular Curriculum Activities

1. Periodic study sessions

2. Silent reading

3. Individual academic counseling

4. Special team projects

5. Special school projects

6. Current events

7. Guest speakers

8. Indoor and outdoor games

9. Intramural contests

10. Club or activity days

11. Holiday celebrations

12. Films or videotapes

13. Community projects

14. Storytime

15. Career exploration

16. School spirit week

17. Student council events

18. School pride events

19. Journal writing

20. Contests

10 PLUS 1 Quotations From Well-Known Figures To Use As Discussion Sparkers

1. *Winston Churchill:* The price of greatness is responsibility.

2. *Charles De Gaulle:* Silence is the ultimate weapon of power.

3. *Albert Einstein:* The most beautiful thing we can experience is the mysterious. It is the source of all true art and science.

4. *Dwight D. Eisenhower:* Leadership is the art of getting someone else to do something you want done because he wants it done.

5. *Henry Ford:* Failure is only the opportunity to begin again more intelligently.

6. *Mahatma Gandhi:* No culture can live if it attempts to be exclusive.

7. *Martin Luther King:* Injustice anywhere is a threat to justice everywhere.

8. *Vince Lombardi:* It's not whether you get knocked down, it's whether you get up.

9. *Margaret Thatcher:* Being powerful is like being a lady. If you have to tell people you are, you aren't.

10. *Golda Meir:* You cannot shake hands with a clenched fist.

11. *John Mosley:* All things are difficult before they are easy.

SOME DISCUSSION QUESTIONS TO CONSIDER:

1. Do you generally agree or disagree with this quotation? Explain.
2. Give an example from history or personal experience to illustrate the idea behind this quotation.
3. Why do you think the author of this quotation chose to say what he or she said?
4. How might you restate the quotation in your own words?

(SAMPLE) STUDENT INTEREST INVENTORY

Write a spontaneous personal reaction to complete each sentence below.

1. The thing I do that I am proudest of is _____
   because _____.

2. My favorite leisure time activity is _____.

3. I would like to make improvement in _____
   because _____.

4. My favorite book is _____.

5. One thing I enjoy doing with my family is _____
   because _____.

6. I think my family's rules are _____
   because _____.

7. One thing I enjoy doing with my friends is _____

8. One thing I would change about my home is _____
   because _____.

9. I would like for my friends to think I am _____
   because _____.

10. When I am an adult I would like to _____
    because _____.

11. One thing I would change about my community is _____
    because _____.

12. When I think of school, I feel _____
    because _____.

13. The thing I like best about school is _____
    because _____.

14. The thing I like least about school is _____
    because _____.

15. The trait I admire most in a teacher is _____
    because _____.

16. I think homework is _____
    because _____.

17. I think our school rules are _____
    because _____.

18. My favorite school subject is _____.

19. One thing I would change about my school is _____
    because _____.

20. I hope **ADVISORY** will help me to _____
    _____.

Adapted from *Advisory Middle Grades Advisee/Advisor Program* by Imogene Forte and Sandra Schurr. Nashville, TN: Incentive Publications, ©1991. Used by permission.

(SAMPLE) STUDENT ADVISORY QUESTIONNAIRE

Please read carefully. Circle the number that best represents your response using this rating scale:

1	2	3	4	5
STRONGLY AGREE	AGREE	UNDECIDED	DISAGREE	STRONGLY DISAGREE

1. My advisory period is important to me. 1 2 3 4 5

2. I look forward to my advisory group time. 1 2 3 4 5

3. My advisor listens to me when I have a problem. 1 2 3 4 5

4. My advisor treats me as an individual of worth in my own right. 1 2 3 4 5

5. My advisor takes time to talk about things that are important to me & my future. 1 2 3 4 5

6. My advisor helps me do better in school. 1 2 3 4 5

7. My advisor believes in & enjoys advisory group time. 1 2 3 4 5

8. We talk about a variety of things in advisory group, such as school problems, study skills, making decisions, & getting along with others. 1 2 3 4 5

9. Advisees are involved in planning advisory group activities and projects. 1 2 3 4 5

10. The lessons planned for my advisory group are interesting. 1 2 3 4 5

11. The activities presented to my advisory group are meaningful to my age group. 1 2 3 4 5

12. The advisory period meets often enough to satisfy my needs. 1 3 3 4 5

13. I would miss advisory time if we didn't have it. 1 2 3 4 5

14. My parents/guardian understand(s) the goals of my advisory program. 1 2 3 4 5

15. My parents/guardian would call my advisor first if I had a problem with one of my classes at school. 1 2 3 4 5

16. The advisory program encourages school spirit. 1 2 3 4 5

17. The advisory program is planned to take advantage of community resources. 1 2 3 4 5

18. The advisory program makes school a better place for most students. 1 2 3 4 5

19. The advisory program helps my parents/guardian know more about & be more involved in the overall school program. 1 2 3 4 5

20. The advisory program helps me get better grades in school. 1 2 3 4 5

21. The advisory program helps me make & keep friends at school. 1 2 3 4 5

Adapted from *Advisory Middle Grades Advisee/Advisor Program* by Imogene Forte and Sandra Schurr. Nashville, TN: Incentive Publications, ©1991. Used by permission.

(SAMPLE)
INSTRUMENT FOR EVALUATING AN ADVISORY PROGRAM'S EFFECTIVENESS
Part One
The Teacher Self-Checklist

This checklist should be completed individually by each advisory teacher. Comments should be written on a separate sheet of paper and attached to this sheet.

		Yes	No
1.	My school, county, or district has developed a comprehensive advisory program complete with philosophy statement, goals, objectives, & activities.		
2.	I have a copy of the full advisory program for my grade level.		
3.	The advisory program in my school, district, or county has a name and a logo.		
4.	Each student in my school has contact with his/her advisory teacher at a regularly scheduled time each day.		
5.	There is a person(s) in my school who supports, coordinates, monitors, and evaluates the advisory program.		
6.	The advisory activities are appropriate for students in my grade level.		
7.	The weekly schedule of events for advisory is appropriate.		
8.	I have ample advisory activities to choose from.		
9.	I am free to deviate from the activities in the advisory manual to take advantage of teachable moments on a timely basis.		
10.	The advisory activities encourage a variety of teaching methods and materials not dependent on paper & pencil activities.		
11.	The advisory period is a "special" and important part of our school day with few interruptions.		
12.	The number of students in my advisory class is appropriate.		
13.	Every certified staff member in my school is an advisory teacher with few exceptions.		
14.	The majority of students appear to find the advisory program meaningful & relevant to their needs.		
15.	The majority of parents give positive support to the advisory program.		
16.	The majority of faculty give positive support to the advisory program.		
17.	I give positive support to the advisory program.		
18.	Effective education is an integral part of my school day.		

Adapted from *Advisory Middle Grades Advisee/Advisor Program* by Imogene Forte and Sandra Schurr. Nashville, TN: Incentive Publications, ©1991. Used by permission.

(SAMPLE)

INSTRUMENT FOR EVALUATING AN ADVISORY PROGRAM'S EFFECTIVENESS

Part Two
The Advisory Class Observation Form

This form should be used when a person is called in to observe an advisory class. The results of this observation can be compared to the teacher's self-checklist. The numbers in parentheses refer to the number of related questions from the team's self-checklist.

	Yes	No
1. The advisory teacher is in possession of a full copy of the advisory program for his/her grade level (1, 2, 3).		
2. Advisory time occurs at a regularly scheduled time during the school day.		
3. The advisory activity for the day seemed appropriate for the age of the students (6, 7).		
4. The activity for the day encouraged a variety of teaching methods and/or materials (8, 10).		
5. There were no unnecessary outside interruptions during this advisory class (11).		
6. The number of students in this advisory class is appropriate (12).		
7. The students in this advisory class appear to find the day's topic and/or activity relevant & meaningful to themselves (9, 14).		
8. The teacher appeared to be positively involved in the activity of the day (17).		
9. The teacher appeared prepared for advisory class (18).		
10. The overall classroom environment appears to reinforce the advisory concept (18).		

Adapted from *Advisory Middle Grades Advisee/Advisor Program* by Imogene Forte and Sandra Schurr. Nashville, TN: Incentive Publications, ©1991. Used by permission.

(SAMPLE)

INSTRUMENT FOR EVALUATING AN ADVISORY PROGRAM'S EFFECTIVENESS

Part Three
Teacher Interview Form

This form should be used by an outside observer to interview selected advisory teachers regarding the effectiveness of the advisory program and the teacher's feelings toward the program.

1. How do you generally feel about the advisory program in your school?

_____

_____

_____

_____

2. If you could change one thing regarding the advisory program at your school, what would you change?

_____

_____

_____

3. Tell me about the type of activities that have been most successful with your students during the advisory period.

_____

_____

_____

4. Tell me about the type of activities that have been least successful with your students during the advisory period.

_____

_____

_____

5. Summarize your feelings about the variety of methods and materials afforded by the present advisory curriculum.

_____

_____

_____

6. How well do you feel the advisory program helps to meet the affective needs of your students?

_____

_____

_____

Adapted from *Advisory Middle Grades Advisee/Advisor Program* by Imogene Forte and Sandra Schurr. Nashville, TN: Incentive Publications, ©1991. Used by permission.

SELECTED RESOURCES FOR DISCUSSION STARTERS AND SESSION SPARKERS FOR ADVISORY SESSIONS

Breeden, T. and Mosley, J. *The Cooperative Learning Companion.* Nashville, TN: Incentive Publications, 1991.
A teacher-friendly collection of aids, bulletin board ideas, reproducible forms and guides, and techniques for teaching cooperative skills.

Cook, S. *180 Days Around The World.* Nashville, TN: Incentive Publications, 1993.
Students "travel around the world," to gain information about important world locations and the people who inhabit them, and to develop valuable research skills.

Cook, S. *Story Journal For Middle Grades.* Nashville, TN: Incentive Publications, 1990.
Seventeen carefully-selected pieces of middle grades literature provide the foundation for a journal of activities and questions based on Bloom's Taxonomy.

Farnette, C., Forte, I., and Loss, B. *People Need Each Other (Revised).* Nashville, TN: Incentive Publications, 1989.
Will help students acquire an understanding of themselves and others as they become aware of the skills and attitudes necessary for satisfying interpersonal relationships.

Forte, I. *Think About It! Middle Grades.* Nashville, TN: Incentive Publications, 1981.
A unique collection of activities, projects, puzzles, and games designed to stimulate thinking skills.

Forte, I. and MacKenzie, J. *Pulling Together For Cooperative Learning.* Nashville, TN: Incentive Publications, 1991.
High-interest basic-skills activities designed to stimulate reading, writing, and reasoning skills with a team learning approach.

Forte, I. *One Nation, Fifty States.* Nashville, TN: Incentive Publications, 1993.
Content-based lessons and projects, "fast fact sheets," maps, and assessment pages will enable students to acquire a background knowledge of the fifty United States.

Forte, I. and Schurr, S. *Operation Orientation.* Nashville, TN: Incentive Publications, 1991.
Motivators, ice breakers, discussion sparkers, and get-acquainted activities to be used at the start of an advisory program, or at the beginning of any middle grades year.

Forte, I. *The Me I'm Learning To Be.* Nashville, TN: Incentive Publications, 1991.
Will help students learn to deal effectively with contemporary problems. Topics include peer pressure, family relationships, jealousy, and loyalty.

Forte, I. and MacKenzie, J. *Writing Survival Skills For The Middle Grades.* Nashville, TN: Incentive Publications, 1991.
Real-life writing activities from the business letter to a job application prepare students for success in tomorrow's world.

Frender, G. *Learning to Learn.* Nashville, TN: Incentive Publications, 1992.
Practical hints, methods, tips, procedures, resources, and tools that will help middle grades students succeed in school and life.

U.S. Social Studies Yellow Pages For Students & Teachers. Nashville, TN: Incentive Publications, 1993.
A time-saving collection of United States social studies information.

World Social Studies Yellow Pages For Students & Teachers. Nashville, TN: Incentive Publications, 1993.
A collection of important world social studies information including facts, charts, lists, and definitions.

ADVISORY TEACHER'S WRAP-UP, À LA BLOOM

KNOWLEDGE
Name three major ideas you consider important in an advisory program.

COMPREHENSION
Give examples of three ways an advisor might make an impact on an advisee's life.

APPLICATION
With a colleague, discuss one idea that both of you consider an essential element of an effective advisory program.

ANALYSIS
Identify five ways the role of advisor is different from the role of instructor.

SYNTHESIS
Brainstorm a list of creative acronyms/names for a school or a district advisor/advisee program.

EVALUATION
Select a statistic, quotation, or fact related to advisory that supports your philosophy of affective education.

COOPERATIVE LEARNING

Cooperative Learning Overview

COOPERATIVE LEARNING IS:
- Mutual success through a collaborative effort.
- Individual accountability and responsibility requiring each group member to contribute to the group's work to successfully meet desired goals.
- Face-to-face interaction.
- Group processing through discussion and evaluation of direction and working relationships.
- Appropriate use of collaborate skills and social skills.

TEACHER'S STEPS TO FOLLOW WHEN SETTING UP A COOPERATIVE LEARNING ACTIVITY:
1. Decide on the task and write out directions and guidelines.
2. Divide class into groups.
3. Assign a role to each group member.
4. Determine which social processing skills will be emphasized.
5. Review and discuss rules for functioning in a group.
6. Select a group and/or individual method for assessing group performance.

STUDENT ROLES FOR COOPERATIVE LEARNING:
- Coordinator/Manager
- Timekeeper
- Secretary/Recorder
- Evaluator
- Encourager
- Artist
- Reader
- Checker
- Praiser
- Go-For

STUDENT RULES FOR COOPERATIVE LEARNING:
- You are responsible for your behavior in your group.
- You are accountable for contributing to the assigned task.
- You must help any group member who wants, needs, or asks for help.
- You will ask the teacher for help only when everyone in the group has the same need.
- You may not "put down" another person in any way.

10 Important Cooperative Learning Questions To Find Answers For

1. What are the benefits of Cooperative Learning for today's middle level students?

2. How do Cooperative Learning groups differ from traditional student work groups?

3. How does a teacher prepare to move into Cooperative Learning?

4. What are some things to consider when moving into Cooperative Learning?

5. What are some things to consider when determining time limits for group activity?

6. What kinds of roles should be assigned to students in groups?

7. What are some preparations teachers can make to promote student Cooperative Learning success?

8. What are some classroom management techniques that can be employed to ensure Cooperative Learning success?

9. What are some things teachers can do to help uncooperative students learn to work effectively in cooperative groups?

10. How can teachers evaluate the work done by Cooperative Learning group members?

10 Definitions Essential To Cooperative Learning Success

1. **Structured Cooperative Learning:** A systematic process whereby the teacher facilitates small groups of students in their achievement of a group goal through collaborative interaction.

2. **The Teacher's Role in Cooperative Learning:** To specify objectives of lesson, determine group sizes and membership, explain task and goal structure, provide task assistance on a need basis, and evaluate students' academic achievements and social processing skills.

3. **The Student's Role in Cooperative Learning:** To work toward positive interdependence within a small group setting so that the group achieves its goal and the individual members are accountable for what is learned both individually and collectively.

4. **Group Processing Skills Necessary for Cooperative Learning:** The social and collaborative skills that will allow a group to work together in a harmonious manner and to maintain positive and effective working relationships while attempting to achieve group goals.

5. **Heterogeneous Groups:** Groups of students with diverse and varied achievement levels, interest/experience levels, and socioeconomic or ethnic backgrounds.

6. **Homogeneous Groups:** Groups of students with like or similar characteristics in such areas as ability levels, achievement levels, interest/experience levels, and socioeconomic or ethnic backgrounds.

7. **Positive Interdependence:** The mutual dependence of group members on one another, accompanied by an understanding that the success of each group member is dependent on the degree of success of the total group.

8. **Individual Accountability:** The valuing and assessment of an individual group member's contributions to total group success in achieving both affective and cognitive goals.

9. **Face-To-Face Interaction:** Sharing information, pooling knowledge, and coordinating past and present experiences to achieve mutual goals.

10. **Interpersonal and Small Group Skills:** The skills necessary for individuals within a small group to interact with one another in an accepting and reinforcing manner to solve problems and achieve mutually-established goals.

10 PLUS 1

Findings From The Published Literature To Document The Need For Cooperative Learning

1. FINDING
William Glasser concludes:

Four needs must be satisfied in order for students to choose motivated behavior. Those needs are to belong and to love, to gain power, to be free, and to have fun. When classrooms are organized in a way that introduces belonging, power, and freedom into the situation, students usually have fun. Learning follows.

Reference: Glasser, William. "Control Theory in the Classroom,"
The International Association for the Study of Cooperation in Education,
newsletter. Volume 8, Numbers 3 & 4, September 1987.

2. FINDING
David Johnson and Roger Johnson state:

What is cooperative learning and how does it differ from competitive and individualistic learning? In the competitive classroom, students work against one another to achieve a goal that only one or a few students can attain. Students are graded on a curve, which requires them to work faster and more accurately than their peers. In the individualistic classroom, students work by themselves to accomplish learning goals unrelated to those of the other students. Individual goals are assigned each day, students' efforts are evaluated on a fixed set of standards, and students are rewarded accordingly. In the cooperative classroom, students work together to accomplish shared goals. Students assigned to small groups learn the assigned material and make sure that the other members of their group learn it also. A criterion-referenced evaluation system is used regularly to ensure that students are learning.

Reference: Johnson, D. and Johnson, R. "Cooperative Small-Group Learning,"
Curriculum Report. Reston, VA: National Association of Secondary
School Principals. Vol. 14, No. 1, October 1984.

3. FINDING
Dewey summarizes:

One important means-ends relationship is the creation of a democratic social and learning environment in order to maintain a maximum degree of continuity between life inside and outside the school. The operational translation of this schools-society continuum in terms of democratic structure is the provision for student participation in planning the nature of the school environment and student learning experiences. These experiences should include an exchange of ideas, opinions, attitudes, feelings, and perceptions through discussions conducted in a systematic fashion among peers to clarify their understanding of their world.

Reference: Dewey, John. "Philosophy of Educational and Cooperative Learning," The International Association for the Study of Cooperation in Education, newsletter. Volume 8, Numbers 1 & 2, March 1987, p. 3.

4. FINDING
Nancy B. Graves and Theodore D. Graves cite:

The effect of cooperative learning on academic achievement now seems clear. There can be no further doubt that cooperative small-group learning methods which incorporate appropriate reward structures are far superior to traditional whole-class lecture/recitation methods in producing the very results which both educators and the public are demanding: improvement in the acquisition of basic academic skills. Consequently, given their psychological benefits for participants and their positive impact on intergroup relations as well, these methods deserve favorable attention from all educators.

Reference: Graves, Nancy B. & Graves, Theodore D. "The Effect of Cooperative Learning Methods on Academic Achievement: A Review of the Reviews," The International Association for the Study of Cooperation in Education, newsletter. Volume 5, Numbers 3 & 4, December 1984, p. 5.

5. FINDING
David Johnson and Roger Johnson summarize:

Teaching students interpersonal and small-group social skills produces both short-term and long-term outcomes. Short-term outcomes include greater learning, retention, and critical thinking. Long-term outcomes include greater employability and career success. If the potential of cooperative learning is to be realized, students must have the prerequisite interpersonal and small-group skills and be motivated to use them. These skills should be taught just as systematically as mathematics, social studies, or any other subject.

Reference: Johnson, D. and Johnson, R. "Social Skills for Successful Group Work," Educational Leadership. Alexandria, VA: Educational Association for Supervision and Curriculum Development, Vol. 47, No. 4, December 1989/January 1990.

6. FINDING

Spencer Kagan writes an answer to the questions:

Isn't the accelerated achievement of low-achieving students in cooperative learning bought at the expense of high-achieving students? Couldn't the high achievers learn more if they were not tutoring?

The research is clear. Studies of cross-age peer tutoring reveal that tutors make substantial academic gains; they learn almost as much as their tutees. There is no evidence that time spent tutoring others is a detriment to learning. The opposite is true. The high achievers profit from cooperative learning in many ways. Leadership skills, self-esteem gains, conflict resolution skills, and role-taking abilities are part of the "new curriculum" inherent in cooperative learning. Ask the parents of the high achiever: "What do you most want your child to do when he or she leaves school?" They will respond by naming a position which involves leadership. Then ask, "If your student doesn't have the opportunity to work with others, how will he or she obtain the necessary leadership skills?"

Reference: Kagan, Spencer. Cooperative Learning. San Juan Capistrano, CA: Resources For Teachers, Inc., 1992.

7. FINDING

Robert E. Slavin stresses:

In addition to motivating students to do their best, cooperative learning also motivates students to help one another. This is important for several reasons.

First, students are often able to translate the teacher's language into "kid language" for one another. Students who fail to fully grasp a concept the teacher has presented can often profit from discussing the concept with peers who are wrestling with the same questions.

Second, students who explain to one another learn by doing so. Every teacher knows that we learn by teaching. When students have to organize their thoughts to explain ideas to teammates, they must engage in cognitive elaboration that greatly enhances their own understanding (see Dansereau 1985).

Third, students can provide individual attention and assistance to one another. Because they work one-on-one, students can do an excellent job of finding out whether their peers have the idea or need additional explanation.

In a traditional classroom, students who don't understand what is going on can scrunch down in their seats and hope the teacher won't call on them. In a cooperative team, there is nowhere to hide; there is a helpful nonthreatening environment in which to try out ideas and ask for assistance. A student who gives an answer in a whole class lesson risks being laughed at if the answer is wrong; in a cooperative team, the fact that the team has a "we're all in this together" attitude means that when they don't understand, students are likely to receive help rather than derision.

Reference: Slavin, Robert E. "Cooperative Learning and the Cooperative School," Educational Leadership. Volume 45, Number 3, November 1987, p. 7.

8. FINDING
Susan S. Ellis and Susan F. Whalen summarize:

A large number of research studies have demonstrated that cooperative learning is more effective than individualistic or competitive structures for increasing students' achievement and promoting their cognitive growth. There are several reasons for this. First is a concept cognitive psychologists call "oral rehearsal," or thinking out loud. To learn, we need to talk about what we are thinking. Through talking, we discover what we know and what we don't yet understand. A second reason is the increase in time-on-task that cooperative groups produce. In small groups, it's much harder for a student to drift off without a group member noticing and pulling the wanderer back into the conversation or activity. Cooperative learning also promotes controversy. When students are regularly confronted with ideas and convictions different from their own, they learn to examine their own thinking and adjust it if necessary. A fourth reason that cooperative learning stimulates achievement is that children often engage in more higher-order thinking than they do in whole class discussions which tend to operate on the knowledge and comprehension levels. Finally, cooperative learning is effective because it promotes the development of children's self-esteem.

Reference: Ellis, Susan S. and Susan F. Whalen, Cooperative Learning: Getting Started. Jefferson City, MO: Scholastic Inc., 1990.

9. FINDING
Robert E. Slavin stresses:

The principal reason that schools are built is to provide students with the knowledge, concepts, skills, and understandings needed for survival in our society. The most important outcome of cooperative learning, and the one that has been most extensively researched, is enhanced achievement. If properly structured, cooperative learning methods can significantly accelerate the learning of all children.

Cooperative learning is also a social method. It involves students working together as equals to accomplish something of importance to all of them. Cooperative learning is also fun, and it engages students in active rather than passive learning. For these reasons, it is logical to expect that cooperative learning has positive effects on social, motivational, and attitudinal outcomes as well as on achievement. Many researchers have studied such outcomes and have found evidence that cooperative learning does indeed have such positive effects.

Reference: Slavin, Robert E. Cooperative Learning: Theory, Research, and Practice. Needham Heights, MN: Allyn and Bacon, 1990.

10. FINDING
James A. Beane and Richard P. Lipka conclude:

Students acquire a great deal from the climate in which learning is to take place. It is evident that in climates that emphasize external control, young people learn to depend on others for direction, whereas in climates that put a premium on self-control, individuals tend to learn to be self-directed.

Too, those schools and classrooms in which competitive reward systems are used seem to have the intention of having large numbers of learners who view themselves as incapable. Such an intention is simply indefensible when we know that viewing oneself as a capable person or successful learner is critical in achieving success. Individual reward systems that place learners in personal competition with themselves also present difficulties since they tend to have an isolating effect, separating individuals from their peers. The fact is that self-perception in youth is largely dependent on social connectedness—the feeling that one is accepted as part of the group. For this reason, those educators who wish to enhance self-perceptions need to make efforts to replace competitive and individual reward systems with cooperative reward structures that emphasize group work.

Reference: Beane, James A. and Richard P. Lipka. Self-Concept, Self-Esteem, and the Curriculum. New York, NY: Teachers College Press, Teachers College, Columbia University, 1986.

11. FINDING

Nancy Schniedewind and Ellen Davidson state:

Cross-cultural studies by anthropologist Ruth Benedict show that the overall structure of a society accounts for the relative degrees of aggression and competition, or nonviolence and cooperation, in that society. Societies that are organized so that individuals get ahead at the expense of others—that is, competitively-structured societies—are more likely to produce aggression. Benedict discovered that aggression is lowest in social orders where the individual, by the same act and at the same time, serves his own advantage and that of the group. These societies are organized so that the group values and rewards the individual for doing what benefits the group. Benedict calls such societies high in synergy, the combination of actions of a number of things or people providing results greater than the sum of the separate actions.

Reference: Schniedewind, Nancy and Ellen Davidson. Cooperative Learning, Cooperative Lives. Dubuque, IA: Wm. C. Brown Company Publishers, 1987.

COOPERATIVE LEARNING AND GLOBAL EDUCATION

Radical shifts in our economy and the increasingly pluralistic nature of our population are forcing a reexamination of what and how we teach. The trend toward an information-based, high-technology, interdependent, rapidly changing economy supports the need for teaching high-level thinking skills as well as the communication and social skills necessary for participation in the increasingly interdependent world. Racial, linguistic, economic, and social diversity call for teaching methods that accommodate heterogeneity in proficiency levels and cultural backgrounds.

The heart of complex organizational life today is collaboration. Words like "we" and "our" replace "I" and "my." The team, not the leader, is viewed as the key to success. Collaboration generates the best ideas and options for running an organization. Allan Cox (1989), a highly respected management consultant, claims that "corporations that do not think teamwork will not prosper." It may seem contradictory, but our hopes to become more competitive in an increasingly interdependent world may well require more emphasis on cooperation.

The world is not just competitive—and in some important respects, it probably must become less so. For example, in many organizations, job-related skills may not be as crucial as interpersonal skills.

The increasingly complex, unpredictable, changing world requires students to be prepared to be flexible so they can recognize and adapt to cooperative, competitive, and individualistic social interactions. It is foolish to prepare students to be only competitive or only cooperative. More attention needs to be given to recent developments in learning, which stress collaboration and teamwork. Cooperative learning methods assume heterogeneity and emphasize interactive learning opportunities. They are better designed to cope with the diverse needs of students and the requirements for success in an interdependent world. Cooperative learning is an important element of global education.

Adapted from "Curriculum Considerations in Global Studies," by James Becker in *Global Education: From Thought To Action, The 1991 ASCD Yearbook,* ed. by Kenneth A. Tye. Reprinted with permission of the Association for Supervision and Curriculum Development, Alexandria, Virginia. Copyright 1990 by the Association for Supervision and Curriculum Development. All rights reserved.

10 Often-Used Student Roles For Cooperative Learning Groups

Reminder: When students are placed in cooperative learning groups, it is important that each group member have a specific role to perform while achieving the group's goal or completing the group's task. Jobs should be rotated from time to time so that each student has an opportunity to play each role.

1. ARTIST — Illustrates and displays projects.

2. CHECKER — Checks for group members' comprehension of material.

3. COMMUNICATOR — Conveys actions and findings of group to other groups.

4. COORDINATOR/MANAGER — Keeps the group on task.

5. ENCOURAGER/PRAISER — Makes sure all group members have their turns and provides positive feedback to group.

6. EVALUATOR — Keeps notes on group processing and social skills.

7. GO-FOR — Gets materials and equipment and runs errands for group.

8. READER — Reads directions, problems, and resource materials to group members.

9. SECRETARY/RECORDER — Writes down group responses.

10. TIMEKEEPER — Keeps track of time allotted for assignments and keeps group on time.

10 Pitfalls To Avoid When Moving Into Cooperative Learning

1. **Moving too fast.** Take time to know each other, to be aware of differences within the group, and to establish mutual trust and acceptance.

2. **Insufficient teacher planning,** with lack of attention to detailed step-by-step lesson plans and to goal expectancies.

3. **Lack of clarification of goals and student expectancies.**

4. **Unrealistic goals** requiring student behaviors and achievements beyond the student's normal performance level.

5. **Poor understanding of role definitions,** with undefined specifications of the expected functions of individual group members.

6. **A lack of balance and cohesiveness** in cognitive and affective activities.

7. **Limited or no access to materials needed for task completion.** For example, materials from the media center may be specified, but the group meets at a time when access to the media center is not possible or at a time that dictates that materials must be collected during valuable group time instead of before the group convenes.

8. **Underestimating the significance of individual differences within groups and neglecting to plan for the effect of these differences.** Blending the serious student, the class clown, the disruptive student, the self-appointed group leader, and the shy and aggressive personalities into a homogeneous group in which cooperative learning can flourish is no easy task.

9. **Lack of flexibility in plans** to allow for the setbacks or teachable moments that appear at the most unexpected times or in the most unexpected ways when people of any age work together with common goals.

10. **Lack of commitment to try, try again** when at first cooperative learning groups are not as smooth and/or productive as hoped. All new approaches to classroom management and student interaction require some "getting used to" and some trial-and-error attempts.

10 Creative Methods For Grouping Students

1. Place stickers or pictures of animals (barnyard, jungle . . .) on index cards. If there are to be four members per group, each card in a four-card set should be given an animal picture that is the same as those on the other three cards. Each student finds his or her cooperative group by making the appropriate animals sound and finding the other "animals" in his or her group.

2. Ask youngsters to line up alphabetically by FIRST NAME without talking. Then divide the class by number into groups of the proper size.

3. To celebrate a holiday such as Valentine's Day, give each student a small signed Valentine from you. Use the Valentines that are alike to group the students.

4. Use playing cards. Group by number and/or suit. Use the Joker as a "wild" card. The one student who has the Joker may select his or her own group (good for days when the number of students in class is not even).

5. Use pieces of a jigsaw puzzle to group students. Pass out some of the puzzle pieces to students, selected to allow students to form the proper groups. For example, if your cooperative groups have four members each, select pieces in interlocking sets of four. Each set will contain pieces that fit with each other, but not with any other puzzle piece. Without talking, students work to fit their pieces together to find their groups.

6. Separate and laminate several different sets of comic strip frames. Distribute randomly. Students find others who complete the comic, decide on the correct sequence, and check with the teacher, who has a "key." The group is formed.

7. On individual index cards or strips of paper, put Title, Author, Setting, Plot, and Characters from novels and/or short stories read in class. Students must put all elements together to form the group. (This group could then become the "expert" on that title.)

8. Display outline maps of individual states (the number of states should equal the number of groups desired), with lines provided for state information such as state name, capital, major city, motto, flower (the number of labeled lines should equal the number of students desired for a group). Each student is allowed to fill in one information line, thus forming the groups.

9. Students find their cooperative groups by identifying equivalent fractions, geometrical shapes, or units of measure.

10. Place pictures of the following types of pets on index cards or print these terms on the cards in the numbers needed: dogs, cats, fish, birds, reptiles, amphibians, rodents, insects, etc. Students find their groups by matching pictures or words (no talking allowed).

10 PLUS 10

Social/Process Skills to Work On In Learning Groups

Reminder: The social skills listed below are essential for students to practice when they are in cooperative learning groups. Teachers should pick only one or two social skills to work on at any given time. They should also think about what each skill might "look like" or "sound like" if kids were practicing them and teachers were observing them. For example, what might kids be saying or doing if they were using the social skill of "taking turns"?

1. Taking Turns

2. Offering Individual Encouragement

3. Accepting Criticism

4. Extending Help

5. Listening To Speaker

6. Compromising

7. Making Sure Everyone Has A Chance To Speak

8. Inviting Others To Give Opinions

9. Clarifying Ideas

10. Using Quiet Voices

11. Explaining Answers

12. Summarizing

13. Giving Directions

14. Encouraging Participation

15. Criticizing Ideas, Not People

16. Expressing Feelings

17. Asking Probing Questions

18. Using Time Wisely

19. Sharing Information And Materials

20. Energizing With Humor And Enthusiasm

10 Affective Activities For Nurturing Group Cohesiveness

1. DEFINING COOPERATION
Directions:
Have the members of your group brainstorm ten words that describe cooperation. Ask someone to write these down. Use these as reminders to help you work together in your next group task or project.

2. COOPERATION SYMBOLS
Directions:
Have your group spend a few minutes designing an original symbol to represent the idea of cooperation in your classroom. What shape, color, or size will it be? What slogan or message will it communicate?

3. COOPERATION PUZZLE
Directions:
Cut a large piece of posterboard into many puzzle-like pieces so that each member of your group has two pieces. On one piece each person writes down a positive skill or talent that he or she brings to the group and on the other piece a rule for the group to follow in completing an assigned task. Each piece is then signed and group members arrange puzzle pieces to make a total group picture.

4. STARTER STATEMENTS
Directions:
Ask the members of your group to respond to each of the following starter statements.

A. Today I am feeling _____ because _____ .

B. A special skill or talent I would like to have is _____ .

C. A pet peeve I want you to know about is _____ .

D. A little-known fact about me is _____ .

5. INTERVIEWS
Directions:

Choose one person in your group to interview and introduce to the rest of the group by asking him or her any five of the following questions.

A. What is your most prized possession?
B. What adult do you admire most?
C. What makes you special or unique?
D. What is a great sight to you?
E. What color best describes you and why?
F. If you could travel anyplace, where would you go?
G. What would you like to be doing ten years from now?
H. If you could be granted one wish, what would it be?
I. What do you like to do in your free time?
J. What bugs you the most?

6. FINISH THE DRAWING
Directions:

Have one member of your group use a crayon or marker to begin drawing on a large piece of drawing paper. He or she is to continue drawing for 1 minute. At the end of the minute, when the teacher says STOP, pass the drawing to the individual on your left. The person who receives the drawing may now add to the picture in any way for one minute until the teacher says STOP. Continue in this manner until all group members have contributed to the drawing. After the activity is completed, allow time for group members to discuss their results and what happened in the work group.

7. GROUP RESPONSES CHART
Directions:

Have each group member fill in the appropriate spaces on a chart like the one below. Discuss how your group members are alike and how they are different.

GROUP MEMBER'S NAME	FAVORITE COLOR	FAVORITE BOOK	FAVORITE TV SHOW	FAVORITE HOBBY / ACTIVITY	FAVORITE FOOD	FAVORITE SUBJECT	FAVORITE MUSIC GROUP

8. COOPERATION COLLAGE
Directions:

Use magazines, newspapers, and a large piece of posterboard to create a group collage. Use pictures and words that show or describe cooperation as your group members understand it.

9. PROVERB DECISION-MAKING
Directions:

Ask group members to agree or disagree with one of the following proverbs and to give reasons for their responses.

A. The more, the merrier.
B. Two's company, three's a crowd.
C. Two heads are better than one.
D. Too many cooks spoil the broth.
E. Many hands make light the work.

10. VARIETY IS THE SPICE OF LIFE
Directions:

Use the piece of paper in the center of your group to write down five things you all like and five things you all dislike. For example, you may all like Michael Jackson or you may all hate to eat spinach. Next, on a 3" x 5" file card, write down 5 things about yourself that are different from other members of your group. For example, you may be the only group member who has traveled to Mexico or who has won a trophy. Place these DIFFERENCE cards around the paper in front of you.

10 MINUS 2

"Warmup" Activities For Cooperative Learning

It is of the utmost importance to help students learn to work together in a positive and harmonious manner to achieve common goals before moving into formalized cooperative learning groups with specific objectives and highly-structured lesson plans. Group experiences within a variety of frameworks affording differing approaches to goal-setting, working arrangements, and evaluative criteria help students develop readiness for the more structured settings. Activities ranging from simple one-session group projects to six-step action research assignments based on Bloom's Taxonomy may be employed to help students acquire the social and academic skills necessary for successful cooperative learning. The following activities are representative of effective warmup projects that can be used for this purpose:

1. Content-Based Unit
See "Organ Transplants,"
page 246.

2. Interdisciplinary Unit
See "The Future Is News To Me,"
page 324.

3. Creative Construction
See "Send the Message,"
page 177.

4. Bloom's-Based Research Activity
See "Biographical Beginnings,"
page 178.

5. Games and Game Construction
See "In Pursuit of Trivia,"
page 179.

6. Project Planning and Implementation
See "Bee Sharp,"
page 180.

7. Reaction Groups
See "A Different Drummer,"
page 180.

8. Content-Based Discussion and Demonstrations
See "For Good Measure,"
page 181.

Sample Cooperative Learning Warmup

Send The Message

PURPOSE: To use a cooperative learning activity to encourage group interaction and group creativity through invention and construction.

CONTENT AREA: Inventing, Combining

PREPARATION:

1. Assemble a box of junk including some of the items listed plus others to be contributed by students.

   - spools
   - twine
   - paper clips
   - paper cups & plates
   - bowls, spoons, forks, & knives
   - spatula
   - straws
   - bottles
   - plastic tablecloth
   - jump rope
   - foam rubber
   - old mirrors
   - egg cartons
   - scissors
   - tape or glue

2. Print the following directions on a study guide and place it beside the box.

Great Inventions

"Necessity is the mother of invention." Can you explain the meaning of this famous saying? You can actually illustrate its meaning by "inventing" a one-of-a-kind, never-seen-before item for the "Great Inventions Museum."

1. Think about how each item in this box of junk might be used together with one or more other items to create an item carrying a message about a cause you believe in.
2. Draw a diagram of the completed item, give it a name, and write a description of it. Add a sentence about the social message it is meant to convey.
3. Add your completed diagram and a description to the GREAT INVENTIONS collection.

---

3. Ask students to work in small groups to follow the directions on the box.
4. After all inventions are completed, reconvene the total group to discuss and evaluate the "inventions."

Adapted from *Pulling Together For Cooperative Learning* by Imogene Forte and Joy MacKenzie. Nashville, TN: Incentive Publications, ©1991. Used by permission.

BIOGRAPHICAL BEGINNINGS

PURPOSE: To use a research-based language activity to encourage brainstorming, group discussion, and communication within the framework of a cooperative learning group.

KNOWLEDGE:

Work together to agree on some famous people whose biographies you would like to read. Choose one person from each of these categories: Sports Figure, Television Star, Explorer, Author, Foreign Leader, and Inventor.

COMPREHENSION:

Put your heads together and define "biography," using your own words. Explain how a biography is different from an autobiography.

APPLICATION:

Select a famous person who is of interest to all members of the group and do some research on him or her. Construct a simple "magazine report" by writing down 6-10 facts from your research and putting each one on a separate piece of paper. Find a magazine illustration to go with each fact and paste it on the appropriate page. Make a cover and title page for your biography booklet.

ANALYSIS:

Work together to select titles of 20 different biographies from the card catalog/microfiche in your media center. Classify these titles/biographies in some way so that you have no fewer than three categories (you may have more). Write a statement for each category telling what each title/biography has in common with the others within that group.

SYNTHESIS:

Working together, create a Name Poem for each of the biography characters from the APPLICATION activity above. Each letter in a name will provide the first letter for a word or phrase. (Write each name in vertical format, leaving space to add a word or phrase to the right of each letter.)

EVALUATION:

Agree on three people you know or admire that you think should have biographies written about them. Be prepared to give reasons for your choices.

Adapted from *Cooperative Learning Guide & Planning Pak For Middle Grades* by Imogene Forte and Sandra Schurr. Nashville, TN: Incentive Publications, ©1992. Used by permission.

Sample Cooperative Learning Warmup
In Pursuit Of Trivia

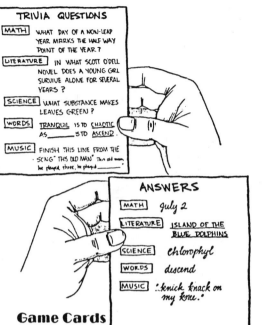

Game Cards

Materials

- trivia game appropriate for students
- textbooks and resource books
- index cards

Romancing

- Have the class play a trivia game. Divide the class into teams of five players each. Each team may consult on each answer.
- After playing, let the students examine several game cards to see how the questions and answers are written. Point out the variety in the kinds of questions and answers.
- Using one textbook (science, for instance), work together to find interesting bits of information. Have the class use the information to write trivia questions.

Collecting

- Agree on five or six categories. Then let students work in pairs to collect facts from textbooks and other resources. Students should write the facts on scrap paper and label each with the appropriate category.

Writing

- Students should use their collected facts to write questions and answers. (You may choose to make changes in the categories.)

Praising

- Each pair trades sheets with another pair of writers. Have the students look for examples which ask questions clearly.
- Point out variety in sentence structure and in the format of questions and answers.

Polishing

- If there are any questions that are too long or confusing, have each pair work to shorten, clarify, or add sufficient information.
- Tell the students to review each question, making sure it is not too obscure or difficult.

Showing Off

- Have each student use index cards to make two trivia cards (questions on one side and answers on the other).
- Have the students put the cards in a box. Now the class has a custom-made trivia game!

Adapted from *Complete Writing Lessons For The Middle Grades* by Marjorie Frank. Nashville, TN: Incentive Publications, ©1987. Used by permission.

Sample Cooperative Learning Warmups

"BEE" SHARP

PURPOSE: Cooperative project planning and implementation.

Divide the class into small groups. Ask each group to select a topic (math, science, current events, history, geography, sports, spelling) for its "bee." Each group should generate a list of questions about its chosen topic. The lists can then be put into a hat to be drawn at random as time permits.

When a list is drawn, the originating group will be responsible for conducting a "bee" in which the entire class will participate. If desired, elements other than questions may be included on the lists: terms to define, concepts to explain, tasks to perform, etc.

A DIFFERENT DRUMMER

PURPOSE: To use "individual differences in human beings" as a topic to encourage cooperative discussion and decision-making.

"IF A MAN DOES NOT KEEP PACE WITH HIS COMPANIONS, PERHAPS IT IS BECAUSE HE HEARS A DIFFERENT DRUMMER. LET HIM STEP TO THE MUSIC WHICH HE HEARS, HOWEVER MEASURED OR FAR AWAY."
—*Henry David Thoreau*

Divide students into groups of three or four to react to this statement by discussing the following questions:
- Do you agree or disagree with this statement? Why?
- Come up with the names of some people who have "stepped to the beat of a different drummer." What effects might this way of living have had on the world? On the individual?
- Is this idea something you hope your own children will believe?

At the conclusion of the small group sessions, one member of each group should be elected (by group vote) to act as spokesperson for the group. The elected spokespersons should then serve as panel members to summarize and present the small group conclusions to the total group.

Adapted from *Cooperative Learning Guide & Planning Pak For Middle Grades* by Imogene Forte and Sandra Schurr. Nashville, TN: Incentive Publications, ©1992. Used by permission.

Sample Cooperative Learning Warmup

For Good Measure

CONTENT AREA: Math/Measurement

PREPARATION:
1. Read aloud to the students the story "The Blind Men and the Elephant."

PROCEDURE:
1. Discuss how blindness causes each man to approach the elephant with a distorted frame of reference.

2. Ask students to conjecture ways in which they could describe objects which could not be handled or felt to persons who cannot see (for example: a train, an acre, features of a person, a large monument, a lion, etc.).

3. Divide students into groups of five or six, and ask them to suppose that there is no uniform system of measurement in existence. Given this problem, each group must devise a new and unique system for measuring height and length that could be used to describe the sizes of buildings, furniture, people, and household objects to someone who has never seen such objects.

4. After the groups have thought of a measurement system, they must plan a demonstration of the use of the new system.

5. Provide time for each group to share results of their thinking and to demonstrate their system.

From *Pulling Together For Cooperative Learning* by Imogene Forte and Joy MacKenzie. Nashville, TN: Incentive Publications, ©1991. Used by permission.

GROUP PLAN AT A GLANCE
(For Teacher And Student Use)

Topic_____ Completion Date_____

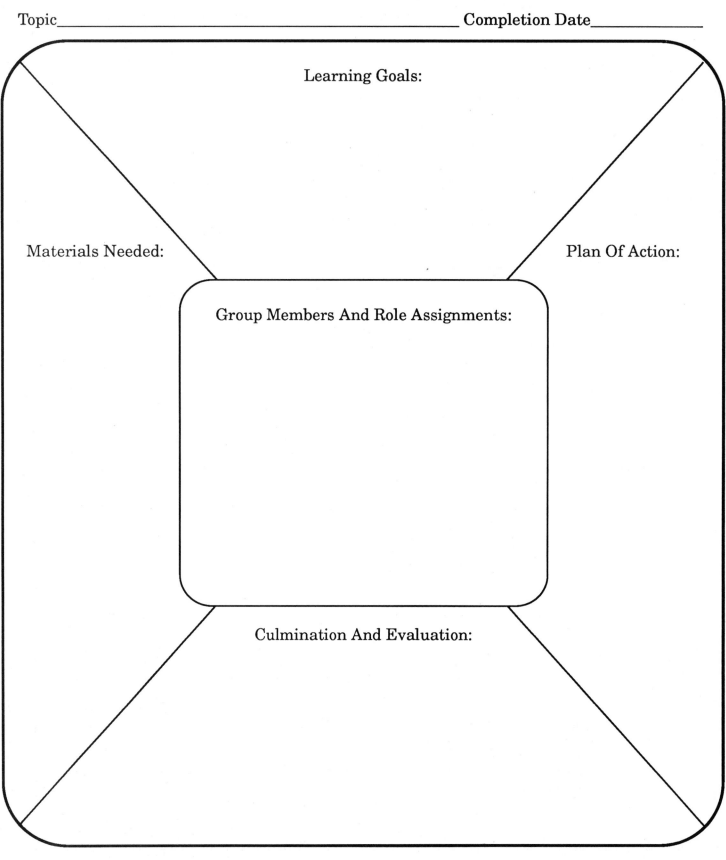

Learning Goals:

Materials Needed:

Plan Of Action:

Group Members And Role Assignments:

Culmination And Evaluation:

182

© 1993 by Incentive Publications, Inc., Nashville, TN.

OFF TO A GOOD START
(Student Planning Worksheet)

What we want to know: _____

_____

_____

What we will do: _____

_____

_____

What we will need: _____

_____

_____

How we will evaluate: _____

_____

_____

How we will define responsibilities:

What?   Who?

_____   _____

_____   _____

_____   _____

_____   _____

_____   _____

_____   _____

_____   _____

183

Behavior Checklist For Observing A Cooperative Learning Activity

Date _____ Teacher _____

School/Grade _____ Subject _____

Physical arrangement _____

Mode of grouping _____ Small group size _____

Type of evaluation _____

Lesson Objectives _____

_____

_____

	Evident	Not Evident	Not Applicable
PHYSICAL			
Rules are posted			
Movement is orderly			
Resources/materials are available			
PROCEDURES			
Roles are assigned			
Objectives are given			
Directions are clear			
Rules are reviewed			
Classroom management is used			
Closure to the lesson is provided			
STUDENTS			
Students are collaborating academically			
Students establish group goals			
Students divide tasks			
Students share resources			
Students perform tasks			
Individual accountability is evident			
Students are cooperating socially			
Learning is taking place			
Students are motivated			
TEACHER			
Moves from group to group			
Is available for resource			
Reinforces positive attitudes			
Observes and facilitates successful elements of cooperative learning			

QUESTIONS/COMMENTS (Use reverse side if necessary) _____

_____

184

10 Discussion Questions For Assessing Social Skills In Group Work

1. How did you feel as you worked with your cooperative group today? Why?
_____
_____

2. What was your major contribution today?_____
_____

3. How would you rank your group on the social skill being observed?
(Scale 1–5, 1=lowest, 5=highest.) Explain your ranking._____
_____

4. How would you rank yourself on the same social skill? Explain._____
_____
_____

5. Was anyone in the group especially helpful? In what way?_____
_____

6. What did your group do well when working together today? _____
_____
_____

7. What might your group do better the next time?_____
_____
_____

8. How might you express your appreciation to the members of your group? _____
_____
_____

9. Did everyone in your group help to complete the assignment? _____
_____
_____

10. What social skill do you think your group should practice next? Why? _____
_____

10 PLUS 1

Ways To Look At Members In My Group

1. The person in my group who contributes the most is . . .
_____

2. The person in my group who is most kind and fair is . . .
_____

3. The person in my group who is most cooperative is . . .
_____

4. The person in my group who has the best ideas is . . .
_____

5. The person in my group who makes a good leader is . . .
_____

6. The person in my group who keeps us on task is . . .
_____

7. The person in my group who is the most fun to work with is . . .
_____

8. The person in my group who works the hardest is . . .
_____

9. The person in my group who helps me the most is . . .
_____

10. The person in my group who keeps peace is . . .
_____

11. The person in my group who sometimes causes problems is . . .
_____ Maybe I could help _____
by _____

10 PLUS 4

Student Measures Of Success

On a scale of 1 to 4 (1=Poor, 2=Acceptable, 3=Good, 4=Best), rank your group's degree of success in working together.

1. Setting achievable goals........................ 1 2 3 4

2. Organizing to work together to meet group goals 1 2 3 4

3. Defining group roles 1 2 3 4

4. Accepting individual responsibility............. 1 2 3 4

5. Listening with respect 1 2 3 4

6. Taking turns to speak 1 2 3 4

7. Using respectful voices 1 2 3 4

8. Encouraging one another 1 2 3 4

9. Avoiding put-downs.................. 1 2 3 4

10. Requesting teacher help only when needed.......... 1 2 3 4

11. Maintaining group order 1 2 3 4

12. Staying in roles 1 2 3 4

13. Success in meeting group goals 1 2 3 4

14. Evaluating group progress....... 1 2 3 4

Summary Statement: On the whole I think our group _____

_____

_____

_____

_____

Name_____

SAMPLE COOPERATIVE LEARNING POST-TEST
(For Three-Member Group)

Name: _____ Date: _____

DIRECTIONS: Each member of your group is to complete his or her own test after each person is designated as Team Member 1, 2, or 3.

1. Write your own definition of cooperative learning by completing this starter statement: Cooperative learning is . . .

_____

_____

_____

2. By yourself, list three advantages of working on assignments cooperatively in small groups. Share your ideas with the other two members of your group and put a circle around your best idea as determined by the three of you.

a. _____

b. _____

c. _____

3. Which of the following social skills is most important to have when working in a cooperative learning setting? Rank order them from 1 to 5 with 1 being least important and 5 being most important. Do this task first by yourself and then with your team members, reaching a consensus.

My rank order is:

_____ open-minded

_____ listening

_____ supportive

_____ enthusiastic

_____ responsible

My group's rank order is:

_____ open-minded

_____ listening

_____ supportive

_____ enthusiastic

_____ responsible

188

4. If you were a team leader of a small group, what would you do in each of the following situations?

Team Member 1: A member of your group is not contributing ideas.

_____

_____

_____

Team Member 2: A member of your group refuses to cooperate or play by the rules.

_____

_____

_____

Team Member 3: A member of your group is having trouble with the assigned task.

_____

_____

_____

5. Does your group agree or disagree with the following statement? "No one is as smart as all of us."

_____ We agree.

_____ We disagree.

Write down one reason for the agreement or disagreement from each team member.

Team Member 1:_____

_____

Team Member 2:_____

_____

Team Member 3:_____

_____

TEACHER'S COOPERATIVE LEARNING WRAP-UP, À LA BLOOM

KNOWLEDGE
In your own words, define Cooperative Learning.

COMPREHENSION
Explain how Cooperative Learning could be used in your classroom to help students work together to achieve learning goals and develop interactive skills.

APPLICATION
Review the research findings and/or what the published literature has to say about Cooperative Learning. Use the facts gained to make a list of "Ten Things Teachers Need To Know Before Moving Into Cooperative Learning."

ANALYSIS
Compare and contrast Cooperative Learning and traditional "group work" groups.

SYNTHESIS
Plan a Cooperative Learning activity appropriate for your class.

EVALUATION
Determine three strengths and three weaknesses of Cooperative Learning. Combine the two lists and rank order the listings according to their importance to group success. Give reasons for your rankings of the first and last on your list.

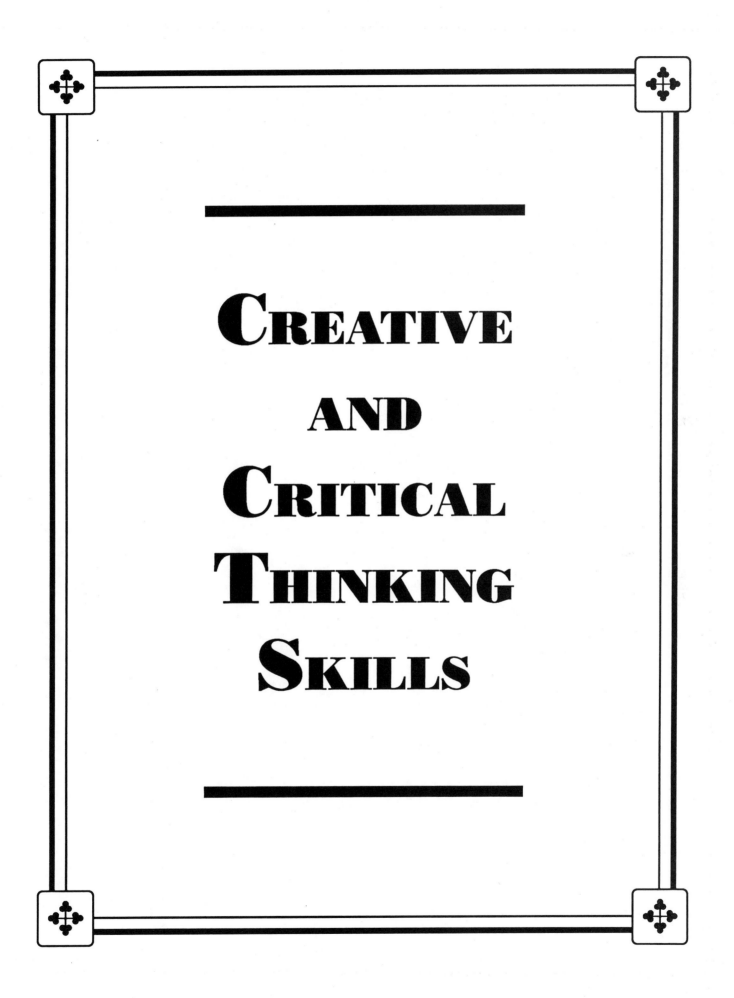

CREATIVE AND CRITICAL THINKING SKILLS

Thinking Skills Overview

TEACHERS CAN INTEGRATE THINKING SKILLS INTO THE CURRICULUM BY:

• Stressing the importance of thinking daily through role modeling, poster/bulletin board displays, and class discussions on the subject.
• Encouraging student interaction through such directives as . . .
   a. Asking a student to elaborate on a statement made by another student.
   b. Encouraging students to "agree" or "disagree" with an idea expressed by another student in the class.
   c. Using questions such as "Who will challenge the response just given by Student X or Student Y?"
   d. Encouraging students to paraphrase, summarize, or critique another student's ideas before adding to the discussion.
• Asking open-ended and extension questions rather than closed and single-response questions.
• Refraining from offering personal opinions, value judgments, or comments on the topic.
• Developing wait time with students through such strategies as . . .
   a. Counting to twenty before calling on a student.
   b. Giving students a short writing assignment to answer a series of questions before calling on them.
   c. Distracting yourself by writing on the blackboard or on an overhead transparency.
   d. Waiting until at least half the class members have their hands up to respond before calling on anyone.
• Keeping a tally of student responses to encourage widespread participation.
• Giving a grade, reward, or extra credit mark for student participation and/or quality of student responses.
• Organizing students into cooperative learning "think tanks" when doing complex-level thinking activities.
• Using Bloom's Taxonomy when structuring discussion questions, worksheets, tests, or assignments so that students are working at all levels of the taxonomy.
• Complimenting all students at the end of a group discussion for the quality of their thinking and of their contributions.

IN SUMMARY:
Thinking skills beneficial to students in career and life can be developed during the teaching of all disciplines through encouragement and rewards, effectively-structured questions, the employment of higher-level thinking taxonomies, and the use of simple teaching strategies.

10 Important Thinking Skills Questions To Find Answers For

1. What are some notable features of high-level thinking skills? How may one distinguish various kinds of high-level thinking skills?

2. How can a teacher evaluate a student's intellectual growth?

3. Why is the development of high-level thinking skills of considerable importance in all areas of life?

4. How can the importance of thinking skills be communicated to students?

5. What are the characteristics of questions which effectively stimulate thinking skills?

6. How can vocabulary usage, especially the use of action verbs, promote higher-level thinking skills?

7. How can one assess the degree of acceptance of creative thinking in one's own school?

8. What are some of the major thinking taxonomies and models for teaching thinking skills in the classroom?

9. How can thinking taxonomies be helpful when structuring classroom activities, discussions, and assignments?

10. How can a selection of teaching strategies be used to integrate thinking skills into any subject area or discipline?

10

PLUS 10

Definitions Essential To Success With Thinking Skills

1. **Analyze:** To separate or break up a whole into its parts according to some plan or reason. Opposite of *synthesize. Structural analysis* is performed in randomly-ordered steps. *Operational analysis* is performed in sequential steps.

2. **Brainstorming:** A group or individual method of generating solution paths for problems. The goal is to produce multiple possible solutions.

3. **Comprehension:** The arrival at the speaker's or writer's intended meaning by a listener or reader.

4. **Convergent thinking:** Thinking that requires a single correct answer to a question or problem. (Compare with divergent thinking.)

5. **Creative thinking:** The action of using one's mind to produce thoughts along new and original lines.

6. **Critical thinking:** Using basic cognitive processes to analyze arguments and generate insight into particular meanings and interpretations; also known as directed thinking.

7. **Decision making:** The process leading to the selection of one of several options after consideration of facts or ideas, possible alternatives, probable consequences, and personal values.

8. **Develop criteria:** To create standards, rules, or tests for judging ways in which one event, item, or person may be differentiated from another one.

9. **Divergent thinking:** The kind of thinking required to generate many different responses to the same question or problem. (Compare with convergent thinking.)

10. **Elaborate:** To expand on concepts or ideas; to give greater detail to the explanation of an idea or description of an object.

11. **Evaluation:** To make an examination or judgment based upon a set of internal or external criteria.

12. **Flexibility:** The ability to take alternate points of view, to present a different perspective with each response, to try several different approaches, and/or to apply concepts, ideas, or rules to a variety of situations.

13. **Fluency:** The ability to list many possible ideas (the more ideas one produces, the more fluent one is); the ability to produce a variety of responses.

14. **Inquiry:** Seeking information about a problem or condition.

15. **Knowledge:** Acquaintance with or theoretical or practical understanding of some art, science, or other area of learning.

16. **Originality:** The ability to generate novel, nontraditional, or unexpected responses.

17. **Problem solving:** Defining or describing a problem, determining the desired outcome, selecting possible solutions, choosing strategies, testing trial solutions, and evaluating the outcome, making revisions where necessary.

18. **Reasoning:** In two forms, deductive and inductive. *Deductive reasoning:* Using knowledge of two or more premises to arrive at a valid conclusion. *Inductive reasoning:* Arriving at an inference or conclusion by working from the particular to the general.

19. **Synthesize:** To unite parts into a whole; to conclude; to move from principle to application; to reason deductively from simple elements into a complex whole.

20. **Thinking:** The mental manipulation of sensory input to formulate thoughts, to reason, or to judge.

10 Findings From The Published Literature To Document The Need For Higher-Order Questioning And Thinking Skills

1. FINDING

Marylou Dantonio writes:

Effective questioning is an innate talent for some teachers. Most of us, however, must work at developing our questioning talent. It stands to reason that the more we know about the nature and function of questions, and the more opportunities we have to practice questioning techniques, the more effective we will become at asking questions. Review of the literature on teacher questioning (Brophy and Good, 1986; Wilen and Clegg, 1986; Georgia, 1987) confirms that keeping students on task during question-and-answer lessons, phrasing questions clearly, providing wait time, providing positive feedback specifically and discriminately, and probing student answers are all important techniques of effective questioning practices.

Reference: Dantonio, M. How Can We Create Thinkers? Questioning Strategies that Work for Teachers. Bloomington, IN: National Educational Service, 1990.

2. FINDING

Barbara Z. Presseisen states:

A focus on metacognition in the classroom emphasizes helping students understand their own responses to thoughtful situations. In the thinking classroom, tacit understandings of a problem situation should be discussed, group interaction encouraged, and learners made aware of the characteristics of the information under scrutiny. Metacognition seeks to make student learning more explicit and the products of classroom experiences more memorable.

Reference: Keefe, J. and Walberg, H. Teaching for Thinking. Reston, VA: National Association of Secondary School Principals (NASSP), 1992.

3. FINDING
Vincent Ryan Ruggiero stresses:

If educators want to persuade students that thinking skills are vital in every area of life, they must show students that those skills are important enough to receive regular attention in every academic discipline. Moreover, if they wish students to have the level of cognitive skill necessary to resist the shallow and specious thinking so prevalent today, they must assist students in reaching that level of skill.

The second reason for teaching thinking across the curriculum is that wherever it is taught, it tends to increase student enthusiasm for a course. The traditional lecture approach and the traditional textbook not only deny students training in analyzing problems and issues, but also suggest to students that the subject of a course is static, inert, dead. Teaching thinking in a course emphasizes the processes that give every subject its vitality—hypothesizing, interpreting, seeking alternative views, raising questions, evaluating, discovering. The emphasis creates excitement and encourages involvement.

Reference: Ruggiero, V. Teaching Thinking Across the Curriculum. New York, NY: Harper and Row, 1989.

4. FINDING
Robert Marzano and his colleagues conclude:

Critical thinking is sometimes defined narrowly and sometimes more globally. Ennis (1985), who at one time preferred the narrower meaning, now defines critical thinking as "reasonable, reflective thinking that is focused on deciding what to believe or do." This broader interpretation, he explains, is more in keeping with general usage and is constant with a view of good thinking as including a generative element. The goal of teaching critical thinking is to develop people who are fair-minded, objective, and committed to clarity and accuracy.

Reference: Marzano, R., Brandt, R., Hughes, C., Jones, B., Presseisen, B., Rankin, S., and Suhor, C. Dimensions of Thinking: A Framework for Curriculum and Instruction. Alexandria, VA: Association for Supervision and Curriculum Development (ASCD), 1988.

5. FINDING
John Barell concludes:

The characteristics of a thoughtful person are drawn from research on teaching and cognitive development. Thoughtful people have confidence in their problem-solving abilities. They persist. They control their own impulsivity. They are open to others' ideas. They cooperate with others in solving problems. They listen. They are empathetic. They tolerate ambiguity and complexity. They approach problems from a variety of perspectives. They research problems thoroughly. They relate prior experience to current problems that may contradict favored points of view. They pose what-if questions, challenging assumptions and playing with variables. They are metacognitive: they plan, monitor, and evaluate their thinking. They are able to transfer concepts and skills from one situation to another. They are curious, and wonder about the world. They ask "good questions."

Reference: Barell, J. Teaching for Thoughtfulness. New York, NY: Longman Publishing Group, 1991.

6. FINDING
Lauren Resnick claims:

It is not difficult to list some of the key features of higher-order thinking:

- Higher-order thinking is non-algorithmic. That is, the path of action is not fully specified in advance.

- Higher-order thinking tends to be complex. The total path is not "visible" (mentally speaking) from any single vantage point.

- Higher-order thinking often yields multiple solutions, each with costs and benefits rather than unique solutions.

- Higher-order thinking involves nuances, judgment, and interpretation.

- Higher-order thinking involves the application of multiple criteria, which sometimes conflict with one another.

- Higher-order thinking often involves uncertainty. Not everything is known ahead of time that bears on the task at hand.

- Higher-order thinking means self-regulation of the thinking process. We do not recognize higher-order thinking in an individual when someone else "calls the plays" at every step.

- Higher-order thinking involves imposing meaning, finding structure in apparent disorder.

Reference: Resnick, L. Education and Learning to Think. Pittsburgh, PA: Learning Research and Development Center, University of Pittsburgh, 1985.

7. FINDING
Robert J. Swartz writes:

Teachers who have taken the time to understand critical thinking based on their own experiences and studies have turned away from prepackaged curriculums in favor of infusing critical thinking into the restructured content of their own teaching.

Reference: Swartz, R. "Restructuring Curriculum for Critical Thinking." Educational Leadership, 43 (8), 1986.

8. FINDING
Daniel M. Purdom stresses:

There are several reasons the Taxonomy of Educational Objectives (Bloom) is considered one of the significant works in education. Most important is that it provides educators with precise descriptions of different kinds of student behaviors and identifies some terms to use which signify distinct differences in behavior.

Reference: Purdom, D. "Why the Taxonomy Is Important." A Simple Guide to Using Bloom's Taxonomy. Tampa, FL: University of South Florida Press, 1986.

9. FINDING
Doris J. Shallcross states:

Creativity is not the exclusive possession of a chosen few, the Mozarts, the Rembrandts, the Einsteins. Their talents might be more obvious and grandiose, but their kind do not have a corner on the market. Creativity is in all of us. It is the ability that raises humanity above the other living species in our world. Creative abilities exist in varying degrees among us, as do other kinds of intelligence. It is a matter of getting those abilities to surface and making them work for us.

Reference: Shallcross, D. Teaching Creative Behavior. Buffalo, NY: Bearly Limited, 1985.

10. FINDING
Roger von Oech emphasizes:

Creative thinking requires an attitude or outlook which allows you to search for ideas and manipulate your knowledge and experience. With this outlook, you try various approaches, first one, then another, often not getting anywhere. You use crazy, foolish, and impractical ideas as stepping stones to practical new ideas. You break the rules occasionally, and hunt for ideas in unusual outside places. In short, by adopting a creative outlook you open yourself up to both new possibilities and to change. Nobel Prize-winning physician Albert Szent-Gyorgyi put it well when he said: "Discovery consists of looking at the same thing as everyone else and thinking something different."

Reference: von Oech, R. A Whack on the Side of the Head: How to Unlock Your Mind for Innovation. New York, NY: Warner Books, 1983.

10 Characteristics Of Intellectual Growth In Students

Below are ten suggested characteristics of intellectual growth which teachers can observe and record. Keeping anecdotal records of a student's acquisition of these types of behaviors provides more usable information about growth in intellectual behaviors than typical norm-referenced, multiple-choice, standardized tests.

1. Persevering when the solution to a problem is not immediately apparent, and growing in their ability to use alternative strategies or problem-solving techniques.

2. Decreasing impulsivity, and deferring judgments until adequate information is available.

3. Flexibility in thinking, and the ability to sustain a process of problem-solving and finding the answer over time.

4. Metacognition: The ability to be aware of what they don't know and to describe what goes on in their heads when they think.

5. Checking for accuracy of their work, contemplating their precision, and taking pride in their accomplishments.

6. Problem-posing, or a shift from teachers asking questions and posing problems toward students asking questions and finding problems for themselves.

7. Drawing on past knowledge and experiences in order to extract meaning from one experience and apply it in the next experience.

8. Transference beyond the learning situation so that school-learned knowledge is translated to real-life situations and content areas beyond that in which it was originally taught.

9. Precision of language so that their speech becomes more concise, descriptive, and coherent.

10. Enjoyment of problem-solving so that they make up problems to solve on their own and submit to others without the teacher's help or intervention.

Adapted from *The School as a Home for the Mind* by Arthur L. Costa. Palatine, IL: Skylight Publishing, 1991. Used by permission.

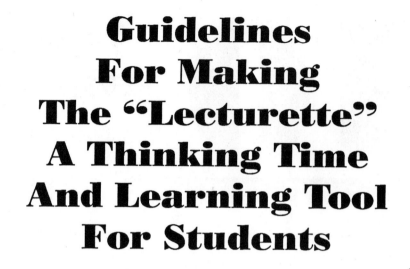

Guidelines For Making The "Lecturette" A Thinking Time And Learning Tool For Students

1. Limit the goal of the mini-lecture to one of the following: introducing or summarizing a unit of study, presenting or describing a problem, providing information otherwise inaccessible to students, sharing personal experiences of the teacher, clarifying important concepts associated with a unit of study, or reviewing ideas necessary for student retention.

2. Develop a set of specific content and process objectives for the mini-lecture.

3. Prepare and use an outline or set of notes for the mini-lecture.

4. Rehearse the delivery of the mini-lecture.

5. Enhance content of mini-lecture with audio-visuals and multisensory stimulation.

6. Lecture for ten minutes and then pause between two and five minutes, allowing time for students to reflect on their notes or discuss their notes with partners.

7. Use vocabulary and examples in the mini-lecture that are familiar to the students and appropriate for their age and ability levels.

8. Provide students with a written outline or study guide of the mini-lecture to serve as advanced organizers of the content to be covered.

9. Make modifications in the mini-lecture for students with special needs.

10. Maintain positive eye contact, body language, and voice pitch during the mini-lecture.

10 PLUS 1 Points To Ponder When Setting Up A Classroom Discussion To Promote Thinking Skills

1. Why is a classroom discussion important to the teaching of this topic or subject?

2. What specific content and process objectives do I have for this discussion?

3. How do I want to physically arrange the room and student seating for this discussion?

4. What ground rules should I establish for student participants before starting this discussion?

5. What plans do I have for dealing with students who dominate the discussion or who will not participate in the discussion?

6. What preparations should the students make before the discussion?

7. What roles will I play throughout the discussion?

8. How can I actively involve all students in the discussion?

9. What classroom activities would be appropriate as a follow-up to this discussion?

10. How long should the discussion last and should students be graded for their participation in class discussion? If so, how?

11. What are the key questions that I should prepare for leading the discussion?

10 Teacher Responses To Incorrect Answers That Encourage Student Thinking

Note: If a wrong answer is given, you can use any of these strategies to turn a negative experience into a positive one.

1. Supply the question that the student actually answered.

2. Allow time for the student to think (6 seconds wait-time) and respond again.

3. Prompt when students have the partial answer.

4. Give differential reinforcement ("That's almost 100 percent correct!").

5. Paraphrase the question.

6. Expand upon the answer and ask the student to repeat it aloud.

7. Tell the student the answer and stress the need for him or her to remember the answer.

8. Ask a fellow student to supply clues.

9. Provide examples of the possible answer.

10. Supply opposites of the answer.

Adapted from *Time Management for Teachers* by Cathy Collins, 1987. Reprinted by permission of the publisher, Parker Publishing/A division of Simon & Schuster, West Nyack, New York.

10 PLUS 10

Examples Of Questions For Student Journal Writing That Are Transitions For Thinking Activities And Follow-up Thinking Lessons

CRITICAL THINKING

INTRODUCTORY QUESTIONS

1. How do you figure things out on your own?

2. How do you clear your thinking when it is confused?

3. How do you make decisions?

4. How do the choices we make influence our lives?

5. What does it mean to think critically?

FOLLOW-UP QUESTIONS

1. In what ways did you work to organize your thoughts for logical thinking?

2. How do you know your answers or conclusions are accurate?

3. Why is reflective thinking important for making wise decisions?

4. How might we use critical thinking to improve our judgments?

5. How might you define and set your own criteria before making judgments or decisions?

CREATIVE THINKING

INTRODUCTORY QUESTIONS

1. What is a creative idea?

2. Why has creative thinking been important to the development of our society?

3. What do we have to let our thinking do so that we can create new ideas?

4. Why is so little time given to developing our creative thinking abilities?

5. What attitudes and emotions can strengthen or inhibit creative thinking?

FOLLOW-UP QUESTIONS

1. Why is imagination important to creative thinking?

2. What kinds of creative thinking did you do for this activity?

3. How does creative thinking help you to be more productive in your learning and school work?

4. Were you able to use your creative thinking when necessary in order to produce better ideas?

5. How might you use creative thinking to help you solve problems in your life?

Adapted from *Effective Questions to Strengthen Thinking* by Marilyn Brown. Hawthorne, NJ: Educational Impressions, Inc., 1989. Used by permission.

10 PLUS 1

Guidelines For Developing Simulation Games To Encourage The Use Of Thinking Skills

1. Determine the overall purpose of the simulation game for the students.

2. Determine the specific content (concepts) and skill (competency) objectives to be addressed as part of the gaming process.

3. Determine the major players, roles, groups, or organizations whose collective decisions will have an impact on the game's actions.

4. Determine the outcomes (influence, knowledge, etc.) desired most by the major players, roles, groups, or organizations.

5. Determine the resources that the major players, roles, groups, or organizations will have at their disposal throughout the game.

6. Determine the sequence of events and the information outlets that will occur among the major players, roles, groups, or organizations.

7. Determine the key guidelines, rules, and decision opportunities that will have an impact on the major players, roles, groups, or organizations.

8. Determine the external barriers or roadblocks that will limit the actions of the major players, roles, groups, or organizations.

9. Determine the rules and criteria by which winners will be selected from the major players, roles, groups, or organizations, making certain to accommodate the application of skills and content mentioned in Guideline Two above.

10. Determine the format and props for implementation of the game.

11. Determine the type of follow-up debriefing session you will have with the major players, roles, groups, or organizations.

10 Selected Models For Teaching Thinking Skills In The Classroom

1. MODEL ONE: BLOOM'S TAXONOMY OF COGNITIVE DEVELOPMENT

Bloom's Taxonomy is a structure for classifying educational objectives so that teachers and students have a common framework for determining the types of desired changes in student behavior as learning takes place. Bloom suggests that there are at least six distinct levels of behavioral outcomes related to thinking and that each level is arranged in a hierarchy from the simplest to the most complex. These levels, defined in simple operational terms, are:

Knowledge Level: Students learn information through remembering content, either by recall or recognition.

Comprehension Level: Students understand information through translation, interpretation, or extrapolation (doing something extra with the material or event being comprehended).

Application Level: Students use information in a context different from the one in which it was taught.

Analysis Level: Students examine (break down) specific parts of the information in order to accomplish such tasks as reading between the lines, finding subtle implications, or completing a logical dissection of a communication.

Synthesis Level: Students do something new and different with information in a process that is directly opposite to that of analysis. Synthesis requires integrating ideas in new and different ways.

Evaluation Level: Students judge information by considering alternatives in making a judgment, establishing criteria for judging those alternatives, and by defending that final judgment among the established alternatives.

It is suggested that teachers use the Bloom Reference Chart with its collection of "verbs" or "behaviors" when designing their lesson plans, their tests, their classroom discussion questions, and their units of study so that students continue "to stretch their minds and tease their imaginations" in the teaching and learning process.

Bloom's Taxonomy (continued)

BLOOM ACTION VERBS FOR CLASSROOM ACTION

KNOWLEDGE: Knowledge is defined as the remembering of previously-learned material. This may involve the recall of a wide range of material, from specific facts to complete theories, but all that is required is the bringing to mind of the appropriate information. Knowledge represents the lowest level of learning outcomes in the cognitive domain.

RELATED ACTION VERBS

acquire	group	name	record
choose	identify	outline	repeat
count	indicate	pick	reproduce
define	know	point	select
distinguish	label	quote	state
draw	list	read	tabulate
fill in	locate	recall	trace
find	match	recite	underline
follow directions	memorize	recognize	write

COMPREHENSION: Comprehension is defined as the ability to grasp the meaning of material. This may be shown by translating material from one form to another (e.g. words to numbers), by interpreting material (e.g. explaining or summarizing), and by estimating future trends (e.g. predicting consequences or effects). These learning outcomes are one step beyond the simple remembering of material and represent the lowest level of understanding.

RELATED ACTION VERBS

account for	draw	infer	reorganize
associate	estimate	illustrate	represent
change	expand	interpolate	retell
classify	explain	interpret	reword
conclude	express in	measure	rewrite
compare	other terms	outline	restate
contrast	extend	paraphrase	show
convert	extrapolate	predict	simplify
demonstrate	fill in	prepare	suggest
describe	find	put in order	summarize
determine	generalize	read	trace (on map
define	give in own words	rearrange	or chart)
differentiate	give examples	recognize	transform
distinguish	group	reorder	translate

Bloom's Taxonomy (continued)

APPLICATION: Application refers to the ability to use learned material in new and concrete situations. This may include the application of such things as rules, methods, concepts, principles, laws, and theories. Learning outcomes in this area require a higher level of understanding than those under comprehension.

RELATED ACTION VERBS

apply	discover	investigate	prove (in math)
calculate	discuss	keep records	put into action
choose	distinguish	locate	put to use
classify	between	(information)	put together
collect	employ	make	record
information	estimate	manipulate	relate
complete	examine	model	restructure
compute	expand	modify	select
construct	experiment	operate	show
construct using	express in a	organize	solve
convert	discussion	participate	track
(in math)	find (implies	perform	(in development,
demonstrate	investigation)	plan	history, process)
derive	generalize	practice	transfer
determine	graph	predict	translate
develop	illustrate	prepare	use
differentiate	interpret	present	utilize
between	interview	produce	

ANALYSIS: Analysis refers to the ability to break down material into its component parts so that its organizational structure may be understood. This may mean the recognition of relationships between parts or the recognition of the organizational principles involved. Learning outcomes here represent a higher intellectual level than comprehension and application because they require an understanding of both the content and the structural form of the material.

RELATED ACTION VERBS

analyze	diagram	group	relate
break down	differentiate	identify	search
categorize	discover	illustrate	select
classify	discriminate	infer	separate
compare	distinguish	inspect	simplify
contrast	divide	make	sort
criticize	draw conclusions	inferences	subdivide
debate	examine	order	survey
deduce	formulate	outline	take apart
detect	form generali-	point out	transform
determine	zations	recognize	uncover

Bloom's Taxonomy (continued)

SYNTHESIS: Synthesis refers to the ability to put together parts to form a new whole. This may involve the production of a unique communication (theme or speech), a plan of operations (research proposal), or a set of abstract relations (scheme for classifying information). Learning outcomes in this area stress creative behavior, with the major emphasis being on the formulation of new patterns or structures.

RELATED ACTION VERBS

arrange	devise	originate	rearrange
blend	develop	organize	reconstruct
build	document	perform	relate
categorize	explain	(in public)	reorganize
combine	form	plan	revise
compile	formulate	predict	rewrite
compose	generalize	prepare	specify
constitute	generate	prescribe	suppose
construct	imagine	present (an	summarize
create	integrate	original report	synthesize
deduce	invent	or work)	tell
derive	make up	produce	transmit
design	modify	propose	write

EVALUATION: Evaluation is concerned with the ability to judge the value of material (a statement, novel, poem, or research report) for a given purpose. The judgments are to be based on definite criteria. These may be internal criteria (organization) or external criteria (relevance to the purpose), and the student may determine the criteria given them. Learning outcomes in this area are highest in the cognitive hierarchy because they contain elements of all of the other categories, as well as conscious value judgments based on clearly-defined criteria.

RELATED ACTION VERBS

appraise	critique	judge	standardize
argue	decide	justify	summarize
assess	defend	interpret	support
award	describe	measure	test
choose	determine	rank	validate
compare	discriminate	rate	verify
conclude	distinguish	recommend	
consider	evaluate	relate	
contrast	grade	select	

Adapted from *Dynamite in the Classroom: A How-to Handbook for Teachers* by S. L. Schurr. Columbus, OH: National Middle School Association, 1989. Used by permission.

2. MODEL TWO:
WILLIAMS' TAXONOMY OF DIVERGENT THINKING AND FEELING

The Williams Model has been widely used in middle level classrooms as a major delivery system in developing creativity in students. The first four behaviors are associated with the cognitive or intellectual domain while the last four behaviors are associated with the affective or feeling domain. The levels of Williams Taxonomy are listed below along with selected pupil behaviors and cue words.

Levels and Learner Expectations   Trigger Words

COGNITIVE

Fluency is a skill that enables the learner to generate lots of ideas, oodles of related answers, scads of options, or a bunch of choices in a given situation.

how many?	oodles
one	a bunch
quantity	scads
a few	lots

Flexibility is a skill that enables the learner to change everyday objects to fit a variety of categories by taking detours and varying size, shape, quantities, time limits, requirements, objectives, or dimensions in a given situation.

variety	detour
adapt	alternatives
different	change
redirect	

Originality is a skill that enables the learner to seek the unusual or not-obvious by suggesting clever twists to change content or arrive at strategies to seek the novel in a given situation.

unusual	clever
unique	not obvious
new	novel

Elaboration is a skill that enables the learner to stretch a topic by expanding, enlarging, enriching, or embellishing a list of finds or possibilities in order to build on previous thoughts or ideas in a given situation.

embellish	stretch
expand	enlarge
upon	enrich
build	add on
embroider	

Williams' Taxonomy (continued)

Levels and Learner Expectations   Trigger Words

AGGRESSIVE

Risk Taking is a skill that enables the learner to deal with the unknown by taking chances, experimenting with new ideas, or trying new challenges in a given situation.

dare	try
estimate	experiment
explore	predict
guess	

Complexity is a skill that enables the learner to create structure in an unstructured setting or to bring a logical order to a given situation.

improve	order
seek	intricate
alternatives	
solve	

Curiosity is a skill that enables the learner to follow a hunch, question alternatives, ponder outcomes, and wonder about options in a given situation.

question	wonder
inquire	puzzle
ask	ponder
follow a hunch	

Imagination is a skill that enables the learner to visualize possibilities, build images in one's mind, picture new objects, or reach beyond the limits of the practical in response to a given situation.

reach	expand
fantasize	wonder
visualize	dream

Adapted from *Creativity Assessment Packet* by Frank Williams. Austin, TX: Pro-Ed Publishers, 1980. Used by permission.

3. MODEL THREE: THE WEB

Webbing is an effective tool for brainstorming. To begin construction of a web, the student or teacher selects a major topic or theme which becomes the focus of the web. Once the main idea has been established, a set of related sub- or second-level points are identified and added to the web using a spider-like diagram. Additional sub- or third-level points can likewise be added, much as one develops a two- or three-level outline. This model provides the student with both a visual and graphic portrayal of ideas and their relationships to one another.

BRAINSTORMING WEB

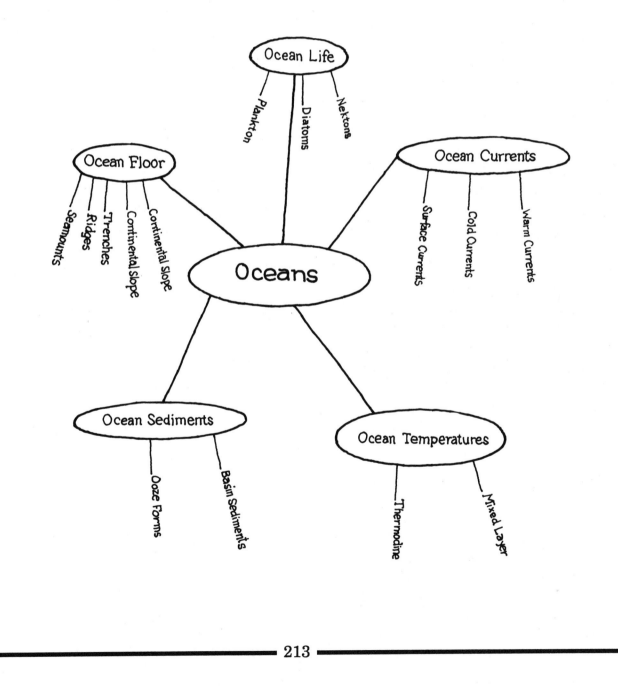

4. MODEL FOUR: RESEARCH, WRITE, AND CREATE MODEL

Another model that nurtures thinking skills in students is referred to by middle level educators as the Research, Write, and Create Model. This strategy can be adapted to any subject area and is designed to integrate thinking skills across the disciplines of science or social studies, language arts, and the fine arts.

The model requires teachers to design a classroom set of activity cards, file folders, or worksheets based on a given science or social studies topic. Each activity card, folder, or worksheet contains a cognitive RESEARCH task, a creative LANGUAGE ARTS task, and an affective FINE ARTS task. It is suggested that the teacher prepare 10 to 20 different activity cards, folders, or worksheets so that they can be used to teach a comprehensive interdisciplinary unit or so they can be used as enrichment or reinforcement opportunities for students. A set of four sample activity cards on the topic of "Health and Disease" follows.

HEALTH AND DISEASE

Research Task: Research to find out if bacteria are helpful or harmful. Present your findings in chart or graph form.

Language Arts Task: Design a magazine ad promoting a product that bacteria need to eat and drink in order to survive.

Fine Arts Task: Create a collage related to good health habits necessary to prevent disease.

HEALTH AND DISEASE

Research Task: Find out everything you can about a virus. Take notes from your reading.

Language Arts Task: Invent a virus. Tell its name, its origin, symptoms of the disease it causes, and the treatment or cure for the disease.

Fine Arts Task: Create a set of viral finger or stick puppets. Use them to share the information from your research.

HEALTH AND DISEASE

Research Task: What are the pros and cons of providing free immunizations to Americans who can't afford them, including flu shots that are not mandatory? Interview at least five people to find out their opinions.

Language Arts Task: Pretend you are Edward Jenner, the man credited with the invention of the smallpox vaccine. Write a series of diary entries he might have recorded while injecting material from cowpox into people.

Fine Arts Task: Create a cartoon showing people at the doctor's office anticipating their inoculations.

HEALTH AND DISEASE

Research Task: Which is more dangerous to the body—alcohol, tobacco, or illegal drugs? Organize a debate to discuss the issue.

Language Arts Task: Design a pamphlet or booklet which warns young children of the dangers of alcohol, tobacco, and drug abuse.

Fine Arts Task: Rewrite the lyrics to a popular song or nursery rhyme to celebrate good health habits.

5. MODEL FIVE: CHART FOR MAKING QUALITY DECISIONS

Many tools can be used to help students solve problems and make decisions more effectively. The chart concept is one effective strategy for students to use in this manner. The first step in developing such a chart is to have students generate a number of relevant criteria that can be used in making a given decision or in choosing a viable solution when solving a problem. Some criteria to consider as springboards might include:

appeal	long-term effect
cost	relevance to student
ease of use	practicality
risk involved	interest level
complexity	creativity required
time involved	most logical
timeliness	most innovative
short-term effect	most challenging

In using a chart of this type, students should list their ideas or alternatives vertically down the left side of the chart and list the criteria horizontally. Any number of criteria can be used and any number of ideas or alternatives can be included. Students might also want to use "weighted criteria" by assigning a point value to each criteria item used as part of the decision-making or problem-solving effort. (See sample on page 216.)

Sample Chart For Making Quality Decisions

Criteria

Alternative Ideas

								Total Scores
1.								
2.								
3.								
4.								
5.								
6.								
7.								
8.								
9.								
10.								

Scoring of Criteria: 3 points = Great
                      2 points = O.K.
                      1 point   = Not So Good

6. MODEL SIX: THE THINKTRIX

The thinking matrix, or "thinktrix," is a device designed to aid teachers and students in generating questions and responses (Lyman, 1987). The vertical axis of the matrix contains symbols of types of thought. The horizontal axis lists categories that give points of departure for inquiry, which vary according to the subject area. For example, using the matrix in language arts, the teacher or student points to an intersection such as *cause/effect* and *event* or *character* and asks a question about the cause of the hero's death. In social studies, the student or teacher could point to the intersection of *idea to example* and *concept or theory* and ask for historical examples of balance of power.

The thinktrix has many uses in the classroom. Students can analyze classroom questions or discourse, or they can create, analyze, and answer their own questions using a desk-size matrix as a game board. Using a poster-size matrix or wheel, teachers can make up their own questions, teach students how to design questions, show students how to respond to information using different thinking strategies, and point out the possible visual representations of each thinking style. In essence, the thinking matrix allows for shared metacognition in which teacher and student have a common framework for generating and organizing thought, as well as for reflecting on it.

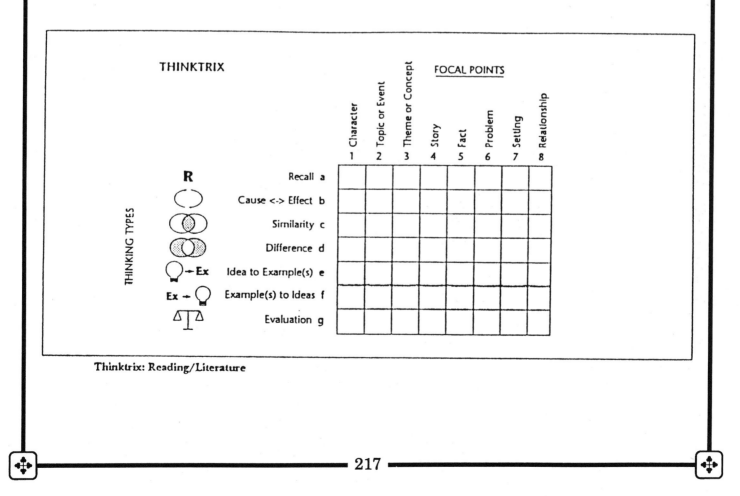

Thinktrix: Reading/Literature

The Thinktrix (continued)

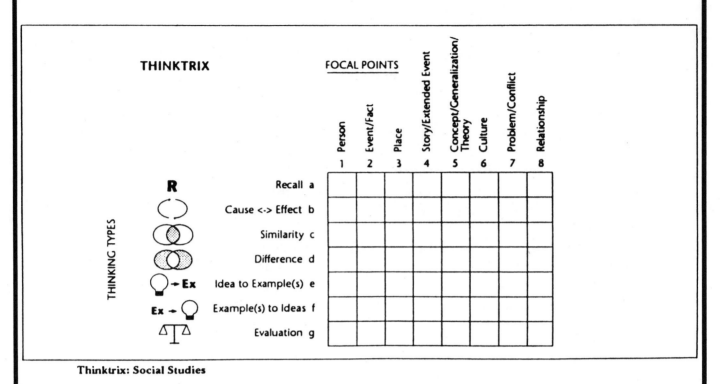

Thinktrix: Social Studies

Adapted from "The Thinktrix: A Classroom Tool for Thinking in Response to Reading" by F. Lyman in *Reading: Issues and Practices*, Yearbook of the State of Maryland International Reading Association Council, L. Gambrell, ed. College Park, MD: University of Maryland Press, 1987. Used by permission.

7. MODEL SEVEN: THINKING ON YOUR FEET

Impromptu speeches can serve as excellent models for teaching students to "think on their feet." To introduce this strategy, encourage students to write or think about such questions as:

1. When do many adults have to give impromptu speeches at home, at work, at play, or in the community?

2. What occupations or careers regularly require the workers to "think on their feet" as part of the job?

3. What skills should one have to be able to give an effective impromptu speech?

4. What do you think is hardest about being asked to "think on your feet"? What is easiest?

5. Why is it a good idea for students to learn the essentials of impromptu speaking?

Suggest to students that they practice "thinking on their feet" by giving a series of impromptu speeches following these guidelines:

1. Students are able to select from a list of topics.

2. Students have approximately three minutes to think about the topic for their impromptu speeches before performing it.

3. Students should limit their impromptu speeches to between one and two minutes in length.

4. Students should be encouraged to give their impromptu speeches some type of simple organization in order to structure their ideas for the listener. A possible outline for an impromptu speech might be:

   a. an opening statement
   b. a series of questions, arguments, factual ideas, or opinions to be addressed
   c. a set of brief details or comments about each question, argument, idea, or opinion
   d. a concluding statement

Thinking On Your Feet (continued)

Topics for impromptu speeches can be specific to a given subject area as a means for reviewing concepts learned, or impromptu speeches may be varied and reflect student interests, attitudes, opinions, and reflections. Some topic suggestions are outlined below:

1. What are ten important things you feel others should know about hurricanes (or computers, or Martin Luther King, or parts of a novel)?

2. What laws would you pass or repeal if you were President of the United States?

3. If you could be principal of your school for a day, what would you want to do and why?

4. Which is more important to you—good health, good looks, good personality, or good grades?

5. What do you think you will be like as a parent?

6. What job or career most appeals to you at this time?

7. What would you do to improve the environment if you had unlimited resources?

8. Can you describe the positive and negative impact of television on your life today?

9. If you could give advice to foreigners visiting your community, state, or country, what would you tell them?

10. What is the most exciting subject, class, or learning experience you have ever had in your school years?

8. MODEL EIGHT:
USING A PATTERN FOR PROBLEM-SOLVING TASKS

Many of the problem-solving models in the literature on thinking skills follow a general pattern requiring the following (or highly comparable) steps in the problem-solving process.

1. **PERCEPTION OF PROBLEM:** Objectively define the problem to be solved from the perspective of all members of the problem-solving group.

2. **DEFINITION OF PROBLEM:** Mutually agree upon a neutral definition of the problem so that group members understand the problem as given.

3. **ANALYSIS OF PROBLEM:** Break down the problem into its component parts so that the group can determine the problem's worst, best, and current states.

4. **GENERATION OF ALTERNATIVE SOLUTIONS:** Brainstorm optional solutions to the problem, looking for both the obvious and the not-so-obvious (novel) solutions without the use of individual criticism, judgment, or evaluation of those ideas generated.

5. **EVALUATION OF ALTERNATIVE SOLUTIONS:** Group members should establish a set of criteria for judging the worth of each alternative solution (or combination of alternative solutions) using a rating scale or ranking system.

6. **DECISION ON ALTERNATIVE SOLUTIONS:** Group members should determine the decision-making process for deciding on the best solution to the problem by looking at a variety of decision-making models such as consensus building, majority vote, delay of decision, or process of elimination.

7. **IMPLEMENTATION OF BEST SOLUTION:** An action plan should be developed by the group to determine who is responsible for what and the milestones or benchmarks to be used in documenting the implementation process. An inventory of resources and support networks should be identified at this time.

8. **EVALUATION OF RESULTS:** An evaluation plan should be established by the group to measure the success or lack of success in the problem-solving project. Celebrations of little successes should be part of this overall evaluation program.

9. MODEL NINE: THE WHY MODEL

A very simple, but effective, tool to use with students in problem-solving is one referred to as the Why Model. Students are presented with a problem question and must answer the it with a series of five "Why" questions given and answered in rapid sequence.

For example, if the problem statement reads "Why did people immigrate to the United States?" then the "Why" process would work like this:

1. *Why did people immigrate to the United States?*
   "Because they wanted to escape from political, religious, and economic discrimination."

2. *Why did they want to escape from political, religious, and economic discrimination?*
   "Most countries had a class system which only allowed selected individuals from wealthy and powerful families to take control of their lives."

3. *Why did most countries have a class system?*
   "The families with wealth and power were the people who made the laws, ran the businesses, collected the wages, and determined the religious preferences. They didn't want to give up either wealth or power, so they made certain that only the elite had opportunities for improving their standard of living."

4. *Why did the elite want to improve their standard of living?*
   "As countries grew in size and population, it took more wealth and power to maintain one's standard of living and to keep other countries that were larger or stronger from conquering those that were smaller and weaker."

5. *Why did larger and stronger countries want to overcome countries who were smaller and weaker?*
   "The ruling class of each country often had an insatiable need for more resources, not only to protect their country from war but also to satisfy their lust for more material goods and riches."

10. MODEL TEN: STARTER STATEMENTS

The following starter statements can serve as springboards for assigning creative and critical thinking tasks. They can be adapted to any content area and can be used in combination with any of the preceding models.

1. **STARTER STATEMENT ONE:** "How about . . . "

   . . . designing a house made of hexagons?

   . . . writing a speech to discuss the dangers of impulse buying?

   . . . developing a new type of snack food that is both tasty and nutritious?

   . . . drawing a picture of the setting in the short story we read in class today?

2. **STARTER STATEMENT TWO:** "What if . . . "

   . . . kids could vote in presidential elections?

   . . . our brains could only retain information for a year?

   . . . you could travel to the moon? Would you want to go and why?

   . . . there were no fractions in the world? What would you no longer be able to do?

3. **STARTER STATEMENT THREE:** "Can you . . . "

   . . . make out a grocery list for a family living in Japan?

   . . . write ten sentences that describe what you learned in our study of rocks and minerals?

   . . . invent a gadget that will help clean up the environment?

   . . . dream up a new design for a fabric that you would like to have made into a blouse or a shirt?

4. **STARTER STATEMENT FOUR:** "What are your feelings about . . . "

   . . . the Persian Gulf War?

   . . . the poetry of Shel Silverstein?

   . . . test tube babies?

   . . . calculators in the math classroom?

5. **STARTER STATEMENT FIVE:** "Will you . . . "

   . . . write some directions for taking a walking tour of your community?

   . . . compose a play about the life of a famous African-American?

   . . . construct a diorama of an underwater city?

   . . . teach me the steps in detecting an acid from a base?

6. **STARTER STATEMENT SIX:** "Do you think . . . "

   . . . you could name the major bodies of water in the world?

   . . . you would know what to do if you were caught in a hurricane?

   . . . you could explain the value of a video arcade to a Martian?

   . . . you can think of ten reasons why someone would want to go without watching television for a year?

Starter Statements (continued)

7. **STARTER STATEMENT SEVEN:** "Why don't you . . . "
   . . . think of something creative to do with 50 broken watches?
   . . . write about your superhero?
   . . . name "seven wonders of the world for the 21st century"?
   . . . make a list of things that make you happy ?

8. **STARTER STATEMENT EIGHT:** "You are a . . . "
   . . . Designer. Create a new fad or fashion for teenagers.
   . . . Landscape Architect. Design the ideal park for kids.
   . . . Poet. Write a series of haiku poems describing your favorite season or outdoor setting.
   . . . Geometrist. Draw a painting that is done only with geometric shapes.

9. **STARTER STATEMENT NINE:** "In what ways . . . "
   . . . is sunlight like jewelry?
   . . . are friends like enemies?
   . . . do butterflies resemble flags?
   . . . are the night sounds of the forest like music?

10. **STARTER STATEMENT TEN:** "Which is . . . "
    . . . sharper—a knife or a broken heart?
    . . . more dangerous—a lie or a mugger?
    . . . softer—a tear or a cotton ball?
    . . . faster—a frown or a smile?

11. **STARTER STATEMENT ELEVEN:** "Are you more like . . . "
    . . . a circle or a square?
    . . . a comma or a period?
    . . . a lake or a mountain stream?
    . . . a beaker or a test tube?

12. **STARTER STATEMENT TWELVE:** "What is . . . "
    . . . the shape of broken friendship?
    . . . the color of hope?
    . . . the texture of a dream?
    . . . the size of disappointment?

10 Ways To Use Questions To Develop Higher-Level Thinking Skills

1. **KNOWLEDGE QUESTIONS** Who, what, when, where, why, and how _____?
Recite, recall, record, or reproduce _____.
Locate, label, or list _____.

2. **COMPREHENSION QUESTIONS** Retell_____in your own words.
Describe, summarize, discuss, or explain the main idea of _____.
Give examples of _____.

3. **APPLICATION QUESTIONS** How is _____ an example of or related to _____?
Distinguish between _____ and _____.
Illustrate the workings of a _____.

4. **ANALYSIS QUESTIONS** What are the parts or features of _____?
Compare and contrast _____ with _____.
Outline, diagram, or web _____.
Draw conclusions or make inferences about _____.

5. **SYNTHESIS QUESTIONS** What would you predict or propose about _____?
What might happen if you combined _____ with _____?
How would you improve a _____?
What creative solutions would you suggest for _____?

6. **EVALUATION QUESTIONS** Rank order _____ according to _____.
What criteria would you use to assess or evaluate _____?
Defend or validate this idea/statement: _____.

7. **PERSONAL QUESTIONS** How do you feel about _____?
Do you think _____?
Where do you stand on the issue of _____?

8. **OBSERVATION QUESTIONS** What seems to be happening in this picture?_____
_____
What might you infer from your observations of _____?

9. **CAUSE/EFFECT QUESTIONS** Why did _____?
What would happen if _____?

10. **VIEWPOINT QUESTIONS** How would this look to a _____?
What would a _____ mean from the viewpoint of a _____?
How would _____view this?

10 Questions To Use To Assess Creativity In Your School

How does your school feel about the role of innovation and creativity in the curriculum and in the assessment process that drives the curriculum? Use this list of questions to determine your school's Creativity Quotient, or C.Q.

1. Is creativity highly regarded by your school's administration and faculty members?

2. Is creativity included in your school's mission statement, goals, and objectives?

3. Are creative ideas implemented quickly in your school setting?

4. Does your school have a "skunk works" or encourage brainstorming sessions as part of its agenda for in-service days?

5. Do you have staff meetings to discuss opportunities and challenges as frequently as those to discuss problems and procedures?

6. Is your school's student assessment program designed to generate qualitative as well as quantitative information about your kids?

7. Do you combine creative enterprises and innovative programs with your best and brightest teachers?

8. Do you maintain the notion that faculty are here first and foremost to meet the creative and critical thinking skill needs of the students?

9. Do you celebrate creativity in your school with ceremony, traditions, and rewards?

10. Are innovators in your school treated like heroes?

10 MINUS 2

Ways To Foster A Creative Climate In The Classroom

1. Encourage students to discuss ideas and problems in groups.
A teacher of poetry may ask students to divide into small groups to discuss and interpret a poem.

2. Ask open-ended questions.
A social studies teacher may ask questions about motivation, historical themes, and student opinions rather than confining questioning to simple facts.

3. Plan innovative and exciting activities that encourage students to investigate the world around them.
A science teacher may arrange a trip to an observatory so that students can observe the planets first-hand.

4. Be careful that you don't adhere too closely to the "one-right-answer-or-procedure" line, even in disciplines that seem to warrant this approach.
A math teacher who asks that students show their work knows that a variation from the "normal" way of arriving at an answer may work as well as a standard procedure and may indicate a high degree of creativity and intuition in the student.

5. Offer time for drawing or other alternative activities that foster creative thinking and novel approaches to problem-solving.
A science teacher may play music during problem-solving time or make drawing a part of a scientific investigation.

6. Provide an atmosphere of acceptance when ideas are being generated, even if an idea seems offbeat and/or unworkable.
A teacher who is teaching thinking skills should never give an immediate negative response to a student's idea unless the teacher's goal is to discourage students from coming up with creative ideas! The deferring of critical judgment until a later time is a creative principle that should be employed by teachers and taught to students.

7. Occasionally give assignments for which "left-brain" rules are relaxed.
A writing teacher may give assignments for which perfect spelling or punctuation is not required (at least in initial drafts).

8. Recognize the value of humor in helping to foster a creative classroom atmosphere.
The use of humor can make students want to learn and can relax students so that their thinking processes become "unstuck"—and a humorous train of thought may inspire some good, workable ideas.

10 Strategies For Smuggling Thinking Skills Into Your Subject Area

1. STRATEGY ONE: THINK SMART TASK CARDS

Think Smart Task Cards are designed for the heterogenous classroom and for use with individual or small groups of students. Each set of task cards is designed based on one of the thinking skill models described on the previous pages. To prepare the task cards, the teacher determines the model of choice and then constructs a series of individual activities based on the behaviors, questions, or stages of that model. For example, if Bloom's Taxonomy is chosen as the model, then a set of no less than twelve and no more than twenty-four individual task cards whose activities reflect each level of Bloom's Taxonomy will be created. The activities are then arranged and coded in order of difficulty so that activities which require Knowledge-level thinking skills appear first, and activities which require Evaluation-level thinking skills appear last. At least two to four different activities for each level should be available in order to provide options and choices for both the teacher and student. All cards are also numbered so that specific tasks or cards can be assigned to specific students. Topic areas for the Think Smart Task Cards should be taken directly from the major concepts and content being taught in a given subject area so that the task cards can function as review, remedial, or enrichment exercises.

A sample set of Think Smart Task Cards for problem-solving in math is included here. Reproduce page 229 in the quantities needed, cut cards apart, then write an activity on the back of each card. This set uses coupon collection as a springboard for designing the Think Smart tasks. Think Smart Task Cards work best when students have a concrete object or springboard from which to work. In math, a meter stick, mail order catalog, or set of tangrams might be used as the springboard. In science, a microscope, set of magnets, or rock collection may be the springboard. A book of poems, a dictionary, or grammar chart might be the springboard for a language arts class.

THINK SMART TASK CARDS

COUPON

CLIP THIS COUPON FOR EXTRA SAVINGS

¼ **ADDITIONAL OFF**
ANY SPECIAL IN THIS AD

Limit one per customer

COUPON

CLIP THIS COUPON FOR EXTRA SAVINGS

¼ **ADDITIONAL OFF**
ANY SPECIAL IN THIS AD

Limit one per customer

COUPON

CLIP THIS COUPON FOR EXTRA SAVINGS

¼ **ADDITIONAL OFF**
ANY SPECIAL IN THIS AD

Limit one per customer

COUPON

CLIP THIS COUPON FOR EXTRA SAVINGS

¼ **ADDITIONAL OFF**
ANY SPECIAL IN THIS AD

Limit one per customer

Think Smart Task Cards (continued)

A. To The Teacher: Make a set of Think Smart Task Cards by reproducing page 229 in quantities needed, cutting cards apart, and writing an activity from the Bloom's Overview section below on the back of each card. A package of assorted supermarket coupons must accompany each set of investigation cards.

Student Directions: Your teacher will determine whether you will investigate individually, in pairs, or in a group. In most instances, you will be required to read all activities and select at least one to complete for each level of Bloom's Taxonomy.

B. **BLOOM'S OVERVIEW**

KNOWLEDGE

1. Alphabetize the name of each item or service found on your package of coupons.

2. List the most common types of information found on coupons.

3. Define these terms using a dictionary:

Coupon	Delivery
Limited	Obligation
Bonus	Personalized
Guarantee	Specify
Brochure	Quality
Consumer	Producer

COMPREHENSION

4. Classify your coupons by type, amount saved, and other criteria of your choice.

5. Summarize the advantages and disadvantages of coupons for both consumer and producer.

6. Put your coupons in some sort of order. Explain your criteria.

Think Smart Task Cards (continued)

APPLICATION

7. Calculate your total savings if you used all of the coupons in your package. Determine how much you must spend in order to save.

8. Interview at least five adults. Ask them about their use of coupons when shopping. Share your findings.

9. Plan a sales campaign for a supermarket which does not accept coupons.

ANALYSIS

10. Draw conclusions about a shopper who saves enough money from coupon use to finance a one-week, four-person family vacation each year.

11. Point out the attention-getting savings terms or layout on your coupons.

12. Discover the coupons which offer the most savings, the least savings, and no savings.

SYNTHESIS

13. Design an original savings coupon for a service you can provide to a parent, a neighbor, or a teacher.

14. Create five math word problems using several of the coupons. Exchange with a friend and solve.

15. Combine at least five of the coupons to make one "super saver coupon."

EVALUATION

16. Rank your set of coupons from those you would most likely use to those you would never use. Explain your first and last selection.

17. Decide on the one coupon which is most pleasant to look at. Defend your choice.

18. Determine who would lose more if coupons were outlawed—the consumer, the store, or the supplier. Justify your answer.

Adapted from *The Cooperative Learning Companion* by Terri Breeden and Janice Mosley. Nashville, TN: Incentive Publications, ©1992. Used by permission.

2. STRATEGY TWO: INDEPENDENT STUDY SHEETS

Students can be motivated through the use of a one-page mini-unit or assignment sheet that is creative and unique in design. Such worksheets can be adapted to most of the thinking skill models and can be illustrated with computer graphics, clip art, border designs, or geometric shapes. The format of these independent study guides requires the teacher to visually arrange a variety of learning tasks in a logical sequence according to complexity of skills/concepts. The end result is a worksheet that looks much like a "maze" of activities which students follow in order to fulfill their requirements. Williams' Taxonomy is an excellent model to use when initiating this strategy with students, although it can be used successfully in most contexts. A sample Independent Study Sheet on "Cars" using Williams' Taxonomy is show below, and a study sheet on "Fads" using Bloom's Taxonomy is on the following page. Notice that all levels of each taxonomy have been used, and simple graphics have been inserted to add interest and novelty.

CARS

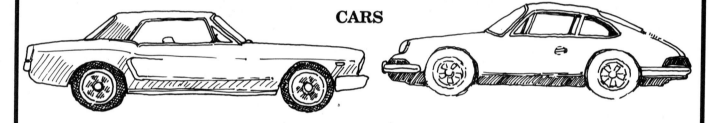

FLUENCY: Name as many kinds of automobiles as you can think of in 60 seconds.

ORIGINALITY: Think up an original ornament for a car.

RISK-TAKING: If you compared yourself to a car, what kind of care would you resemble? Give three reasons why you are like that car.

COMPLEXITY: Describe an object or machine that you could make from a heap of car parts. Tell what its function would be.

FLEXIBILITY: Classify those cars listed in the Fluency exercise by something other than foreign or domestic make, price, or color.

ELABORATION: Explain what you think our society would be like today if the automobile had never been invented.

CURIOSITY: If you could meet an automotive engineer, what would you want to know about car design?

IMAGINATION: Imagine that cars could talk. What would they say about people?

SAMPLE STUDY SHEET

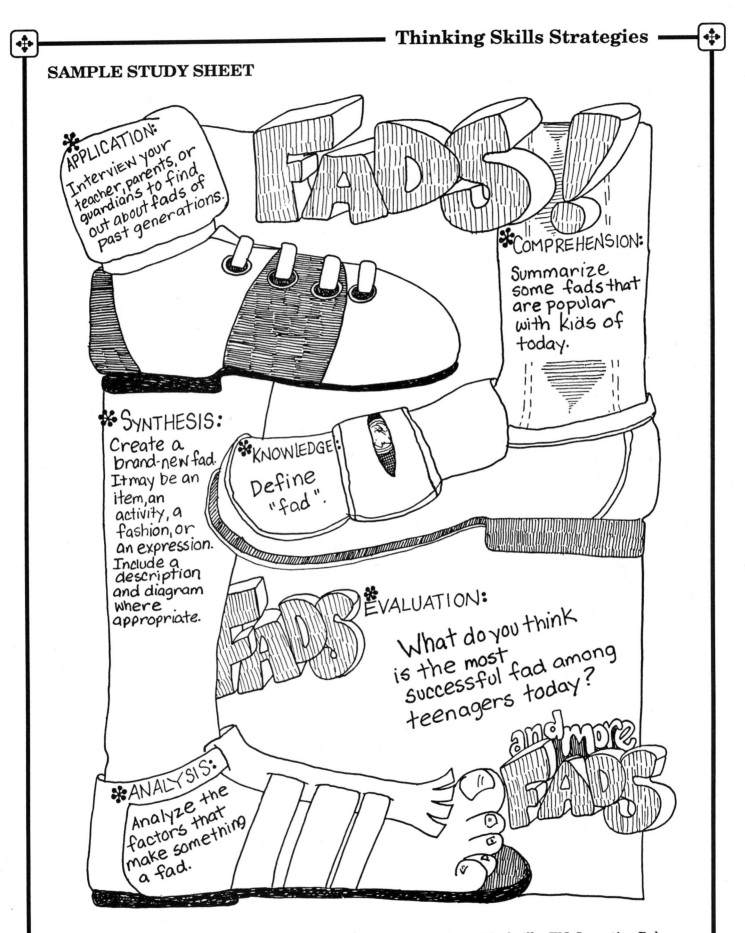

APPLICATION: Interview your teacher, parents, or guardians to find out about fads of past generations.

FADS!

COMPREHENSION: Summarize some fads that are popular with kids of today.

SYNTHESIS: Create a brand-new fad. It may be an item, an activity, a fashion, or an expression. Include a description and diagram where appropriate.

KNOWLEDGE: Define "fad".

FADS

EVALUATION: What do you think is the most successful fad among teenagers today?

and more FADS

ANALYSIS: Analyze the factors that make something a fad.

From *Operation Orientation* by Imogene Forte and Sandra Schurr. Nashville, TN: Incentive Publications, ©1991. Used by permission.

3. **STRATEGY THREE: COMMERCIAL POSTERS**

Commercial posters are popular teaching tools with middle level students. All kids love posters. Collections of posters of art, wildlife, sports, space, national parks, special events, superstars, and many other subjects make excellent springboards for applying critical and creative thinking skills. A teacher may select one or more posters and design a set of questions or tasks relating to the poster according to the models given in this section. Another way to use the posters is through cooperative learning groups. Give each small group of students a collection of five to eight posters. The posters may have the same theme or they may reflect several different themes in a given content area. Students are asked to complete any of the "poster tasks" outlined below, using the poster collection as the foundation for the activities. Good sources of posters are travel agencies, bookstores, inserts in teacher magazines, student book clubs, poster catalogs, or the students themselves. Asking each student to bring in his or her favorite poster for a classroom activity is truly a motivating invitation.

Bloom Activities Based On Commercial Posters

KNOWLEDGE

1. Measure the length and width and compute the area of each poster. What is the combined length of the posters? Combined width? Combined area?

2. Arrange the posters in a grouping that makes sense to you. Record your scheme or the logic behind your grouping.

3. List all the different types or subjects of posters that you can think of.

COMPREHENSION

4. Describe how posters might be used to . . .
   a. inform.
   b. entertain.
   c. inspire.
   d. decorate.

5. In your own words, summarize the content of each poster.

6. Give examples of subject matter and information which would lend itself to a poster format and examples that would not.

Commercial Posters (continued)

APPLICATION

7. Collect 8–10 posters. Write ten words to describe each one. Ask a friend to match each poster with each group of words.

8. Write a story that has one of the following titles:
   The Missing Poster
   The Poster That Changed The World
   A Poster Competition
   The Scandalous Poster

9. Prepare a set of quality questions to go with each poster.

ANALYSIS

10. How is a poster like and unlike a photograph? a portrait? a postcard?

11. Defend this statement: A poster is a form of art.

12. Compare and contrast any two of the posters.

SYNTHESIS

13. Make up an original title or caption for each poster.

14. Imagine what each of the following objects might say to a poster: a billboard, a masterpiece in an art museum, a magazine cover, a kindergarten drawing.

15. Survey the students in your class to determine their favorite poster. Graph your results.

EVALUATION

16. Develop a set of criteria for judging the appeal of a poster. Apply this set of criteria to each poster in your collection. Rank order your posters from the most appealing to the least appealing.

17. Diagram a flow chart for constructing a poster on any topic of your choice.

18. Argue for or against the idea that "a poster is worth a thousand words."

4. STRATEGY FOUR: REPORTS

Most students with limited reading or writing skills find assignments that require report writing to be time-consuming, redundant, uninteresting, and non-motivating. One way to overcome these students' reluctance to complete assigned reports is to provide them with some alternative writing formats that are creative, manageable, and relevant to their particular needs. One or more of the thinking skill models should form the basis of the lesson in order to help students infuse higher-order thinking into the content of their reports. Guidelines for three different types of reports are outlined below. Any one of these formats can be adapted for a variety of ability levels and interest areas.

Guidelines for Developing Magazine Reports

Magazine-driven reports are designed to provide students with a vehicle for writing reports on people, places, or things that does not demand a great deal of writing but that does demand intelligent application of thinking skills. Once a topic has been decided upon (such as biographies in English, historical landmarks in social studies, ecology in science, or computers in math), the student makes a list of the ten most important facts or key ideas and restates them into a set of sentences. Each fact or group of sentences is carefully printed, written, or typed on a single page of paper, one idea per page. Students then search through magazines, catalogs, booklets, newspapers, etc. and select illustrations to accompany each idea. These are then pasted on the page, and a booklet is made when all work is completed. Students should add a title page, a dedication page, and a bibliography page as well. Students may also want to embellish their work with their own drawings and diagrams if time and talent permit. A simple quiz might also be included as an appendix at the back of the booklet.

Guidelines for ABC Reports

In ABC reports, students use the alphabet as the basic structure for organizing their ideas on a central theme or topic. Although a report using this format requires 26 paragraphs (one for each letter of the alphabet), students often find it a manageable and straightforward format. Once a topic has been chosen for the report, the student selects a key term, concept, event, person, or situation that begins with each letter of the alphabet or that contains a key descriptive word for each letter of the alphabet. The student then writes a short expository paragraph of three to five sentences elaborating on that

Reports (continued)

main idea and using transition words, symbols, or graphics to make the ideas flow from one paragraph to another. When approaching less commonly used letters such as Q, X, or Z, students may improvise by coming up with variations. For example:

> X is for "eXamples of . . . "
>
> Q is for "Quick hints for using . . . "
>
> Z is for "Zest for . . . "

Guidelines for Question and Answer Reports

Question and Answer reports are also popular with students because they provide a structure that is both simple in design and comprehensive in content.

One such Question and Answer report uses the six reporter's questions of How? What? When? Where? Who? and Why? as its basic structure. When using this report format, a student decides on a general topic, such as tornadoes, and then formulates six questions about tornadoes based on the six reporter's questions. The student then researches each question and writes a six-paragraph report. A variation on this format would be to use the six questions as springboards for writing about several different weather-related subjects, provided that each paragraph responds consistently to any one of the six questions. For example, a "Why?" report might answer the questions: "Why do hurricanes form in the warm months?" "Why do tornadoes make a circular or spiral motion?" "Why does fog appear so dense?"

5. STRATEGY FIVE: INVESTIGATION KITS

Another way to enrich the curriculum is through teacher- or student-constructed Investigation Kits. Each kit is based on one of the thinking skill models and is designed to teach a specific topic in any of the disciplines. For example, in a science class, an investigation kit's topic might be endangered species. The topic of an investigation kit in a social studies class might be famous battles. In a math class, investigation kits might have students explore optical illusions, while the topic of a language arts investigation kit might be poetry forms. Each kit is designed to be self-contained and service a small group of students, and can be packaged in a shopping bag, a cardboard box, a basket, a plastic portfolio, or similar container. Inside the kit, the student would find several items, including:

1. An information card containing a substantive overview and discussion of the major concepts associated with the topic.

2. An objective card stating the kit's desired learning outcomes.

3. A vocabulary card giving the major terms and definitions associated with the topic.

4. A task card outlining a series of mini-investigation activities for students to complete.

5. A project card providing directions for completing a variety of individual project options.

6. A take-home written text for demonstrating skills and concepts learned upon completing the Investigation Kit.

7. A kit evaluation form for assessing how well the kit met the objectives of the teacher and the needs and interests of the student.

8. A bibliography of the kit's resources as well as a list of additional references available in the school's media center.

6. STRATEGY SIX: DESKTOP LEARNING STATIONS

Creating a series of portable desktop learning stations is another way to infuse thinking skills into any given subject area, as well as to provide a means of differentiating instruction within the heterogeneous classroom. These mini-learning stations are inexpensive to make, easy to store, adaptable to a variety of student ability levels, and appealing to students. The desktop format allows the teacher to construct several stations on the same subject or to construct several stations on a wide range of subjects, depending upon whether the objective is for enrichment, reinforcement, or remediation. These learning stations are three-sided, free-standing cardboard sections cut from boxes or purchased from office supply stores. Students complete the assigned tasks according to directions given. Sample learning stations are shown below.

C is for CELEBRITY CARDS

MY THOUGHTS ON CELEBRITIES

1. A celebrity is someone who . . .
2. A celebrity who impresses me is . . . because . . .
3. Some synonyms for "celebrity" are . . .
4. If I were a celebrity, I would never . . .
5. The best and worst things about being a celebrity must be . . .

CELEBRITY APPLICATION ACTIVITIES FOR ME TO COMPLETE

Baseball cards celebrate the members of baseball teams or leagues, and collecting baseball cards is a popular hobby with young people. With your classmates, create a set of baseball-card-style celebrity cards for one of the following types of heroes:

Language Arts:	Famous authors or literary characters
Social Studies:	Famous presidents or world leaders
Math:	Famous mathematicians or world record-holders
Science:	Famous scientists or inventors

G is for GREETING CARDS

MY THOUGHTS ABOUT GREETING CARDS

1. Greeting cards are a big business today because . . .
2. People like to send and receive greeting cards when . . .
3. Unusual types of greeting cards I've seen are those that . . .
4. Greeting cards should always be . . .
5. Greeting cards can be especially popular if . . .

Desktop Learning Stations (continued)

GREETING CARD APPLICATION ACTIVITIES

Design a series of original greeting cards that contain varied rhyming patterns, puns, similies, metaphors, and plays on words or ideas. Use the following suggestions as springboards for your creative efforts.

Language Arts: Design a birthday card for a character in a nursery rhyme, fairy tale, legend, tall tale, or myth.

Social Studies: Design a *bon voyage* card for an explorer.

Math: Design an anniversary card for the marriage of the English and the metric measurement systems.

Science: Design a get-well card for a broken microscope, balance scale, or beaker.

P is for PICTURE POSTCARDS

MY THOUGHTS ABOUT PICTURE POSTCARDS

1. Postcards are good souvenirs to buy because . . .
2. People enjoy sending or receiving postcards from trips because . . .
3. Collecting postcards could be a good hobby if . . .
4. Postcards can be good advertisements for a place when . . .
5. A time I bought and/or sent a postcard was . . .

PICTURE POSTCARD APPLICATION ACTIVITIES

Design a set of five postcards as a format on which to complete a report on one of the following topics. Make your postcards from large file cards or cut them from manila file folders. Make sure your postcards feature a picture or illustration on one side and a short descriptive paragraph, a message, and an address/stamp section on the other.

Language Arts: Settings from short stories

Social Studies: American symbols

Math: Symmetry in nature

Science: Local flora and fauna

7. STRATEGY SEVEN: FACT AND ACTIVITY FILE FOLDERS

Another popular format for differentiating instruction in the classroom is the adaptation of file folders as learning tools. Specifically, once a thinking skills model has been selected by the teacher as the structure for designing a set of instructional tasks, he or she can use the following "Fact and Activity" format to put together file folder assignments. Again, content information becomes the springboard for creating a wide variety of unique or unusual reading or writing tasks for students to complete.

To use this format, teachers select five to ten important concepts related to a unit of study. Each fact is simply stated in paragraph form. Each student is given a challenging task that reflects an idea presented in one of the concept paragraphs. Each paragraph and its corresponding follow-up activities are typed or written on an 8½" x 11" sheet of paper, which is pasted or stapled on the inside covers of a file folder. The title of the paragraph is printed with magic marker on the outside cover of the file folder while a bibliography of classroom/library readings and resources is written on the outside back cover.

Fact and Activity Folders in which content is merged with critical and creative thinking objectives are popular with middle level students because they are short, simple, challenging, and open-ended. Teachers can construct multiple copies of a few Fact and Activity Folders or they can construct a larger number of different Fact and Activity Folders. Numbers, levels, stages, or codes can be added to the file folders as management tools for the teacher when assigning specific file folder titles to students. File folders are convenient for storing student work as it is completed for the teacher to collect and grade. Sample Fact and Activity file folder pages on the subject of Botany are included on the following pages.

BONING UP ON BOTANY

Teacher Talk

Purpose:
To recognize the importance of plants in our environment.

Materials Needed:
- Copy of Facts To Review sheet for each group
- Copy of Activity page for each group
- Paper and pencils

Suggested Group Size:
Four

Suggested Group Roles:
Coordinator, Recorder, Reader, and Checker

Suggested Social Skills:
Speaking and listening, and developing respect. for differing opinions

Suggested Methods Of Accountability:
Individual — Ability to explain the importance of plants in our environment
Group — Satisfactory completion of all activities

Directions:
- You will be teaching one another about plants by brainstorming and completing the activities as a group.
- To stimulate creative thinking, first read the information on the Facts To Review sheet.

BONING UP ON BOTANY

Facts To Review

1. Botany is the science or study of plants. A botanist examines plants—how they are structured and how they function.

2. Every plant is a living laboratory in which chemical reactions take place. Heat and light often stimulate these chemical reactions.

3. Early physicians used plants as remedies for their patients. They had to know how to distinguish between useful and poisonous plants.

4. Explorers sailing to new parts of the world found many unknown plant species. The resulting growth in demand for plant products (such as foods, fibers, drugs, and dyes) led to an increase in trade.

5. The study of plants is important to humans because most of our food comes from plants. Through the science of botany, humans can improve these vital food sources.

BONING UP ON BOTANY

Activities

1. Imagine a world without plants. List ten ways in which life would be different in such a world.

2. Pretend you are a plant suffering from too much light or heat. Describe how you feel and what is happening to you.

3. Assume you have been incorrectly labeled as a plant poisonous for humans. Compose a protest speech declaring your innocence.

4. You are a miracle plant who has just been discovered by an explorer. Write a series of diary entries: What is your name? Where were you found? Who discovered you? Why are you important?

5. Create a lunch or dinner menu, including many of your favorite "plants." Describe your dishes in mouth-watering terms.

Adapted from *The Cooperative Learning Guide & Planning Pak For Middle Grades: Thematic Projects And Activities* by Imogene Forte and Sandra Schurr. Nashville, TN: Incentive Publications, ©1992. Used by permission.

8. STRATEGY EIGHT: LEARNING LOGS AND DIALOGUE DIARIES

Another meaningful method of smuggling thinking skills into daily classroom events is through the continued and programmed use of learning logs and dialogue diaries maintained by students as an integral part of any study unit. This strategy is excellent for merging several of the thinking models into one integrated program. The key to making log and diary entries successful with middle grades students is to make certain that the logs or diaries are evaluated and counted as part of the overall grade for the unit of study, receiving equal weight with other program components such as textbook readings and questions, tests, homework assignments, and classroom tasks. Daily log/diary questions, starter sentences, reaction statements, or short writing exercises that are structured according to any of the thinking skills models should be provided as well. Some sample student questions and directives based on the various models follow.

1. Use logs and diaries for self-assessment by writing entries to evaluate one's individual progress in a given subject area.

2. Use logs and diaries to explore personal reactions and responses to lectures, readings, viewings, recordings, and simulations.

3. Use logs and diaries to reflect on one's contributions to a class project, assignment, discussion, or field trip.

4. Use logs and diaries to record questions, observations, and insights in preparation for a student-teacher conference.

5. Use logs and diaries to keep track of one's independent research, reading, and study activities.

6. Use logs and diaries to maintain personal dialogues between oneself and the teacher or peers.

7. Use logs and diaries as source books for writing ideas for reports, research projects, writing assignments, and self-study topics.

8. Use logs and diaries as places for integrating subject matter and commenting on ideas or concepts learned.

9. Use logs and diaries for describing specific incidents and impressions arising from special events, challenges, opportunities, and excursions.

10. Use logs and diaries as sounding boards or trial runs for writing for a variety of purposes and a wider audience.

9. STRATEGY NINE: INTERDISCIPLINARY UNITS

An effective means for strengthening thinking skills is provided through the use of the interdisciplinary unit. With this approach, the thinking skills themselves, exhibited as student behaviors or stages, are used to link disciplines (ordinarily, subject matter concepts serve to link disciplines). The following unit on Organ Transplants is an excellent example of this way of smuggling thinking skills into the curriculum.

Sample Interdisciplinary Unit

ORGAN TRANSPLANTS

Purpose: To use Bloom's Taxonomy as a structure for examining implications of organ transplants.

Materials Needed:
• Copies of student worksheets for each group
• Paper and pencils

Suggested Group Size:
Four

Suggested Group Roles:
Facilitator, Timekeeper, Checker, Recorder

Suggested Group Social Skills:
Sharing materials and ideas

Suggested Methods Of Accountability:
Individual—Oral response to Evaluation Task
Group—Quality of "Science Fair Fun" Plan

Directions:
• Working as a group, read, discuss, and contribute information and ideas to each level of the Group Overview Worksheet.
• Share information and jointly complete the five tasks (one worksheet *only* to be completed by each group).
• Turn in completed Worksheets to the teacher.

ORGAN TRANSPLANTS

 KNOWLEDGE

Write the dictionary definition of transplant, organ, and donor.

 COMPREHENSION

Give at least three examples of when an organ transplant might be the only solution to a serious medical situation.

 APPLICATION

Suppose that you are a transplant candidate waiting for a kidney. Predict what criteria would be used in deciding whether you would be the recipient of the next available organ.

 ANALYSIS

To maintain a person on dialysis (a kidney machine) for one year costs $30,000. A kidney transplant operation also costs $30,000. When would dialysis be the best procedure to follow and when would a kidney transplant be the best procedure to follow?

 **SYNTHESIS**

Hundreds of thousands of people around the world are waiting for transplants, but there are very few organs or organ donors available. Organize a very creative campaign to promote the idea of becoming an organ donor.

EVALUATION

Do you think that organ donations should be mandatory for individuals who die prematurely? Be able to support your opinion with at least three good arguments.

247

ORGAN TRANSPLANTS

NAME _____   DATE

Make a list of body organs which can be transplanted.   _____

Why are organ transplants often called "the gift of life" or
"an ordinary miracle"?   _____

Pretend that you are to interview a potential organ donor.
Design interview questions and answers to demonstrate
how one goes about becoming an organ donor.   _____

Compare what is involved in a cornea transplant with
what is involved in a liver transplant. Show your findings
in outline form.   _____

Design a donor card for organ donors. What information
would you need or want to know about a donor?   _____

SPARE PARTS FOR PEOPLE

Would you like to meet a bionic boy or girl? Perhaps you already have! The word "bionic" describes any artificial body part that's designed to work exactly like the real thing. Today there are many people whose worn-out or damaged body parts have been replaced by artificial ones.

Pretend that you are a bionic boy or girl living in the year 2050. Write an autobiography telling about your bionic body and your life. The outline below will help you.

Date and place of birth: _____

List of damaged or worn-out body parts and causes of problems:

_____

_____

_____

List of electronic parts or organs obtained:

_____

_____

_____

List of unusual facts, activities, interests and hobbies relating to your mechanical body parts:

_____

_____

_____

249

LETTERS TO THE EDITOR

Someday doctors will have the medical knowledge enabling them to transplant organs of any type to recipients of any age or sex. Write a letter to the editor describing your feelings, concerns, and expectations surrounding the extensive use of organ transplant banks.

Dear Editor,

_____

_____

_____

_____

_____

_____

_____

_____

_____

_____

_____

_____

_____

_____

_____

THE BUSINESS OF ORGAN TRANSPLANTS

You have been hired to improve the operation of a human organ transplant bank. Write a description of the improvements you plan to make in each of the following areas.

Procedures for organ donors:

_____

_____

_____

_____

Procedures for organ recipients:

_____

_____

_____

_____

Procedures for organ storage, identification and transportation:

_____

_____

_____

_____

Procedures for marketing organ transplant services:

_____

_____

_____

_____

SCIENCE FAIR FUN

Plan a project for the science fair on organ transplants. Combine creative flair with scientific facts to create an outstanding exhibit. Use the questions below as a guide in structuring your project.

From what sources will you get your facts and information?

_____

_____

_____

_____

What type of project will you prepare? (notebook, filmstrip, diorama, model, poster, etc.)

_____

_____

What kind of graphics and illustrations will you use? (charts, graphs, lists, original drawings, pictures, etc.)

_____

_____

_____

How will you evaluate your project? _____

_____

_____

_____

From *Science Mind Stretchers* by Imogene Forte and Sandra Schurr. Nashville, TN: Incentive Publications, ©1987. Used by permission.

10. STRATEGY TEN: GAMES

Educational games play an important role in the middle-level classroom because kids have an inherent passion for games. When playing games, kids can constructively interact with one another, apply their communication and decision-making skills in a nonthreatening environment, and participate regardless of their ability level. They are evaluated by the outcome of the game and not by grades or body language of the teacher. One interesting way to get students to apply thinking skills from any of the models is to assign them the task of constructing a game as the culmination of a unit of study. It is important to provide students with an outline of what should be included in this gaming project; some suggestions for this are given below. Make certain that students know that they must use one of the thinking skill models as the basis for designing all game questions, events, tasks, or challenges. Encourage them to include an outline of the thinking skill model as part of the game's directions.

Requirements for Your Game Project

DIRECTIONS: You are to construct a game on a topic of your choice that is related to our recent unit on _____. Your game must require its players to use their best creative and critical thinking skills throughout the playing time. Before you actually begin creating your gaming masterpiece, you must decide on a thinking skill model as the foundation for your game design.

Your game should include:
1. An unusual title
2. Number of players
3. Learning outcomes and/or purposes of the game
4. Specific topic, theme, or subject from your recent study of _____.
5. Dice, spinner, or other method for specifying turns
6. Playing pieces for players
7. Question, task, statement, or activity cards
8. Chance or special direction cards
9. Answer key or booklet
10. Rules and directions for play
11. Playing board, deck of cards, or equivalent
12. Special container or package for game contents

10 Characteristics Of Five Varied Learning Styles

1. TEN CHARACTERISTICS OF AUDITORY LEARNERS

1. Auditory learners like to be read to.
2. Auditory learners sit where they can hear.
3. Auditory learners are most likely to read aloud or subvocalize when they read.
4. Auditory learners enjoy music.
5. Auditory learners acquire information primarily through sound.
6. Auditory learners are easily distracted by noises.
7. Auditory learners may not coordinate colors or clothes, but can explain what they are wearing and why.
8. Auditory learners enjoy listening activities.
9. Auditory learners enjoy talking.
10. Auditory learners hum or talk to themselves or others when bored.

2. TEN CHARACTERISTICS OF VISUAL LEARNERS

1. Visual learners like to read.
2. Visual learners take copious notes
3. Visual learners often close their eyes to visualize or remember.
4. Visual learners are usually good spellers.
5. Visual learners like to see what they are reading.
6. Visual learners tend to value planning and organization.
7. Visual learners are meticulous, neat in appearance.
8. Visual learners notice details.
9. Visual learners find something to watch when bored.
10. Visual learners find quiet, passive surroundings ideal.

3. TEN CHARACTERISTICS OF KINESTHETIC LEARNERS

1. Kinesthetic learners enjoy using manipulatives.
2. Kinesthetic learners speak with their hands and with gestures.
3. Kinesthetic learners remember what was done but have difficulty recalling what was said or seen.
4. Kinesthetic learners will try new things.
5. Kinesthetic learners rely on what they can directly experience, do, or perform.
6. Kinesthetic learners are outgoing and expressive by nature.
7. Kinesthetic learners tend to be messy in habits and dress.
8. Kinesthetic learners are uncomfortable in classrooms where they lack hands-on experience.
9. Kinesthetic learners like physical rewards.
10. Kinesthetic learners need to be active and in motion.

4. TEN CHARACTERISTICS OF RIGHT-BRAIN LEARNERS

1. Right-brain learners think intuitively and respond well to open-ended activities.
2. Right-brain learners have a common-sense approach to problems.
3. Right-brain learners remember faces.
4. Right-brain learners make subjective statements.
5. Right-brain learners are spontaneous, impulsive, flexible, and creative.
6. Right-brain learners solve problems through synthesis.
7. Right-brain learners are free with feelings.
8. Right-brain learners prefer essay tests.
9. Right-brain learners lack a strong sense of time and structure.
10. Right-brain learners "see the forest."

5. TEN CHARACTERISTICS OF LEFT-BRAIN LEARNERS

1. Left-brain learners are rational, logical, and verbal.
2. Left-brain learners like facts and knowledge.
3. Left-brain learners remember names.
4. Left-brain learners make objective judgments.
5. Left-brain learners respond to structure, order, and rules.
6. Left-brain learners solve problems through analysis.
7. Left-brain learners control feelings, emotions.
8. Left-brain learners prefer multiple-choice tests.
9. Left-brain learners like schedules and lists and have a well-developed sense of time.
10. Left-brain learners "see the trees."

TEACHER'S THINKING SKILLS WRAP-UP, À LA BLOOM

KNOWLEDGE
List ways thinking skills can be taught.

COMPREHENSION
Give examples of things teachers can do to encourage creative thinking through interdisciplinary instruction.

APPLICATION
Plan a presentation for faculty in-service on "Strategies For Developing Higher-Level Thinking Skills."

ANALYSIS
Compare and contrast three major taxonomies and/or models for teaching or strengthening thinking skills in the classroom.

SYNTHESIS
Create a lesson plan, classroom activity, or assignment designed to teach thinking skills at one or more levels.

EVALUATION
Summarize in three sentences or less your interpretation of the phrase "smuggling thinking skills into the classroom."

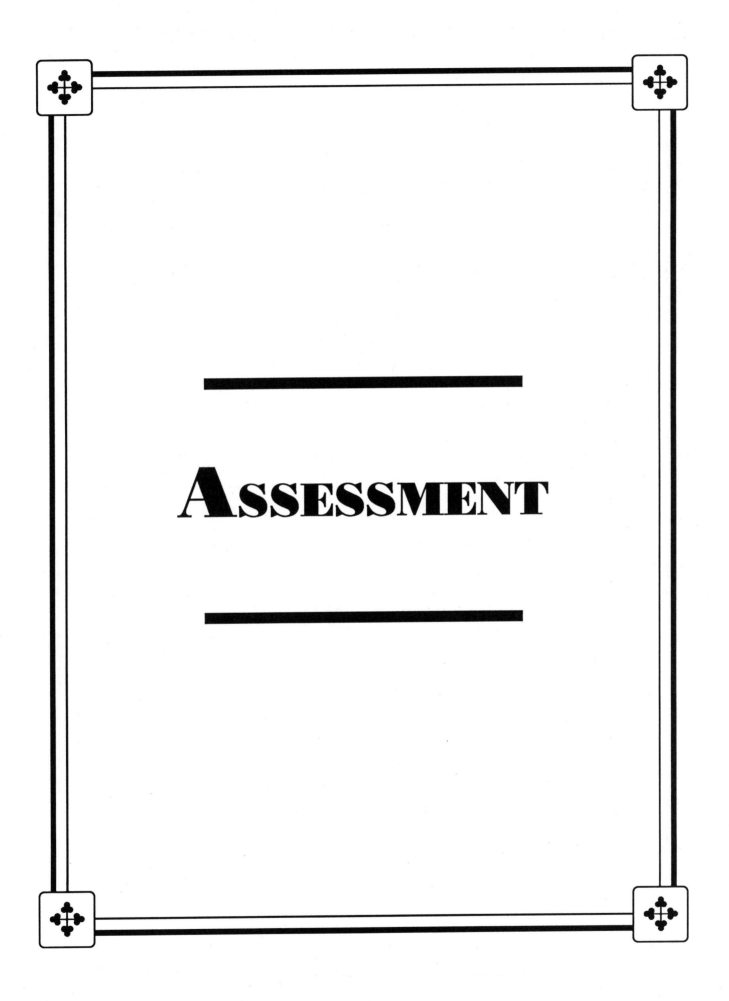

ASSESSMENT

Assessment Overview

ASSESSMENT IS:
- The testing or grading of students according to a given set of criteria.
- Referred to as authentic when methods of assessing achievement or performance are as close to real-life situations as possible.
- Valuable to both teachers and students as feedback on the effectiveness of classroom delivery systems and outcome expectancies.

MEANINGFUL ASSESSMENT SHOULD BE PLANNED TO TAKE INTO ACCOUNT:
- The use of a wide variety of methods and techniques, avoiding overuse of any one testing strategy.
- The need to assess individual student growth in both cognitive and affective areas.
- The use of tests, quizzes, products, portfolios, and performance assessments to stimulate student interest, enthusiasm, quest for knowledge, and improved self-esteem.
- Provisions for prompt, accurate, and concise feedback to students and parents.
- A nonthreatening environment and avoidance of personally embarrassing situations.
- New and different approaches to provoke student interest and positive behavior.
- Measurement of innovative delivery systems such as cooperative learning, peer tutoring, exploratory and mini-courses, and thematic and research- and literature-based units as well as teacher-directed lessons and lectures.

EFFECTIVE ASSESSMENT DEVICES CHARACTERISTICALLY:
- Identify both strengths and weaknesses.
- Make provisions for student involvement in a personal sense in the overall assessment process.
- Take into account differences in student learning styles, attitudes, interests, and talents.
- Honor all student efforts and neither downgrade nor glorify varying exceptionalities at either end of the grading spectrum.
- Make provisions when feasible for collaborative efforts while taking into account individual differences within the group.
- Employ a multifaceted scoring procedure rather than one rigid grading system while avoiding "fuzzy and unclear" terminology or evaluative criteria that has little actual meaning for any stakeholder in the assessment process.
- Provide timely and specific feedback for teacher evaluation and future planning.
- Contribute to the student's sense of self-worth and academic achievement.

10 PLUS 10

Important Assessment Questions To Find Answers For

1. Under what circumstances are teacher-made tests more effective than standardized tests? Explain your answer and give at least one example of an occasion when just the opposite would be true.

2. What are some advantages and some disadvantages of the use of true-false questions as a measure of major concepts and understandings gained and processed?

3. What are some guidelines for developing matching and/or sentence completion questions?

4. What are some common pitfalls to avoid when developing and using multiple-choice questions?

5. What can teachers do to make sure that assessment results are reported and interpreted in a manner that is actually meaningful and useful to parents and students?

6. What are some major guidelines for writing and scoring essay tests?

7. What are some commonalities of portfolio, performance, and product assessment? Explain the strengths and weaknesses of each and give one example of a situation in which each would be a valid means of assessment.

8. How would you define outcomes-based education? In your own words, explain an effective approach to outcomes-based assessment.

9. What are some ways middle level students can be prepared for taking essay tests?

10. What are some advantages of portfolio assessment over traditional testing? Give at least three advantages for the student.

11. Why are student products good assessment tools? How can they be used to encourage creativity?

12. What are some things to keep in mind when designing, scoring, and using performance tests and evaluating their results?

13. What are some major advantages of including student self-evaluation as an ongoing part of a structured assessment program?

14. What are the most valuable components of a student portfolio as viewed by the teacher?

15. What are the most valuable components of a student portfolio as viewed by the student?

16. How can teachers assigned to the same team work together to develop a plan to more effectively assess individual students within the group?

17. What steps can teachers take to become more proficient in selecting, administering, recording, and making use of assessment tools and results?

18. How can total group assessment devices be tailored to acknowledge and make positive application of differences in individual learning styles?

19. What are some informal methods of assessing student understanding of material covered during instruction?

20. How can assessment be used to help students develop a positive self-image and capitalize on individual strengths and weaknesses?

10 Definitions Essential To Assessment Success

1. **Authentic Assessment** refers to methods of assessing student achievement or performance that are as close to real-life situations as the setting allows.

2. **Assessment** is the testing or grading of students according to a given set of criteria.

3. **Evaluation** is the process used to determine the general value or worth of programs, curricula, or organizational settings.

4. **Measurement** implies the assignment of a numerical quantity to a given assessment or evaluation procedure.

5. **Metacognition** stresses the consciousness of one's own thinking process.

6. **Outcomes-Based Education** focuses curriculum, instruction, and measurement/assessment on the desired student outcomes—the knowledge, competencies, and qualities students should be able to demonstrate when they finish school.

7. **Outcomes-Based Assessment** is assessment in the context of outcomes-based education. It is those skills, competencies, experiences, talents, and attitudes which the student is intended to have after graduation for the purpose of employment or personal human development which are assessed.

8. **Validity** refers to the extent to which a test measures what it was intended to measure.

9. **Reliability** is the consistency of performance on the test from one taking of the test to another by the same individual.

10. **Portfolio, Performance, and Product Assessment** are three different forms of authentic assessment. A portfolio is a meaningful collection of student work that exhibits the student's overall efforts, progress, and achievements in one or more areas. Performance assessment is based on the professional judgment of the assessor through observation of the student performing a predetermined task. Product assessment is an assessment that requires a concrete end result such as a display, videotape, learning package, experiment, script, production, manual, or exhibit.

10 MINUS 1

Findings From The Published Literature To Document The Need For Alternative Assessment Methods

1. FINDING
Glen Fielding and Joan Shaughnessy state:

Despite the visibility of testing and its obvious importance, testing generally is a weak aspect of secondary school instruction. Classroom tests tend to focus on lower-order knowledge and skills at the expense of broad understanding and meaningful applications (Fleming and Chambers, 1983). That which teachers emphasize on tests, moreover, often appears out of line with that which they have emphasized during instruction (Haertel et al., 1984). Finally, teachers rarely use test information as a guide to improving instruction, and students rarely use test results to help them decide how to do better (Rudman et al., 1980). The gap between the potential of testing as a teaching-learning tool and the reality of current testing practices is wide.

Reference: Fielding, G. and Shaughnessy, J. Improving Student Assessment: Overcoming the Obstacles. NASSP Bulletin. Reston, VA: National Association of Secondary School Principals, November 1991, p. 91.

2. FINDING
The editor of *Instructor Magazine* writes:

The older the students, the less likely are they to believe that their scores on standardized tests reflect their actual abilities, a new study reports. Scott Paris, a professor of education at the University of Michigan, surveyed 900 Arizona, Michigan, California, and Florida students in grades 2–11 and found:

- Seventy-five percent of second-graders, but only five percent of eleventh-graders, agreed that "test scores show how intelligent you are."
- Ninety-five percent of second-graders, but only forty percent of eleventh-graders, agreed that "most students try to do their best on tests."

Reference: Editor. "Teachers Are Talking About." Instructor Magazine, May 1991, p. 14.

3. FINDING

Vito Perrone summarizes:

In documenting the "process of learning," teachers in a school might wish to include information about a child's originality, responsibility, initiative, and independence of effort. In relation to the "content of learning," they might wish to consider materials a child produces (writings, drawings, projects), evidence that instruction deals with important concepts as well as necessary skills, and evidence that a child finds meaning in learning, that it is not merely rote. And in relation to the "context of learning," they might consider the basic human relationships that exist—child to child, child to teacher, and teacher to teacher—and see how much respect there is for the efforts and feelings of others.

Reference: Perrone, V. The Abuses of Standardized Testing. Bloomington, IN: Phi Delta Kappan Educational Foundation, 1977, p. 33.

4. FINDING

R. E. Sarnacki writes:

Although test-wise examinees may use their general test-taking skills on all types of tests, it is safe to say that "test-wiseness" more readily manifests itself on multiple-choice tests, where maximum item-writing skills are required. Indeed, the majority of test-wiseness research has centered around the recognition of secondary-item cues that occur in flawed multiple-choice items. For example, one item fault known as "absurd options" allows the test-wise examinee to eliminate one or more of the alternatives because of logical inconsistencies with the stem.

More important to the individual test-taker, individual differences in test-wiseness may exaggerate differences in observed scores, perhaps leading to erroneous conclusions concerning levels of content knowledge. And Ebel (1971) has pointedly noted that "more error in measurement is likely to originate from students who have too little, rather than too much, skill in taking tests." This problem is compounded daily, due to the ever-increasing use of multiple-choice tests, new multiple-choice item types, and an increasingly heterogeneous pool of prospective test-takers.

Reference: Sarnacki, R. E. "Test-wiseness." From The International Encyclopedia of Educational Evaluation, edited by Walberg, H. J. and Haertel, G. D. Elmsford, NY: Pergamon Press, Inc., 1990.

5. FINDING
Rexford Brown writes:

That which needs to change in order to make room for more thoughtfulness in the schools is not just the taking of tests—which clearly does not require students to create, construct, negotiate, and communicate meaning—but the whole concept of testing itself. The concept that testing is initiated externally from the student, separate from the learning process, and primarily aimed at determining whether inert knowledge is in students' short-term memories exercises far too much influence over school people today. The goals of thoughtfulness are that students internalize capacities to evaluate their learning, do so as they learn, and do so in ways that exhibit their capacity to be performing thinkers, problem-solvers, and inquirers. The dominant technology neither tells us whether those goals are being met, nor encourages anyone to find out, nor models a kind of inquiry into achievement that students and teachers might profitably imitate.

Reference: Brown, R. Testing and Thoughtfulness. Educational Leadership. Alexandria, VA: Association for Supervision and Curriculum Development, April 1989, p. 33.

6. FINDING
Cathy Vatterott says:

Consider the following cycle of behavioral cause and effect: When a school's social climate fails to meet students' emotional needs, they tend to feel "disconnected" from the school (Strahan, 1989). That sense of disconnectedness produces apathy, which results in less effort, which causes poor performance, which in turn produces a lack of teacher motivation to continue to meet student needs. This lack of teacher involvement fuels further student apathy. Middle schools must take the initiative to break that cycle. As teachers and schools attempt to be more responsive to students' needs, students become more motivated to please the teacher. If learning is designed with sufficient attention to the social and emotional climate in which it occurs, students motivation and performance should improve.

Reference: Vatterott, C. "Assessing School Climate in the Middle Level School." Schools in the Middle: Theory into Practice. Reston, VA: National Association of Secondary School Principals, April 1991, pp. 1–2.

7. FINDING
Allan C. Ornstein says:

Knowledge should be applicable to the real world. Book knowledge that cannot be applied to everyday life is meaningless, easily forgotten, and does not help the learner participate productively in society. The school must resist the teaching of theory that cannot be applied to practice; good theory means that it can be applied to practice.

Reference: Ornstein, A.C. Knowledge as a Source of Change: An Essay. NASSP Bulletin. Reston, VA: National Association of Secondary School Principals, April 1988, p. 73.

8. FINDING
Rexford Brown writes:

The literacy of thoughtfulness calls for a new concept of testing, one that reflects the active nature of learning. Innovation in testing and assessment is following four paths:

1. Expanding existing tests and data-gathering instruments.
2. More innovative analysis and packaging of test information.
3. Adapting and legitimizing evaluation schemes and instruments used in other fields.
4. Breaking new ground through computer testing, video evaluation, tying evaluation to learning, student-created tests/assessments/evaluations/research projects, climate assessment tools, and input from the community. With all of these possibilities, no one should claim that outcomes "cannot" be assessed.

Reference: Brown, R. "Testing and Thoughtfulness." Educational Leadership. Alexandria, VA: ASCD, April 1989.

9. FINDING
Grant Wiggins reports:

Designers of performance assessments should use these eight basic design criteria:

1. Assessment tasks should be, whenever possible, authentic and meaningful—worth mastering.
2. The set of tasks should be a valid sample from which apt generalizations about overall performance of complex capacities can be made.
3. The scoring criteria should be authentic, with points awarded or taken off for essential successes and errors, not for what is easy to count or observe.
4. The performance standards that anchor the scoring should be genuine benchmarks, not arbitrary cut scores or provincial school norms.
5. The context of the problems should be rich, realistic, and enticing with the inevitable constraints on access to time, resources, and advance knowledge of the tasks and standards appropriately minimized.
6. The tasks should be validated.
7. The scoring should be feasible.
8. Assessment results should be reported and used so that all customers from the data are satisfied.

Reference: Wiggins, G. "Creating Tests Worth Taking." Educational Leadership. Alexandria, VA: ASCD, May 1992.

10 Commandments Of Testing In Middle Grades

1. Thou shalt not overuse any one testing strategy.

2. Thou shalt not spring surprise tests on students.

3. Thou shalt not administer tests without adequate preparation on the part of students.

4. Thou shalt not use a test as a threat to motivate or discipline students.

5. Thou shalt not avoid using tests as feedback to teachers on the effectiveness of classroom delivery systems.

6. Thou shalt not use paper-and-pencil tests as the only means of student evaluation.

7. Thou shalt not overlook the importance of measuring growth in both affective and cognitive areas of student development.

8. Thou shalt not fail to provide adequate feedback to students on test results.

9. Thou shalt not neglect to reduce test anxiety among students.

10. Thou shalt not limit test questions to the lower levels of Bloom's Taxonomy.

From *The ABC's of Classroom Evaluation* by Sandra Schurr. Columbus, OH: National Middle School Association (NMSA), 1992. Used by permission.

10 Questions Students Need To Have Answered Before A Test
And
Ten Ways Students Can Use Test Time Wisely

QUESTIONS:

1. Is this going to be a quiz, test, or exam?

2. What type of quiz/test/exam will it be? (Take-home, oral, collaborative, individual, or open book?)

3. What kind of questions will it have? (Multiple choice, essay, fill-in-the-blank, true/false, or short answer?)

4. How much time will I be given to complete the quiz/test/exam?

5. How long will it be? How many questions will it have?

6. What information will be covered? (Notes, textbook, lecture, outside readings, discussions?)

7. Do the answers have to be written in complete sentences and will spelling count?

8. Can I hand in the test as soon as I finish?

9. How can I best review for the quiz/test/exam?

10. How will the test be graded or scored?

WAYS TO USE TEST TIME:

1. Read through the entire test before you begin writing the answers.

2. Budget your time by setting time limits for each section of the test.

3. Complete all questions you know first. Then go back and work on questions of which you are not so certain.

4. Underline or circle key words and phrases in each set of directions on the test.

5. Use intelligent guessing strategies for those questions you don't know. Try not to leave any questions unanswered unless there are penalties for making a "best guess."

6. Never go back and change an answer unless you are absolutely sure you made a mistake.

7. Allow a few minutes at the end of the test to go back and review all questions and answers.

8. Be sure your name is on each page of the test.

9. Don't worry about what other students are doing on the test or how they are pacing their time.

10. If you had to transpose answers from one place to another on the test or answer sheet, doublecheck to make sure you were not careless in doing so.

10 Guidelines For Improving Teacher-Made Tests

In preparing effective tests, teachers should keep the following guidelines in mind:

1. Identify the specific learning outcomes before writing the test items.

2. Match the content of the test with your instructional material.

3. Design item formats parallel to that of the instructional material.

4. Develop and follow test administration procedures consistently and precisely.

5. Ensure that test scoring was done correctly.

6. Develop your own test-rating criteria before administering the test.

7. Write clear, unambiguous test items.

8. Write test items at a level of difficulty that is reasonable for your students.

9. Provide students with a distraction-free test environment.

10. Help students become test-wise.

Adapted from *Assessing Relevance and Reliability to Improve the Quality of Teacher-Made Tests* by Philip A. Griswold. NASSP Bulletin. Reston, VA: National Association of Secondary School Principals, February 1990. Used by permission.

10 Things For Teachers To Consider When Evaluating A Lesson Plan

When preparing successful lesson plans, teachers should keep the following questions in mind:

1. Do you have clearly-stated instructional objectives for both the skills and the content you wish to teach?

2. Are the lesson plans' subject matter and concepts appropriate for the grade level and the cultural diversity of the group?

3. Is the instructional plan feasible in terms of available time and resources?

4. Does the lesson plan accommodate a variety of learning styles and/or modalities of students?

5. Does the lesson plan actively engage students and motivate them to want to learn the materials?

6. Does the lesson plan meet the essential needs and characteristics of the middle level students physically, socially, emotionally, psychologically, and intellectually?

7. Does the lesson plan relate to real-life situations so that the students sees some relevance and practicality in its objectives?

8. Do evaluative criteria exist for determining how much students have learned from the lesson?

9. Do evaluative criteria exist for giving feedback to the teacher on how well the objectives were accomplished?

10. Does the lesson plan have a clearly-stated introduction, body, and conclusion so that the student experiences a sense of completeness when the lesson is over?

10 Guidelines To Consider When Writing Quality Test Items

1. Relate each test item to a specific content or skill (instructional) objective from the curriculum.

2. Keep each test item simple, clear, and well defined.

3. Make certain each test item is age- and grade-appropriate for the student.

4. Doublecheck each test item for any spelling, grammar, and typing errors.

5. Write each test item so that it calls for information that is both relevant and useful to the student.

6. Design each test item to stand on its own, independent of all other test items.

7. Write each test item so that it reflects a factual and objective statement rather than an opinion or subjective statement.

8. Write each test item so that it is free from textbook jargon or formal "teacher talk."

9. Whenever possible, write each test item as a simple and/or compound sentence rather than a complex sentence.

10. Write each test item in a style that matches the style of the desired response.

10 PLUS 5

Hints For Writing Better Objective Test Items

TRUE/FALSE TEST ITEMS

1. Each test item should reflect only one major concept or idea.

2. Each test item should be written with a positive and not a negative focus.

3. Each test item should avoid use of trick or trivial statements, use of double negatives, and use of determiners such as all, never, entirely, absolutely, only, or nothing.

4. Each test item, whether true or false, should contain approximately the same number of words, and tests should consist of approximately equal numbers of true and false statements.

5. Each test item should be totally true or totally false without qualifications.

MULTIPLE CHOICE TEST ITEMS

1. The stem of a multiple choice test item should be brief, concise, stated positively, and should be either a direct question or an incomplete statement.

2. As much of the item as possible should be included in a multiple choice test stem so that students can avoid rereading the same information over and over again when deciphering alternatives.

3. The "best" or "most correct" alternative should be included in a multiple choice test item as well as those that "could be" feasible responses to a student who is not prepared for the test.

4. The correct use of grammar and punctuation between stems and the corresponding alternatives should be observed.

5. The alternatives of a multiple choice test item should be written to be of equal length, sequenced in a random order, and free of such ambiguous options as "none of the above" or "all of the above."

ESSAY TEST ITEMS

1. Create test items that use higher-level thinking skills rather than simple recall of factual information. Encourage questions that highlight creative thought and problem-solving skills.

2. Include test items that outline a specific task or set of tasks that can reasonably be completed by the student in the time allotted. Each test item should specify amount of time to be spent on each question/topic as well as the points to be awarded.

3. Test items should cover the key concepts of the course content, but design them so that students may write quality responses in a single sitting.

4. Write test items that require information from the student that is specific enough for common agreement by teachers on what is an acceptable or an unacceptable response. Each test item should have a list or checklist of informational points/ideas that are important to include in a satisfactory response.

5. Do not include optional questions or opinion questions which can detract from the overall mission of the test and fragment the student's thinking and the teacher's ability to "test" students in the same content areas.

10 (Plus 10, Plus 10) Essay Direction Words

IF YOU ARE ASKED TO:	YOU SHOULD DO THE FOLLOWING:	EXAMPLES:
Analyze	Break down or separate a problem or situation into separate factors and/or relationships. Draw a conclusion, make a judgment, or make clear the relationship you see based on your breakdown.	Analyze the main story line in Chapter 2 and how it sets the stage for Chapter 3.
Categorize	Place items under headings already labeled by your teacher.	Categorize the items on the left under the proper headings on the right.
Classify	Place items in related groups; then name or title each group.	Listed below are 20 items. Classify them in 4 main groups; then name each group.
Compare	Tell how things are alike; use concrete examples.	Compare the American government system with that of the German government.
Contrast	Tell how things are different; use supporting concrete examples.	Contrast the writing styles of Shakespeare and Bacon.
Criticize	Make a judgment of the work of art or literature and support your judgment.	Criticize the use of cigarette advertising in magazines.
Deduce	Trace the course; derive a conclusion by reasoning.	Deduce the following logic problem to arrive at one of the conclusions listed below...
Defend	Give enough details to prove the statement.	Defend the statement "innocent until proven guilty."
Define	Give the meaning.	Define plankton.

IF YOU ARE ASKED TO:	YOU SHOULD DO THE FOLLOWING:	EXAMPLES:
Diagram	Use pictures, graphs, charts mind maps & flow charts to show relationships of details to main ideas.	Diagram the offices of the federal government.
Discuss	Consider the various points of view by presenting all sides of the issue.	Discuss the use of chemotherapy in the treatment of cancer.
Distinguish	Tell how this is different from others similar to it.	Distinguish the three types of mold we have studied in class.
Enumerate	List all possible items.	Enumerate the presidents of the United States since Lincoln.
Evaluate	Make a judgment based on the evidence and support it; give the good and bad points.	Evaluate the use of pesticides.
Explain	Make clear and plain; give the reason or cause.	Explain how a natural disaster can help man.
Illustrate	Give examples, pictures, charts, diagrams or concrete examples to clarify your answer.	Illustrate the use of a drawbridge.
Interpret	Express your thinking by giving the meaning as you see it.	Interpret the line "Water, water everywhere and not a drop to drink."
Justify	Give some evidence by supporting your statement with facts.	Justify the decision to bomb Nagasaki, Japan.
List	Write in a numbered fashion.	List 5 reasons to support your statement.
Outline	Use a specific and shortened form to organize main ideas supporting details and examples.	Outline the leading cause of World War II.

IF YOU ARE ASKED TO:	YOU SHOULD DO THE FOLLOWING:	EXAMPLES:
Paraphrase	Put in your own words.	Paraphrase the first paragraph of the Gettysburg Address.
Predict	Present solutions that could happen if certain variables were present.	Predict the ending of the short story written below.
Prove	Provide factual evidence to back up the truth of the statement.	Prove that the whaling industry has led to almost extinction of certain varieties.
Relate	Show the relationship among concepts.	Relate man's survival instincts to those of animals.
Review	Examine the information critically. Analyze and comment on the important statements.	Review the effects of television advertisements on the public.
State	Establish by specifying. Write what you believe and back it with evidence.	State your beliefs in the democratic system of government.
Summarize	Condense the main points in the fewest words possible.	Summarize early man's methods of self-defense.
Synthesize	Combine parts or pieces of an idea, situation or event.	Synthesize the events leading up to the Civil War.
Trace	Describe in steps the progression of something.	Trace the importance of the prairie schooner to the opening of the West.
Verify	Confirm or establish the truth of accuracy of point of view with supporting examples, evidence and facts.	Verify the Declaration of Independence.

From *Learning To Learn: Strengthening Study Skills and Brain Power* by Gloria Frender. Nashville, TN: Incentive Publications, 1990. Used by permission.

10 Ways To Prepare Middle Level Students For Taking Essay Tests

1. Communicate your expectations early and clearly. Explain to students why you think writing is important and how you plan to use it on classroom tests. Give students some samples of simple essay questions you used the year before.

2. At the beginning of the year, conduct a formative assessment of student writing ability. Give students a short reading assignment and then have them write responses to 2–3 short essay questions.

3. Provide an in-class lesson on what constitutes good writing for essay questions. Working with the class members, review, critique, and rewrite students responses to essay questions from previous task.

4. Assign short, sequenced in-class writing activities frequently. The instructional benefits of using writing to enhance both thinking and subject-matter retention have now been well established. Introduce, for example, a five-minute writing task to launch a mini-lecture or to conclude an instructional task.

5. Provide students with written resources that can help improve their writing skills. Prepare a simple checklist which students can use to evaluate their essays before turning them in.

6. Identify media center and school resources that are available to help students improve their writing skills. Make certain that students know about out-of-class assistance provided by community agencies or self-help books from the school/community library including software tutorial programs.

7. Write essays of your own in the environment in which you expect your students to write. It is beneficial for teachers to do some assignments with their students.

8. Create peer-critiquing exercises. Provide students with written guidelines that describe the specific characteristics of a helpful critique and give them the opportunity to apply these criteria to one another's work.

9. Teach students to reflect upon and critique their completed assignments. For example, after returning a student's essay test or set of questions, have him or her identify the primary strengths and major limitations of the writing assignment just completed. You might even give extra credit for those who rewrite their responses and choose to resubmit them.

10. Provide students with essay questions before the test is given. This affords them the opportunity to plan and research their replies; it will also make the job of correcting errors and providing feedback more pleasant.

Adapted from "Preparing Freshmen to Take Essay Examinations Successfully" by D. Holt and J. Eison. *Journal of the Freshman Year Experience*, Vol. 1, No. 2, 1989. Used by permission.

10 Good Starter Verbs/Behaviors For Assessing Student Achievement Using The Levels Of Bloom's Taxonomy

KNOWLEDGE LEVEL VERBS OR BEHAVIORS

1. List
2. Match
3. Identify
4. Record
5. Who, What, When, or Where
6. Name
7. Find
8. Label
9. Write
10. Recall

COMPREHENSION LEVEL VERBS OR BEHAVIORS

1. Summarize
2. Describe
3. Tell in your own words
4. Explain
5. Give examples of
6. Show
7. Conclude
8. Generalize
9. Rewrite, Reword, Retell, or Restate
10. Express in other terms

APPLICATION LEVEL VERBS OR BEHAVIORS

1. Apply
2. Collect information
3. Construct
4. Demonstrate
5. Experiment
6. Perform
7. Practice
8. Model
9. Put to use
10. Solve

ANALYSIS LEVEL VERBS OR BEHAVIORS

1. Compare and Contrast
2. Deduce
3. Draw conclusions
4. Form generalizations
5. Discover
6. Examine
7. Infer
8. Uncover
9. Formulate
10. Diagram

SYNTHESIS LEVEL VERBS OR BEHAVIORS

1. Create
2. Combine
3. Design
4. Devise
5. Organize
6. Produce or Present
7. Invent
8. Build
9. Imagine
10. Prescribe

EVALUATION LEVEL VERBS OR BEHAVIORS

1. Argue
2. Criticize or Critique
3. Defend
4. Evaluate
5. Grade
6. Judge or Justify
7. Rank
8. Recommend
9. Validate or Verify
10. Support

10 Characteristics Of Authentic Tests

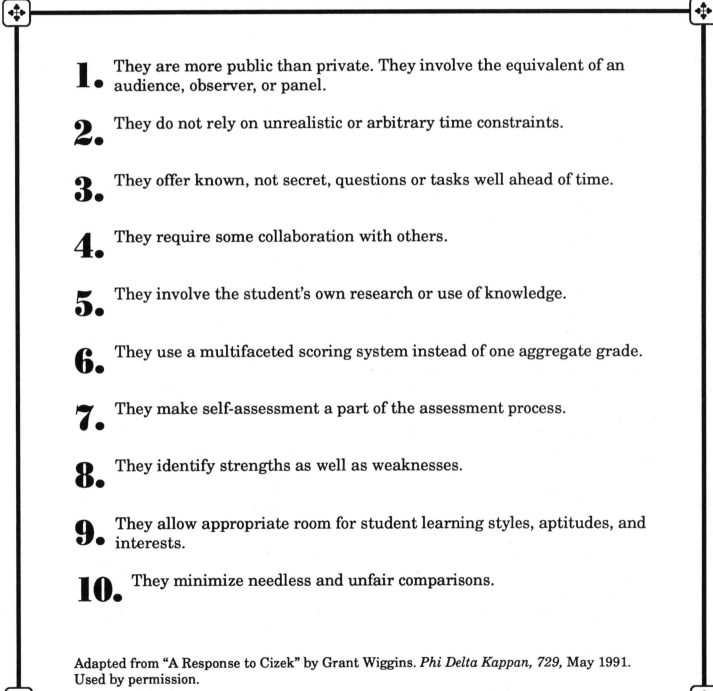

1. They are more public than private. They involve the equivalent of an audience, observer, or panel.

2. They do not rely on unrealistic or arbitrary time constraints.

3. They offer known, not secret, questions or tasks well ahead of time.

4. They require some collaboration with others.

5. They involve the student's own research or use of knowledge.

6. They use a multifaceted scoring system instead of one aggregate grade.

7. They make self-assessment a part of the assessment process.

8. They identify strengths as well as weaknesses.

9. They allow appropriate room for student learning styles, aptitudes, and interests.

10. They minimize needless and unfair comparisons.

Adapted from "A Response to Cizek" by Grant Wiggins. *Phi Delta Kappan, 729,* May 1991. Used by permission.

10 MINUS 2

Guidelines For Realizing The Power Of The Portfolio

Portfolios have the potential to reveal a lot about their creators. They can become a window into the students' minds, a means for both staff and students to understand the educational process at the level of the individual learner. They can be powerful educational tools for encouraging students to take charge of their own learning.

Portfolios allow students to assume ownership in ways that few other instructional approaches allow. Portfolio assessment requires students to collect and reflect on examples of their work, providing both an instructional component to the curriculum and offering the opportunity for authentic assessments. If carefully assembled, portfolios become an intersection of instruction and assessment.

Fulfilling the potential of portfolios as an intersection of instruction and assessment is neither simple nor straightforward. We must find new ways for the two processes to work together. Doing so involves answering a question that has no simple answer: "What makes a portfolio a portfolio?" The portfolio is a concept that can be realized in many ways. Portfolios are as varied as the children who create them and as the classrooms in which they are found. However, to preserve those aspects of the portfolio that give the concept its power, we offer this list of guidelines:

1. Developing a portfolio offers the student an opportunity to learn about learning. Therefore, the end product must contain information that shows that a student has engaged in self-reflection.

2. The portfolio is something that is done *by* the student, not *to* the student. Portfolio assessment offers a concrete way for students to learn to value their own work and, by extension, to value themselves as learners. Therefore, the student must be involved in selecting the pieces to be included.

3. The portfolio is separate and different from the student's cumulative folder. Scores and other cumulative folder information that are held in central depositories should be included in a portfolio only if they take on new meaning within the context of the other exhibits found there.

4. The portfolio must convey explicitly or implicitly the student's activities, for example, the rationale (purpose for forming the portfolio), intents (its goals), contents (the actual displays), standards (what is a good and not-so-good performance), and judgments (what the contents tell us).

5. The portfolio may serve a different purpose during the year from the purpose it serves at the end. Some material may be kept because it is instructional, for example, partially finished work on problem areas. At the end of the year, however, the portfolio may contain only material that the student is willing to make public.

6. A portfolio may have multiple purposes, but these must not conflict. A student's personal goals and interests are reflected in his or her selection of materials, but information included may also reflect the interests of teachers, parents, or the district. One purpose that is almost universal in student portfolios is showing progress on the goals represented in the instructional program.

7. The portfolio should contain information that illustrates growth. There are many ways to demonstrate growth. The most obvious is by including a series of examples of actual school performance that shows how the student's skills have improved. Changes observed on interest inventories, records of outside activities such as reading, or on attitude measures are other ways to illustrate a student's growth.

8. Finally, many of the skills and techniques that are involved in producing effective portfolios do not happen by themselves. By way of support, students need models of portfolios, as well as examples of how others develop and reflect upon portfolios.

There are a considerable variety of portfolio assessment projects appearing in schools, reflecting the fact that portfolio assessment is a healthy and robust concept. We recommend, however, that when designing programs or purchasing commercial portfolio assessment materials, educators reflect on the eight aspects of the portfolio that we believe give the concept its power. We offer our list as a way of initiating thoughtful critiques.

From "What Makes a Portfolio a Portfolio?" by F. Leon Paulson, Pearl Paulson, and Carol Mayer. *Educational Leadership 43, 3:30–33.* Reprinted with permission of the Association for Supervision and Curriculum Development. Copyright 1991 by ASCD. All rights reserved.

10 MINUS 5

Decisions To Be Made For Portfolios Plus Five Reasons To Consider Portfolio Assessment

Portfolio Decisions

1. What do you want your student portfolios to look like? What format, structure, or organizational scheme is best for your class, school, or district?

2. What do you want your students to include in their portfolios? What artifacts will best represent the diverse abilities, interests, cultures, and work of your class, school, or district?

3. When and how should your students select the items for their portfolios? What type of timeline, assignments, tasks, and products should be developed for documenting the learning process of your class, school, or district?

4. How will you and your students evaluate their portfolios? What outcomes, performance standards, or criteria will you establish in your class, school, or district for judging their worth and effectiveness?

5. How will you forward or pass on the portfolio from year to year? What methods, procedures, or guidelines will you establish in your class, school, or district for moving the portfolios on throughout a student's career?

Reasons To Consider Portfolio Assessment

1. Portfolio assessment nurtures developmental stages of young adolescents and allows for individual differences in growth patterns and changes.

2. Portfolio assessment encourages the individual student to assume more responsibility for his or her learning because it is more individualized, more personalized, and depends more on choice through self-reflection and self-selection than traditional testing methods.

3. Portfolio assessment emphasizes reflective thinking, critical thinking, and creative thinking on the part of the student because it is dependent upon self-discovery, self-motivation, and self-initiating behaviors.

4. Portfolio assessment is likely to have more long-term benefits for the student than traditional testing methods because it is more authentic, more diversified, and more relevant from the student's perspective.

5. Portfolio assessment helps the student become more involved in his or her own learning because it demands that the student be more task-oriented and more results-oriented.

10 Reasons Student Products Make Good Assessment Tools

Student products refer to work that students have generated. Products may include journal writing, video- or audiotapes, computer demonstrations, dramatic performances, bulletin boards, debates, formal presentations, student designs and inventions, investigation reports, simulations, physical constructions, or role-playing scenarios.

Advantages of student products include the following:

1. They can show originality that goes beyond what is taught.

2. They can demonstrate knowledge in an effective and attractive manner.

3. They can reflect growth in social and academic skills and attitudes that are not reflected in paper-and-pencil tests.

4. They can engage students who are otherwise unenthusiastic about school.

5. They can bring education to life, making it memorable for students.

6. They can demonstrate to the community what students are achieving in concrete terms.

7. They can allow for the integration of reading/writing/speaking skills with other subject areas.

8. They can give students more flexible time to do thoughtful work.

9. They can permit students to work cooperatively with others.

10. They can encourage creativity.

Adapted from *Assessment Alternatives in Mathematics: An Overview of Assessment Techniques that Promote Learning* by Jean Stenmark. Berkeley, CA: Equals and Assessment Committee of the California Mathematics Council, Regents University of California, 1989. Used by permission.

Bloom Project Chart

	Optional Project Format	Verbs
KNOWLEDGE	Flash cards, rebus story, scrapbook, drawing, puzzle, tape recording, mobile, collage	Define, draw, identify, label, list, locate, match, name, recite, select, state
COMPREHENSION	Puppet show, picture dictionary, pamphlet, news story/report, diagram, essay, bulletin board, diary	Classify, demonstrate, describe, explain, generalize, give examples, group, paraphrase, put in order, retell, rewrite, show, summarize
APPLICATION	Chart/graph, model, peep show, display, interview, survey experiment, mini-center	Apply, compare/contrast, debate, diagram, draw conclusions, discover, examine, interview, investigate, keep records, make, construct, predict, produce, prove, track, translate
ANALYSIS	Textbook, transparency, oral report, movie, scroll, collection, guest speaker, letter	Analyze, deduce, determine, examine, infer, relate, compare, contrast, uncover
SYNTHESIS	Poem/song, game, speech, play, gallery/museum exhibit, choral reading	Combine, create, design, develop, imagine, invent, make up, perform, prepare, present (an original piece of work), produce, revise, tell, synthesize
EVALUATION	Written report, scroll, book cover, poster, project cube, photo/picture essay, advertisement, editorial, debate	Argue, award, choose, criticize, critique, defend, grade, judge, justify, rank, rate, recommend, support, test, validate

10 Steps For Designing Performance Tests In Core Curricular Areas

1. Identify the program/curriculum content area to be assessed. Determine the level of factual and conceptual understanding you wish to measure.

2. Identify the process/inquiry/thinking skills to be assessed. Do not develop a performance task for skills/concepts that can be better tested by a paper-and-pencil item.

3. Write a behavioral objective for the task to help focus the specific skills and materials as well as to help establish the scoring parameters.

4. List the materials/resources required for the task. These should be easily obtained, inexpensive, safe to use, and be regular components of the program.

5. Develop a series of questions for each task. Questions must be focused on a particular process skill for each task. They must be written clearly and balanced to fit the time allotted the task.

6. Write directions. Pay special attention to the placement and sequence of directions to lead the student efficiently through the task.

7. Use graphics where appropriate to assist students with clarity.

8. Determined the reading level of students being tested. Vocabulary should be geared one year below grade level of students. However, terms should be consistent with content and process of the program.

9. Develop scoring procedures. Performance, not content, should be the focus of the task and must be reflected in the scoring. Consider using a point system that gives students a range of points for each task/question.

10. Administer a trial test. Students used in trial testing situation should represent different intellectual abilities, socioeconomic backgrounds, ethnic and racial groups, and should be gender balanced.

Adapted from "Hands-on Evaluation: A How-to Guide" by R. Doran and N. Hejaily. Reprinted with permission from NSTA Publications, copyright March 1992, *Science Scope*, National Science Teachers Association, 1742 Connecticut Avenue, NW, Washington, DC 20009-1171.

10 Benefits Of Self-Evaluation For Students

Self-evaluation:

1. Places the assessment burden on the individual.

2. Answers students' two most basic questions: "How am I doing?" and "Where do I go from here?"

3. Provides the basis for agreement between student and teacher on academic priorities.

4. Improves effectiveness, as opposed to efficiency, in the schooling process.

5. Encourages objective analysis of one's own attitudes and aptitudes.

6. Relates progress to performance by answering such questions as "Are we doing the right things?" and "Are we doing the right things right?"

7. Assists in preparation for added growth and responsibility.

8. Promotes a feeling of personal accomplishment.

9. Encourages individual goal-setting.

10. Acknowledges differences in learning styles.

10 PLUS 1

Types Of Questions To Ask When Gathering Assessment Data

1. **Problem Comprehension**
Can students understand, define, formulate, or explain the problem or task? Can they cope with poorly-defined problems?

• What is this problem about? What can you tell me about it?
• How would you interpret that?
• Would you please explain that in your own words?
• What do you know about this part?
• Do you need to define or set limits for the problem?
• Is there something that can be eliminated or that is missing?
• What assumptions do you have to make?

2. **Approaches and Strategies**
Do students have an organized approach to the problem or task? How do they record? Do they use tools (manipulatives, diagrams, graphs, calculators, etc.) appropriately?

• Where would you find the needed information?
• What have you tried? What steps did you take?
• What did not work?
• How did you organize the information?
• Do you have a record?
• Did you have a system? a strategy? a design?
• Have you tried (tables, trees, lists, diagrams, etc.)?
• Would it help to draw a diagram or to make a sketch?
• How would it look if you used these materials?
• How would you research that?

3. Relationships

Do students see relationships and recognize the central idea? Do they relate the problem to similar problems previously completed?

- What is the relationship of this to that?
- What is the same? What is different?
- Is there a pattern?
- Let's see if we can break it down. What would the parts be?
- What if you moved this part?
- Can you write another problem related to this one?

4. Flexibility

Can students vary the approach if something is not working? Do they persist? Do they try something else?

- Have you tried making a guess?
- Would another recording method work as well?
- What else have you tried?
- Give me another related problem. Is there an easier problem?
- Is there another way to (draw, explain, say, etc.) that?

5. Communication

Can students describe or depict the strategies they are using? Do they articulate their thought processes? Can they display or demonstrate the problem situation?

- Could you reword that in simpler terms?
- Could you explain what you think you know right now?
- How would you explain this process to a younger child?
- Could you write an explanation of how to do this for next year's students (or some other audience)?
- Which words were most important?

6. Curiosity and Hypotheses

Is there evidence of conjecturing, thinking ahead, checking back?

- Can you predict what will happen?
- What was your estimate or prediction?
- How do you feel about your answer?
- What do you think comes next?
- What else would you like to know?

7. Equality and Equity

Do all students participate to the same degree? Is the quality of participation opportunities the same for all students?

- Did you work together? In what way?
- Have you discussed this with your group? with others?
- Where would you go for help?
- How would you help another student without telling the answer?
- Did everybody get a fair chance to talk?

8. Solutions
Do students arrive at a result? Do they consider other possibilities?

- Is that the only possible answer?
- How would you check the steps you have taken, or your answer?
- Other than retracing your steps, how can you determine if your answers are appropriate?
- Is there anything you have overlooked?
- Is the solution reasonable, considering the context?
- How did you know you were finished?

9. Examining Results
Can students generalize, prove their answers? Do they connect the ideas to other similar problems or to the real world?

- What made you think that was what you should do?
- Is there a real-life situation where this could be used?
- Where else would this strategy be useful?
- What other problem does this seem to lead to?
- Is there a general rule?
- How would your method work with other problems?
- What questions does this raise for you?

10. Mathematical Learning
Did students use or learn some mathematics from the activity? Are there indications of a comprehensive curriculum?

- What were the mathematical ideas in this problem?
- What was one (or more) thing(s) you learned?
- What are the variables in this problem? What stays constant?
- How many kinds of mathematics processes were used in this investigation?
- What is different about the mathematics used in these two situations?
- Where would this problem fit on our mathematics chart?

11. Self-Assessment
Do students evaluate their own processing, actions, and progress?

- What do you need to do next?
- What are your strengths and weaknesses?
- What have you accomplished?
- Was your own group participation appropriate and helpful?
- What kinds of problems are still difficult?

Adapted from *Assessment Alternatives in Mathematics: An Overview of Assessment Techniques that Promote Learning* by Jean Stenmark. Berkeley, CA: Equals and Assessment Committee of the California Mathematics Council, Regents University of California, 1989. Used by permission.

10 Guidelines To Follow When Organizing A Student Study Group

1. Recognize the benefits of forming a study group. A study group can:

   a. Reinforce what you already know.

   b. Provide you with an opportunity to practice and review.

   c. Allow you to meet other students and enjoy studying in an atmosphere that is fun.

   d. Enable you to learn new information from others.

   e. Promote a better understanding of confusing or new concepts.

   f. Allow for better coverage of the material to be learned.

2. Notice who is in your class and think about those who are closest to you in ability and motivation.

3. Find five or six interested students and discuss the purpose and benefits of a study group.

4. Contact the students to arrange a meeting time and place for the first study group session.

5. Plan the following agenda for the first session:

   a. Exchange names and telephone numbers.

   b. Set specific goals for the group with reasonable time lines.

   c. Discuss:
- Instructor's teaching style.
- Overview of the subject matter.
- Quality of one another's notes and understandings.
- Possible test questions.

6. Test each other.

7. Review any weak spots.

8. Make a "plan of action" for getting additional help if needed.

9. Set up a followup session if needed.

10. Give out assignments between sessions to make the study time more productive for study group members.

Adapted from *Learning To Learn: Strengthening Study Skills and Brain Power* by Gloria Frender. Nashville, TN: Incentive Publications, 1990. Used by permission.

Sample Student Study Guide
YOU CAN DO IT!

I. CLASSIFY YOUR INFORMATION
Write all like things together on one sheet of paper.

Example: When classifying for a history test, you might have a page for each of the following:

names	superlatives (most, best, first, last, etc.)
places	definitions
vocabulary	dates (in order!)
main ideas	events (what, who, when, where?)
cause & effects	things that can be compared, contrasted

II. WRITE TO REMEMBER
(So you can take mental photographs!)

• Write on only ONE side of the page (easier to find).
• Use different colors of paper or pen (helps to visualize).
• Always put dates or events in chronological order.
• Group things that go together and leave space between groups.
• Put groups of single words in an easy-to-remember order.

Example: You might arrange lists of prepositions or chemical elements in alphabetical order.
To remember the names of the six New England states, you could make up a silly sentence or an acrostic:

M**E** any N**H** asty V**T** ampires M**A** ay C**T** ause R**I** iots.

A very old example is remembering how to spell the word "geography" by using this sentence:
<u>G</u>eorge <u>E</u>lliott's <u>o</u>ld <u>g</u>randfather <u>r</u>ode <u>a</u> <u>p</u>ig <u>h</u>ome <u>y</u>esterday!
This method of remembering things is called "mnemonics." (That's pronounced "nee-mon-icks.")

As you review your study sheets, **highlight, underline, star, color-code,** etc., ANYTHING to help picture it in your mind!

III. TEST YOURSELF – *over and over...*
Use your study sheets to:
LOOK and SAY – **Look** at the term, **say** the definition.
COVER and PEEK – **Cover** part of the list and say it; **peek** to check!
PARTNER QUIZ – Trade study sheets and "test" with a classmate.
MAKE MENTAL SNAPSHOTS – Close your eyes. See if you can visualize the group of words on the page and say them aloud to yourself. (It helps to hear them, too!)

Adapted from *Writing Survival Skills for the Middle Grades* by Imogene Forte and Joy MacKenzie. Nashville, TN: Incentive Publications, ©1991. Used by permission.

10 PLUS 2

Informal Methods Of Assessing Student Understanding Of Material Covered During Instruction

1. IN BASKET

Ask each student to write at least one good question on a 3" x 5" file card about a key topic or set of concepts previously taught in class. Place each of these cards in a box or envelope and randomly select one card at a time to read aloud to the class. Students volunteer to respond to the questions presented and earn "points" for each correct answer. Students may gain additional points for embellishing or adding to someone else's response as well. Several of these student-generated questions could be used on a test to be given at a later date.

2. GROUP PROFILE

Distribute one file card to each student and have each record a number from 1 to 10 that best describes how well he or she understands ideas recently taught during a lecture, discussion, textbook reading assignment, videotape, homework task, etc. Provide students with at least three benchmarks on the rating scale to use in making their decisions. For example, one continuum might look like this:

1   2   3   4   5   6   7   8   9   10

  1 = I don't understand much of anything I read or heard.

  5 = I understand about half of the ideas presented.

 10 = I understand the material well enough to take a test on it or to teach it to someone else.

Collect the file cards (no names on them, please) and record all responses on the board, a transparency, or a piece of chart paper. Use this to determine the percentage of the class that has knowledge of the material that was assigned or taught.

3. SMALL GROUP CONSENSUS REPORT

Divide students into small groups of three or four. Instruct them to reach consensus on the five most important facts they have learned and should remember from the day's lecture, discussion, or assigned reading. Have each group write responses on a large piece of newsprint and post around the room for all to see. Ask each group's recorder to share his or her small group's responses and justify its choice of five facts. Look for similar responses from each group and reach a large-group consensus on the most important information recorded on the charts. Have students copy these in their notebooks to study for a test at a later date.

4. PICTURE CARDS

Provide each student or small group of students with a duplicate set of Picture/Symbol Cards which you have prepared in advance. Picture/Symbol Cards can be made by drawing, pasting, or printing a series of individual pictures or symbols on 3" x 5" cards or sections of card stock. Possible pictures or symbols for this activity might include: a heart, eagle, dollar sign, hourglass, flag, globe, light bulb, bell, star, firecracker, etc. Have students select one or more picture/symbol cards from the group and use them as springboards or catalysts for use in expressing feelings or emotions in any given area. This works well in getting students to use analogies when making informal judgments about people, places, or things. For example, one might instruct the students to select a picture/symbol card from the group that represents their feelings about a recent court decision, about an editorial from the newspaper, about a historical event from the textbook, or about an incident from a novel.

5. STUDENT PANEL

Divide students into small groups and have them generate a list of tasks in school that they find difficult to do and a list of tasks they find easy to do. Have them graph the results of their brainstorming. Share graphs with the entire class. Next, choose a task with which many students have difficulty. Form a panel of students from the class who felt the task was easy for them and use this group to share concrete ideas about how they mastered this task. Allow time for the class to ask questions of this "panel of experts."

6. CONVINCE THE PANEL OF EXPERTS

Each student is instructed to prepare for class one good summary paragraph stating his or her position or collection of facts on a key concept, issue, idea, problem, or situation related to a given unit of study. Each person reads or shares the paragraph with a panel of "student experts" (three selected class members). The panel "rates" the information on prepared flashcards (1–10, with 10 being high). The teacher tabulates each total and announces the "best performances" at the end of the time period. This activity should be followed with a large-group discussion using such questions as:

a. How many students gained at least one new idea or perspective today?

b. Did this process spark any additional ideas in your minds?

c. What criteria were used by the "panel of experts" to judge the summary paragraphs?

d. How could we help each other on our presentations so that all would receive 10s?

7. CAKE WALK

Prior to this activity, write ten important questions about a topic being studied in the classroom. These questions are written on a blackboard, transparency, or large piece of chart paper so they are visible to everyone in the room. Students then form two concentric circles in which each person of the outer circle faces another person of the inner circle to form pairs. Instruct the students in each group to move counterclockwise to one another while background music is being played. When the music stops, the students also stop moving and face one another. They then have two minutes to discuss the answer to the first question on the board, overhead, or chart paper. When the music starts again, the students move counterclockwise until the music stops and they are facing a new partner. This time they are to discuss the answer to the second question given. The process is repeated until all ten questions have been addressed. This makes an excellent review activity at the end of a unit of study.

8. EQUATION QUIZ

The teacher prepares a series of equations that represent a variety of important concepts being studied as part of an instructional unit. Students are given the equations and asked to use their notes, textbooks, or worksheets to figure them out. If time permits, students should also be given the opportunity to create their own equations representing information that they think is important. Examples of equations for several content areas are given below.

Math Examples

2000 = P. in a T. (2000 = Pounds in a Ton)

90 = D. in an R.T. (90 = Degrees in a Right Triangle)

23 Y. - 3 Y. = 2 D (23 Years minus 3 Years = 2 Decades)

32 = D.F. at which W.F. (32 = Degrees Fahrenheit at which Water Freezes)

Social Studies Examples

T. = L.S. State (Texas = Lone Star State)

7 = W. of the A.W. (7 = Wonders of the Ancient World)

M. + M. + N.H. + V. + C. + R.I. = N.E. (Maine + Maryland + New Hampshire + Vermont + Connecticut + Rhode Island = New England)

S. + H. of R. = U.S. C. (Senate + House of Representatives = United States Congress)

9. RESPONSE CARDS

Provide each student with a set of color-coded feedback cards. One set of cards should have True on one card and False on another. A second set of cards should have an A on one card, a B on a second card, a C on a third card, a D on a fourth card, and an E on a fifth card. Inform the class that the cards will be used to provide the teacher with feedback in response to his or her questions. The teacher then proceeds to make a series of True/False statements, and the entire class should hold up the appropriate alphabet card signifying their best response of the choice offered. Variations of this activity are to use other card options such as sets of blank cards on which students should write responses to short-answer questions or alphabet cards for matching questions.

10. ALPHABET REPORTS

Students are given a piece of paper with the 26 letters of the alphabet printed vertically down one side. They are directed to select 26 related concepts, terms, events, or persons that show what they have learned about a given topic. Each item should begin with a different letter of the alphabet and students should be encouraged to think of more than one word for each letter as they record their ideas. Next, students should try creating meaningful phrases with each cluster of words recorded next to the appropriate letter of the alphabet so that the reading of the report flows like a free verse poem.

11. CONCEPT PUZZLES

Students are instructed to select the most important terms, concepts, or ideas associated with a textbook chapter or teaching unit. They are to develop brief definitions or identifying phrases for each, as well. Next, students are told to construct a crossword puzzle that incorporates each of the items and fill in the appropriate numbers, crossword-puzzle style. These can be exchanged among peers to "test" one another on their understanding of information taught.

12. BINGO BONANZA

Students are directed to generate a set of 25 questions and answers that are important to their understanding of a completed textbook chapter, lecture, assigned reading, or instructional unit. The questions should be organized or sorted into five major categories, and students should create some identity for each category name using the letters B, I, N, G, and O. Next, BINGO cards should be designed according to one of these formats:

(A) Generic cards (like traditional BINGO cards) using a 5" x 5" matrix with numbers in the 24 designated cells and the FREE spot designated in the center. In this case, the teacher reads a question with an associated number, and if the student has the number and can correctly write in the answer, he or she fills in the appropriate cell.

(B) Specific cards with the cells previously filled in using 24 of the key concepts, ideas, terms, etc. If the student believes that one of the answers on the card fits the question being read, he or she writes the question number next to it. As in BINGO, the first student to complete the answers in a row horizontally, vertically, or diagonally calls out BINGO and wins the game!

10 PLUS 3

Statements To Assess "The House We Live In"

REMINDERS: Your teacher wants to know what you think about the way your classroom looks and feels. Is it a good place to work and learn? How can we make it better? Please complete the following statements as honestly as possible.

1. The most exciting part of this classroom is . . .

2. The least exciting part of this classroom is . . .

3. The most comfortable place to work is . . .

4. The least comfortable place to work is . . .

5. What is most convenient to use is . . .

6. What is most difficult or inconvenient to use is . . .

7. One thing about this room that is boring is . . .

8. Another room in this school that looks like an interesting, pleasant place to work and learn is . . .

9. The most pleasant place to sit in this room is . . .

10. The one thing I would most like to change is . . .

11. This room is a good place to learn because . . .

12. One other thing I would like to say about this room is . . .

13. One thing I think I could do to make this room a better place is . . .

TEACHER'S ASSESSMENT WRAP-UP, À LA BLOOM

KNOWLEDGE:
Recall three to five important pieces of information from the literature on assessment. State their implications for testing in the middle grades.

COMPREHENSION:
Summarize the important concepts associated with outcome-based education and authentic assessment.

APPLICATION:
Construct a set of true/false, matching, sentence completion, and essay questions on a topic of your choice, using the guidelines presented for writing effective questions in this module.

ANALYSIS:
Compare and contrast product, performance, and portfolio assessment methods for measuring student growth.

SYNTHESIS:
Design plans for conducting a "Test Pep Rally" for your school that could be used before administering important standardized tests to students.

EVALUATION:
Defend or criticize this statement: "Grades have become more important to parents and students than the learning process."

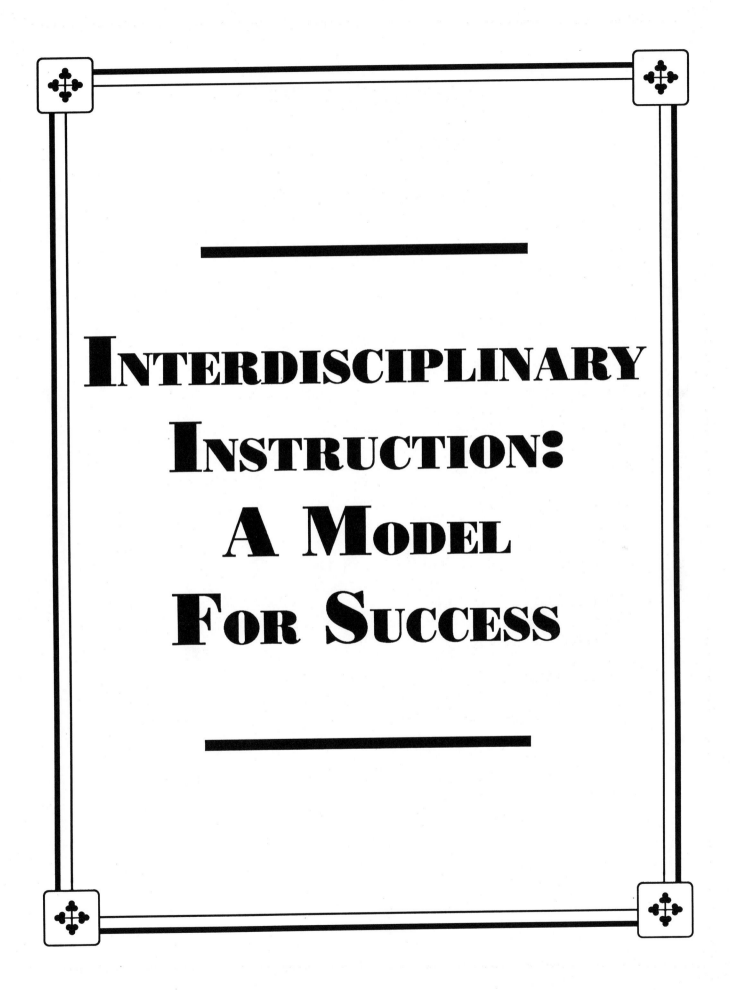

INTERDISCIPLINARY INSTRUCTION: A MODEL FOR SUCCESS

Interdisciplinary Instruction Overview

INTERDISCIPLINARY INSTRUCTION IS VALUABLE BECAUSE:
- It reduces the fragmentation of learning which can result from a traditional junior high school schedule.
- It facilitates the teaching of thinking and interpersonal skills that are often overlooked in conventional instruction.
- It helps students develop a unified view of their education.
- It empowers teachers by providing opportunities to work together.
- Students learn and remember best when learning is connected.
- The world around us is an interdisciplinary world; life is not divided into separate disciplines!

AN INTERDISCIPLINARY UNIT CAN BE:
- Variable in duration.
- Created and conducted by any number of teachers, including an individual.
- Drawn from any number or combination of subject areas.
- Offered once in a while, as it is not intended to be the primary mode of instruction.

AN INTERDISCIPLINARY UNIT INCLUDES THE FOLLOWING ESSENTIAL ELEMENTS:
- A high-interest theme that gives rise to a selection of creative activities.
- Background information that will launch the unit effectively.
- A selection of skills and content from two or more subject areas.
- Supportive materials such as a glossary of key terms, a bibliography, or a list of resources.
- A post-test and/or final project that will serve as an evaluation of the unit.

IN SUMMARY:
Interdisciplinary instruction enhances the learning experience of students because it provides a way of teaching that reflects the interconnectedness of the real world, provides interest and excitement for students and teachers, and allows for many ways to integrate the curriculum so that student needs are most effectively met.

10 Important Interdisciplinary Instruction Questions To Find Answers For

1. What are some advantages of interdisciplinary instruction over the conventional academic-centered, separate-subject approach?

2. What are the major elements of an interdisciplinary unit?

3. How can a traditional teaching team begin to work together to become an effective interdisciplinary team?

4. In what ways can community resources be utilized in interdisciplinary instruction?

5. In what ways can interdisciplinary instruction contribute to student self-esteem?

6. What factors need to be taken into account when selecting themes for interdisciplinary units?

7. How can enrichment activities, homework, and extracurricular projects be incorporated into an interdisciplinary unit?

8. What are some evaluation strategies that can be used effectively in interdisciplinary instruction?

9. What are some broad-based themes for interdisciplinary units that would be of high interest to today's middle graders?

10. What are some pitfalls to look for when planning an interdisciplinary unit?

10 Definitions Essential To Interdisciplinary Instruction Success

1. **Curriculum** is the formal and predetermined plan of systematic skills and content areas to be mastered by the learner. The curriculum is highly structured and emphasizes ends in themselves, not means to those ends.

2. **Instruction** focuses on pedagogy or varied classroom practices and procedures for teaching the curriculum. Instruction encourages alternative delivery systems and emphasizes the means to the ends.

3. **Webbing** suggests a process whereby a general subject-area theme is presented as a concept (such as conflict, trees, or poetry) and related topics or ideas are generated as an outgrowth of this theme.

4. **Concept** is a general idea or collection of understandings derived over time from a specific set of examples, occurrences, or thoughts. To establish concepts, teachers must let students examine an idea from varied perspectives in order to establish relationships and draw conclusions.

5. **Disciplines** refers to separate content or subject areas. Teachers often provide instruction solely within a given branch of knowledge such as math, science, art, English, or social studies.

6. **Curriculum Matrix** consists of a chart that visually represents the relationships or connections between a set of curricular topics within any given subject area and its corresponding skills, attitudes, or concepts.

7. **Simulations** are instructional strategies that offer working models or selected representations of physical and/or social phenomena incorporating gaming techniques. Players assume roles, interact with other players, and make decisions based on those rules and interactions.

8. **IDU's** are interdisciplinary units that interface two or more different disciplines or content areas into a given assignment or task. They are designed to overcome fragmentation of subjects by revealing the interconnectedness of knowledge.

9. **Integrated Learning** is a term applied to the type of learning in which a student tries to see and internalize the logical relationships and interfacings of similar concepts, skills, and attitudes which exist across varied subject areas.

10. **Theme** is a generic or principal term for a series of related topics of discussion, ideas, points of view, or perceptions showing cross-curricular connections within a given classroom or school setting.

10 Findings From The Published Literature About Interdisciplinary Instruction In The Middle School

1. FINDING
Lounsbury states:

Interdisciplinary teaching is central to the middle school concept. Whether conducted by one teacher in a largely self-contained class, by a team through cooperative planning and thematic units, or even via a school-wide effort focused on a particular objective, attempts to reduce the fragmentation of learning created by the conventional high school schedule are recommended by most middle school advocates.

Because interdisciplinary teaching is not included in most teacher education programs, faculties are frequently hesitant to try it; yet, the ultimate success of the middle school movement is heavily dependent upon the implementation of interdisciplinary teaching. Efforts to assist faculty growth in this area, then, have tremendous importance, and most staff development programs for middle level teachers should include an emphasis on this topic.

Reference: Vars, Gordon F. Interdisciplinary Teaching in the Middle Grades. Columbus, OH: National Middle School Association, 1987.

2. FINDING
Bondi and Wiles point out:

There are four essential requirements in order to develop interdisciplinary units of instruction:

1. A staff committed to the interdisciplinary approach as a means of serving the needs of students.
2. Positive interpersonal and professional relationships among all members of the staff.
3. Common team planning time.
4. Sufficient planning time.

Reference: Bondi, J. and Wiles, J. The Essential Middle School. Columbus, OH: Charles Merrill Publishing Company, 1981.

3. FINDING
Heck stresses:

If educators are really searching for an educationally viable plan for teaching children, then they must commit themselves to procedures that encourage children to investigate the world around them in interesting and pleasurable ways. The world around them is an interdisciplinary one. Life is not separated into discrete subject areas. It has a conceptual framework. Unfortunately, teachers often have difficulty arranging an effective sequence of activities for programs based on concepts. They find it difficult to help children see order and pattern in experience.

Reference: Heck, Shirley. "Planning: The Key to Successful Interdisciplinary Teaching." Kappa Delta Pi Record, April 1979, pp. 116-121.

4. FINDING
Hursh, Haas, and Moore summarize:

Curriculum designers are hard-pressed to cite any theory of learning that advances certain disciplines as being necessary—in whatever proportions—to intellectual development. Most general education curricula appear to be formed more by political struggles among academic departments than by struggles among advocates of competing educational theories. This process may account for the relative sameness of the debates (and the curriculum) year after year. The traditional discipline-based recipe continues as the dominant paradigm, even in the more recent of the so-called general education reforms.

Reference: Haas, Hursh, and Moore. Journal of Higher Education, Vol. 54, No. 1, 1983, pp. 42-43.

5. FINDING
The North Carolina Department of Public Instruction concludes:

For many years, leaders in education have pointed to the fragmentation of the school curriculum, highlighting the need for more integrated programs. Several perspectives are listed below:

1. Over three decades ago, Tyler (1949) stated that integration of the curriculum was one of three criteria needed to build an effective schema for the organization of learning experiences. He defined integration as "the horizontal relationship of curriculum experiences" and viewed it as a "must" to help students gain a unified view of their learning.

2. Boyer (1986) criticized schools for presenting segmented, isolated subjects. For the future, he called for a curriculum that helped students understand a complex, integrated world. He maintained that students need a program that allows them "to see relationships that add up to life."

3. Humpry and others (1981) observed that school subjects are typically taught as discrete entities. There is little sense of connectedness among school subjects or among parts of the day. "Children are conditioned in the name of learning to the idea that knowledge and skills are conveyed through the means of separate subjects." Educators seem to assume that students will fit it all together, but, unfortunately, they tend to learn what we teach them and never make such connections.

Reference: *Integrated Learning: What-Why-How, Instructional Services Curriculum Series, No. 1. Raleigh, NC: North Carolina Department of Public Instruction, 1987.*

6. FINDING
Gordon F. Vars summarizes:

Skill development within an interdisciplinary unit employs many of the techniques used by effective teachers in all subjects, but relates them to the problem or topic under study. Skills taught as they are applied are learned more effectively and are more likely to be carried over into real life. Moreover, an interdisciplinary unit makes it possible to stress thinking and interpersonal skills that are too often overlooked in conventional instruction.

Reference: *Vars, Gordon F. Interdisciplinary Teaching in the Middle Grades. Columbus, OH: National Middle School Association, 1987.*

7. FINDING
James A. Beane stresses:

It is apparent that the academic-centered, separate-subject approach is not an appropriate way to conceptualize the middle school curriculum. Moreover, it has other features that call it into question: its historical relations with cultural and intellectual elites, its roots in questionable learning theory, its myopic view of what makes for a "good life," its tenuous claims about effective learning outcomes, and its narrow view of how people generally use subject matter in their real lives. A more appropriate curriculum for the middle school would derive its central themes from the intersection of early adolescent concerns and compelling issues in the larger world.

Reference: *Beane, James. A. A Middle School Curriculum from Rhetoric to Reality. Columbus, OH: National Middle School Association, 1990.*

8. FINDING
Heidi Hayes Jacobs writes:

Interdisciplinary curriculum experiences provide an opportunity for a more relevant, less fragmented, and stimulating experience for students. When properly designed and when criteria for excellence are met, the students break with the traditional view of knowledge and begin to actively foster a range of perspectives that will serve them in the larger world.

Reference: Jacobs, Heidi Hayes, Ed. Interdisciplinary Curriculum: Design and Implementation. Alexandria, VA: Association for Supervision and Curriculum Development, 1989.

9. FINDING
Nancy Doda emphasizes:

The classic interdisciplinary unit often involves all core subjects in planning and works through a single theme. It is important to caution teams that many thematic units run the risk of being more entertaining than instructional. Too often, clever themes can obscure instructional substance. If the theme makes it possible for students to enrich and deepen their understandings of the proposed concepts and ideas or to master the projected outcomes, then it has potential. Otherwise, it is best to dig deeper for another theme which will work to instruct as well as entertain.

Reference: Lounsbury, John H., Ed. Connecting the Curriculum through Interdisciplinary Instruction. Columbus, OH: National Middle School Association, 1992.

10. FINDING
Ron Brandt concludes:

Teachers in forward-looking schools are joining in multidisciplinary teams, tackling the tough questions about what sorts of things their students will need to be able to do to live satisfying, productive lives. The basic school subjects won't disappear; they represent different modes of understanding that human beings have found to be enormously useful. Many of the most urgent and interesting curriculum topics, and a good many of the outcomes we value most, however, do not fit neatly into a single subject area.

Reference: Brandt, Ron. "The Outcomes We Want," Educational Leadership, Vol. 49, No. 3, 1991.

10 MINUS 4

Myths About Interdisciplinary Instruction

1. **Myth: There is a single correct definition of interdisciplinary instruction.** (Truth: Integration of the disciplines can be of any duration, can be any combination of subject areas, and can be done by any number of teachers, including a single individual.)

2. **Myth: An interdisciplinary unit must be a comprehensive, one-month-long affair.** (Truth: It can be as short as one day or as long as one marking period.)

3. **Myth: Interdisciplinary instruction should be the primary mode of teaching a given subject area's content or concepts.** (Truth: Interdisciplinary instruction can satisfy the needs of both teachers and students if it is planned and conducted only once in a while—at the end of the semester, the two weeks before Christmas vacation, or to introduce the school year.)

4. **Myth: Interdisciplinary instruction involves all subject areas simultaneously.** (Truth: Integrating the disciplines can be limited, as to math and science, or social studies and language arts, or art and music.)

5. **Myth: Interdisciplinary instruction involves the lengthy development of a multi-page instructional packet.** (Truth: The teacher can provide a simple, one-page outline showing the overlap of skills or subject matter as typified by the Bloom Task Sheets.)

6. **Myth: Interdisciplinary instruction should be limited to joint planning ventures on the part of teachers over an extended period of time.** (Truth: Interdisciplinary instruction can and should occur as a result of "teachable moments" or spontaneous springboards. Two teachers who become excited about a current event, a new set of materials, or an instant brainstorm should feel free to leave traditional lesson-plan books and use their classes to approach the topic or subject from two different subject matter perspectives.

Adapted from *Integrated Learning: What-Why-How, Instructional Services Curriculum Series*, No. 1, pp. 3-4. Raleigh, NC: North Carolina Department of Public Instruction, 1987. Used by permission.

10 MINUS 5

Reasons To Integrate The Disciplines

1. **The "real world" is integrated.**
Although learning is a natural, integrated process, in order to organize school time educators have often defined getting an education as having separate and unrelated experiences in different disciplines. Despite this arrangement, one relies on the interrelatedness of learning in one's work and everyday life. Individuals do not purchase a car, cast a vote, or listen to a symphony performance with the knowledge and skill of a single discipline. In the real world, we mesh what we know and do.

2. **Students do best when learning is connected.**
Recent research in the areas of effective teaching, reading in the content areas, and writing across the curriculum suggests that students learn and remember best those things that are reinforced and integrated in more than one curricular area. Students respond when one subject area supports another. School subjects are also more meaningful to students if they are shown to have contact outside their own spheres (Sigurdson, 1981).

3. **Students become the focus of learning, not the teacher.**
Students first get hooked by a topic or focus that has a sense of wholeness. Because of the process-orientation of the approach, students are actively involved as decision-makers and problem-solvers. They have choices and can work with their peers. Although there is recognition of involvement at different ability and interest levels, a sense of group effort is still fostered (Johnston and others, 1988). Integrated units or programs create an air of enthusiasm among teachers, students, and the community. Students often consider such study "not like school" and a "real break from textbooks."

4. **Integrated programs are useful in tracking other areas of concern.**
Individual teachers or the entire professional staff have other goals that can be addressed successfully through an integrated curriculum approach (Sigurdson, 1981). Some additional reasons to integrate: integrating the disciplines broadens a teacher's knowledge and understanding of all disciplines and goals at a particular grade level, links a successful program with a less successful one, draws on the strength of master teachers to assist less capable teachers, improves group achievement test scores in a particular area, increases community involvement, and improves school spirit and a sense of belonging in students.

5. **It is difficult to teach subjects and skills in isolation during a 5½-hour instructional day.**
Integrated learning activities can contribute to the efficient use of time, and program offerings can be expanded and strengthened if students can work on two or more subject-area objectives simultaneously. Integrated units between subjects and skills can provide instances of the same piece of work being marked from the perspective of several different subjects.

10 Things To Think About When Selecting A Unit Theme

1. It should incorporate content/skill objectives from all disciplines represented.

2. It should be of interest to every team member.

3. It should be relevant to student needs, interests, and abilities.

4. It should be motivating to both students and teachers.

5. Its length should be appropriate for the subject matter taught.

6. It should focus on active, not passive, learning experiences.

7. It should be a new topic or subject for teachers.

8. It should focus on creative, unique, and uncommon themes not traditionally found in textbooks.

9. It should include resources readily available and accessible to both teachers and students.

10. It should be fun.

10 Steps For Beginning To Integrate The Disciplines

1. Step One: Each teacher on a team should develop a workable definition of interdisciplinary instruction as he or she understands it. All team members compare and discuss individual interpretations of interdisciplinary instruction. Finally, the team synthesizes the best ideas from all team members and comes up with a workable definition for the group.

2. Step Two: Each team member brainstorms a wide variety of possible topics for interdisciplinary instruction that would most easily incorporate their core subject areas. Team members meet to share their respective lists, to eliminate duplicates or overlaps, and to compile a master list that appeals to all team members.

3. Step Three: Each team schedules a formal meeting to select any one of the designated themes for future implementation. Team members brainstorm related topics for each of the core subject areas. Next, teams locate resource materials on the topic and look for activities that lend themselves to science, social studies, math, or language arts.

4. Step Four: The fourth step involves a series of team meetings that requires team members to complete an outline for teaching the interdisciplinary topic agreed upon in Step Three. Each teacher determines the key skills or concepts that are important parts of the interdisciplinary process.

5. Step Five: Team members exchange classes for a least one period, teaching one another's subject areas according to prepared lesson plans. For example, the science and math team members teach each other's classes for a session while the social studies and language arts team members do the same.

6. Step Six: Next, team members set aside the textbook in their subject area for a minimum of three consecutive days. Emphasis is placed on the use of other resources and delivery systems for teaching required basic skills and concepts. This requires team members either to practice using other types of reproducible materials for instruction with students or to develop individual activities of their own using varied tools and techniques to differentiate instruction.

7. **Step Seven:** Team members spend at least three days practicing the art of "creative questioning" within their disciplines. This approach encourages students to tease their minds and stretch their imaginations. Using the same types of higher-order questions in different subject areas can help the young adolescent to see the connectedness of both content and thinking skills.

8. **Step Eight:** Team members decide upon an individual skill such as drawing conclusions or the concept of measurement and develop a short lesson in science, math, social studies, and language arts to present to their students for one week. This activity will provide each team with a chance to approach a skill or concept from several interdisciplinary points of view.

9. **Step Nine:** The team composes a letter to parents or guardians outlining plans for the interdisciplinary unit and the involvement of the family. The content of the letter includes specific information about theme, purpose, length, objectives, varied activities, and projected outcomes. In addition, the letter invites parents to become involved in a variety of ways. The team members should also prepare their homeroom or group of assigned students for this interdisciplinary adventure, making certain that all stakeholders understand its purposes.

10. **Step Ten:** Finally, the interdisciplinary unit is field tested by team members with their students. The team designs a simple student evaluation form for assessing the unit's effectiveness. The evaluation form includes questions about all aspects of the interdisciplinary unit including appropriateness of the subject matter, activities, time span, team teaching, and learning resources.

10 Points for Teachers And Teams To Ponder When Defining Interdisciplinary Curriculum And Instruction

DIRECTIONS: Take a few minutes as an interdisciplinary team to complete each of these starter statements or tasks related to the integration of the disciplines:

1. To us, interdisciplinary instruction means . . .

2. To us, one major advantage of interdisciplinary instruction for the teacher is . . .

3. To us, one key problem or barrier associated with the integration of the disciplines is . . .

4. To us, the most important advantage of interdisciplinary instruction for the student is . . .

5. To date, the closest we have come to integration of subject matter is . . .

6. One big question we have about interdisciplinary instruction in the middle school is . . .

7. One opportunity we had this week to integrate two or more of our subjects as a team was when . . .

8. One experience we had in school this week that showed us how life is indeed integrated and interdisciplinary was . . .

9. Our team feels that the following people in our school would be very supportive of our plans to develop an interdisciplinary unit . . .

10. Through the use of the matrix on the next page, we have discovered the following overlaps/changes which could be easily worked into an interdisciplinary unit(s) . . .

Building An Interdisciplinary Planning Matrix

DIRECTIONS: With your team, sit down and list all the major concepts, units, skills, or topics each of you will be covering during the school year. Try to record by subject area and by month. Look for overlaps or changes which could be easily worked into interdisciplinary units.

	SEPT	OCT	NOV	DEC	JAN	FEB	MAR	APR	MAY
SCIENCE									
MATH									
SOCIAL STUDIES									
LANGUAGE ARTS									
EXPLOR.									
P. E.									

10 PLUS 1

Springboards For Intersection Of Curriculum Themes With Personal And Social Concerns

James A. Beane suggests that "curriculum themes should emerge from the natural overlaps between the personal concerns of early adolescents and the larger issues that face our world. In the intersections between these two categories, we may discover a promising way of conceptualizing a general education that serves the dual purpose of addressing the personal issues, needs, and problems of the early adolescents and the concerns of the larger world, including the particular society in which they live."

Intersections of Personal and Social Concerns			
	EARLY ADOLESCENT CONCERNS	CURRICULUM THEMES	SOCIAL CONCERNS
1.	Understanding personal changes	TRANSITIONS	Living in a changing world
2.	Developing a personal identity	IDENTITIES	Cultural diversity
3.	Finding a place in the group	INTERDEPENDENCE	Global interdependence
4.	Personal fitness	WELLNESS	Environmental protection
5.	Social status	SOCIAL STRUCTURES	Class systems
6.	Dealing with adults	INDEPENDENCE	Human rights
7.	Peer conflict and gangs	CONFLICT RESOLUTION	Global conflict
8.	Commercial pressures	COMMERCIALISM	Effects of media
9.	Questioning authority	JUSTICE	Laws and social customs
10.	Personal friendships	CARING	Social welfare
11.	Living in the school	INSTITUTIONS	Social institutions

From *A Middle School Curriculum: From Rhetoric to Reality* by James A. Beane. Columbus, OH: National Middle School Association, 1990. Used by permission.

10 Essential Elements Of An Interdisciplinary Unit

1. **THEME:** Make it broad enough to:
   a. Include objectives from several subject areas
   b. Motivate and interest students and teachers
   c. Include several creative activities
   d. Accommodate small and large group instructional strategies
   e. Last from 3 to 5 days

2. **TITLE:** Make it creative and fun!

3. **OBJECTIVES:** List at least two objectives for each subject area: Language Arts, Social Studies, Math, Science, Industrial Arts, Art, Music, and Physical Education.

4. **BACKGROUND INFORMATION ON TOPIC FOR STUDENT:** Write a one-page overview of the subject areas that provide students with the appropriate background or springboard information to effectively launch the unit.

5. **GLOSSARY:** Prepare a glossary of key terms, vocabulary, or concepts that are important to the mastery of the material.

6. **STUDENT RECORD SHEETS:** Maintain record sheets to keep track of student progress, or have students keep track of their own progress.

7. **ACTIVITIES IN EACH DISCIPLINE:** Use the same format in preparing your activities, including:
   a. Title
   b. Objective
   c. Materials Needed
   d. Procedure
   e. Evaluation

8. **HOMEWORK AND/OR ENRICHMENT IDEAS:** Create a list of tasks that could be assigned as homework or enrichment for students.

9. **POST-TEST/PROJECT PRESENTATION:** Include a post-test and/or directions for a final project to serve as the evaluation for the unit in addition to those used as part of the activities.

10. **BIBLIOGRAPHY:** List resources/references for follow-up or for use during the unit.

10 Elements That Make A Great Interdisciplinary Unit

1. Relevant topics. Students enjoyed units more if they perceived a direct relevance to their lives. Solicit student input on topics, and involve them in planning units.

2. Clear goals and objectives. Student perceptions of learning correlated positively with the degree of organization and structure in each unit. The more clearly the goals and objectives were conveyed to students, the more they felt they learned. Keep the use of time flexible, however.

3. Variety in topics, activities, grouping. Structure each unit differently. Integrate a variety of activities into the unit, such as individual/group research, project construction, simulations, guest speakers, field trips, presentations, interviews, and surveys. Provide for individual, large, and small group activities.

4. Choice in topics, projects, groupings. Include opportunities for student input and options, thereby increasing motivation and fostering a sense of responsibility for one's learning.

5. Adequate time. Allow sufficient time to explore and incubate ideas, practice skills, and complete all work with pride.

6. Processes and/or products. Weave skill development into unit topic (for example, developing, administering, tabulating, and graphing a survey on attitudes toward work in a World of Work Unit). Use products as vehicles for further student exploration of a topic.

7. Field Trips. Take students on field trips that enable them to "experience" the topic. Assist them in seeing opportunities for learning beyond school walls.

8. Group cooperation. Incorporate group work. Possible ways to facilitate positive peer interaction include: committee work (planning for and assisting at open house), group projects, group tasks (survey design, administration, and analysis), and group sharing.

9. Sharing. Have students share their knowledge/projects with others by inviting another team, an elementary class, or parents to view their final work. Public sharing encourages quality work, reinforces learning, and conveys that all contribute to the teaching/learning process.

10. Community involvement. Involve parents and community members as resource people, chaperones, and aides. This expands students' views of learning, allows greater flexibility of grouping and structure, and builds a bridge between school and community.

Adapted from *Connecting the Curriculum through Interdisciplinary Instruction* by John H. Lounsbury, Ed. Columbus, OH: National Middle School Association, 1992. Used by permission.

10 PLUS 10

Favorite Themes For Interdisciplinary Units

SCIENCE-BASED THEMES

1. Change

2. Power

3. Earth's Secrets

4. Mysteries

SOCIAL STUDIES-BASED THEMES

5. Trailblazers

6. Revolution

7. Conflict

8. Interdependence

MATHEMATICS-BASED THEMES

9. Time

10. Problem-Finding and Problem-Solving

11. Measurement

12. Magic of Numbers

LANGUAGE ARTS-BASED THEMES

13. Communication

14. Relationships

15. Power of Words

16. Media Magic

MISCELLANEOUS THEMES

17. Chocolate

18. Color

19. Futuristics

20. Humor

10
PLUS 8

Sample Tasks/Assignments For An Interdisciplinary Unit On Measurement

LANGUAGE ARTS EMPHASIS

1. Find the many different measurement systems we use now or have used in the past. Choose one and write a descriptive paragraph that includes a topic sentence, a direct quote, and a rhetorical question.

2. Pretend you are a tape measure. Imagine what you might say to the following: a carpenter, a large man, a seamstress, a yardstick.

3. Outline how you would schedule and run a measurement tournament or contest for your school.

4. Explain why and how mathematics is a language.

MATH EMPHASIS

5. Invent ten new symbols for our measurement system.

6. Make a list of objects around each of which you could tie a one-meter string.

7. Think of many possible measurement-related questions that would have the answer "one decimeter."

8. Design a flow chart to show how you would measure the area of your bedroom.

SCIENCE EMPHASIS

9. Think up several ways to verify the temperature on a thermometer.

10. Search for something which is measured in degrees, in square meters, in feet, in decibels, and in light years.

11. Do you think a glass is half filled or half empty? Explain your answer.

12. Write down as many things as you can think of that cannot be measured.

SOCIAL STUDIES EMPHASIS

13. Give some examples of occupations that require the frequent use of standard measurement devices. Show your occupation examples and devices in chart form.

14. Propose a new task to measure intelligence.

15. Of all the measurement devices people commonly use, which one is used most by a teacher, an architect, a mother, a dieter, a student, a builder? Give reasons for your choices.

16. Determine all of the reasons that you think someone invented the compass. Rank them in order from the most important reason to the least important reason.

OTHER EMPHASES

17. Prepare a list of song titles that refer to measurement in some way. Classify your list into at least two groups. Share your classification system with others.

18. Design a meter stick that is also some other object. Draw what it will look like and tell what kinds of things it would do besides measure.

Ten Views For Integrating The Curricula

1

Fragmented
Periscope—one direction; one sighting; narrow focus on single discipline

Description
The traditional model of separate and distinct disciplines, which fragments the subject areas.

Example
Teacher applies this view in Math, Science, Social Studies, Language Arts OR Sciences, Humanities, Fine and Practical Arts.

2

Connected
Opera glass—details of one discipline; focus on subtleties and interconnections

Description
Within each subject area, course content is connected topic to topic, concept to concept, one year's work to the next, and relates idea(s) explicitly.

Example
Teacher relates the concept of fractions to decimals, which in turn relates to money, grades, etc.

3

Nested
3-D glasses—multiple dimensions to one scene, topic, or unit

Description
Within each subject area, the teacher targets multiple skills: a social skill, a thinking skill, and a content-specific skill.

Example
Teacher designs the unit on photosynthesis to simultaneously target consensus seeking (social skill), sequencing (thinking skill), and plant life cycle (science content).

4
Sequenced
Eyeglasses—varied internal content framed by broad, related concepts

Description
Topics or units of study are rearranged and sequenced to coincide with one another. Similar ideas are taught in concert while remaining separate subjects.

Example
English teacher presents an historical novel depicting a particular period while the History teacher teaches that same historical period.

5

Shared
Binoculars—two disciplines that share overlapping concepts and skills

Description
Shared planning and teaching take place in two disciplines in which overlapping concepts or ideas emerge as organizing elements.

Example
Science and Math teachers use data collection, charting, and graphing as shared concepts that can be team-taught.

6

Webbed
Telescope—broad view of an entire constellation as one theme, webbed to the various elements

Description
A fertile theme is webbed to curriculum contents and disciplines; subjects use the theme to sift out appropriate concepts, topics, and ideas.

Example
Teacher presents a simple topical theme, such as the circus, and webs it to the subject areas. A conceptual theme, such as conflict, can be webbed for more depth in the theme approach.

7
Threaded
Magnifying glass—big ideas that magnify all content through a metacurricular approach

Description
The metacurricular approach threads thinking skills, social skills, multiple intelligences, technology, and study skills through the various disciplines.

Example
Teaching staff targets prediction in Reading, Math, and Science lab experiments while Social Studies teacher targets forecasting current events, and thus threads the skill (prediction) across disciplines.

8
Integrated
Kaleidoscope—new patterns and designs that use the basic elements of each discipline

Description
This interdisciplinary approach matches subjects for overlaps in topics and concepts with some team teaching in an authentic integrated model.

Example
In Math, Science, Social Studies, Fine Arts, Language Arts, and Practical Arts, teachers look for patterning models and approach content through these patterns.

9

Immersed
Microscope—intensely personal view that allows microscopic explanation as all content is filtered through lens of interest and expertise

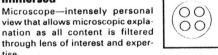

Description
The disciplines become part of the learner's lens of expertise; the learner filters all content through this lens and becomes immersed in his or her own experience.

Example
Student or doctoral candidate has an area of expert interest and sees all learning through that lens.

10
Networked
Prism—a view that creates multiple dimensions and directions of focus

Description
Learner filters all learning through the expert's eye and makes internal connections that lead to external networks of experts in related fields.

Example
Architect, while adapting the CAD/CAM technology for design, networks with technical programmers and expands her knowledge base, just as she had traditionally done with interior designers.

From *The Mindful School: How to Integrate the Curricula* by Robin Fogarty. ©1991 by IRI/Skylight Publishing, Inc., Palatine, IL. Reprinted with permission.

10 PLUS 6 -Item Team Checklist For Evaluating The Interdisciplinary Unit And Development Process

DIRECTIONS: Use this checklist to assess the quality of your interdisciplinary unit.

Our interdisciplinary unit . . .

____ **1.** features a central theme that is of high interest and high content.

____ **2.** has a specific audience and goal beyond the teacher and a grade to make it more real and meaningful.

____ **3.** is a result of cooperative planning by all involved staff members and, when possible, by students.

____ **4.** includes a written set of directions which serves as an overview and schedule. These directions can inform parents, walk students step-by-step through the project, list deadlines, decipher explanations, and help monitor progress.

____ **5.** is based on concepts and skills from each involved discipline area.

____ **6.** focuses on higher-level thinking skills that can be applied across the curriculum to a degree impossible in single disciplines.

____ **7.** places a high priority on student research skills through the structuring of research tasks that require data from multiple sources.

____ **8.** has organizational skills built into its design so that students can take on greater responsibility for planning their own work.

____ **9.** involves cooperative learning groups with an emphasis on affective and social skill development.

____ **10.** stresses individual and small group components which allow students to explore personal interest topics within a larger framework.

____ **11.** offers a variety of presentation formats so teachers can evaluate students using a wide range of modalities.

____ **12.** features simulation of real-world experiences and skills to enhance the meaning of projects for students as well as to bridge the gap between the classroom and the real world for students.

____ **13.** considers relevance to the community at large by the inclusion of real people, resources, and problems which help students to see the significance of what they are learning.

____ **14.** includes morale-, spirit-, and team-building activities to break the "work as usual" routine of school.

____ **15.** has post-project recognition beyond a simple grade to acknowledge achievement, enhance individual esteem, or give a sense of belonging to the team, class, and school.

____ **16.** seeks publicity in the local newspaper to help demonstrate the significance of their work to students, enhance the esteem of individual students, and let the community know what is happening in our school.

Adapted from *Interdisciplinary Units in New England's Middle Schools: What and Why?* by Sam Lewbel, Rowley, MA: New England League of Middle Schools, ©1991. Used by permission.

The Interdisciplinary Team (IDT) Test

DIRECTIONS: Work with three colleagues who teach subject areas different from yours to complete this interdisciplinary quiz. Try to first answer all of the questions by yourself, and then meet with your colleagues to pool your expertise. Did you do better by integrating subject-matter backgrounds or by answering alone?

TWO, THREE, OR FOUR HEADS ARE BETTER THAN ONE

1. What genus of flower was named for German naturalist Leonard Fuchs?

2. What target sport got its name from the Norwegian word for "shoot"?

3. What waterway did the United States officially open to traffic on August 15, 1914?

4. What color is most often used to symbolize truth?

5. What mid-western state can show you the most underground caves?

6. How many sides does a dodecagon have?

7. What "Batman" television villain leads the Molehill Mob?

8. What former United States President hit the jogging paths to enhance his athletic image and, sporting number 39, almost collapsed during a road race?

9. What was the first state to secede from the union on December 20, 1860?

10. Where in the body is the septum linguae?

11. What spaced-out television show bit the cosmic dust after 78 episodes were filmed?

12. What is a syllogism?

13. What country is home to the plains of Jericho?

14. What Shakespeare character tells Ophelia: "Get thee to a nunnery?"

15. What artificial organ was first developed by Gordon Murray?

16. The sum of the squares of two numbers is four less than the sum of one hundred plus half a hundred. What are the two numbers?

ANSWER KEY

1. *fuschia*
2. *sheet*
3. *Panama Canal*
4. *blue*
5. *Missouri*
6. *12 sides*
7. *The Riddler*
8. *Jimmy Carter*
9. *South Carolina*
10. *on the tongue*
11. *"Star Trek"*
12. *deductive reasoning consisting of a major premise, a minor premise, and a conclusion*
13. *Jordan*
14. *Hamlet*
15. *the artificial kidney*
16. *5, 11*

Sample Interdisciplinary Unit:
A Model For Success
"The Future is News To Me"

PURPOSE OF THE UNIT

The purpose of this interdisciplinary unit is to combine the study of the local newspaper as a tool for communicating information today with a study of futuristics as a tool for functioning in the world of tomorrow. Specifically, the student will examine basic journalism concepts using the format of the typical newspaper as the primary vehicle for exploring a series of future-oriented ideas and trends.

OBJECTIVES OF THE UNIT

One set of objectives is based on the newspaper, and the other set of objectives focuses on the study of the future.

Newspaper Objectives

The student will be able to . . .

1. compare and contrast the four major purposes or duties of a newspaper and give an example of each.
2. define a minimum of ten common newspaper terms.
3. explain the six criteria for judging whether an event is newsworthy or not.
4. apply the 5 W (Who? What? When? Where? Why?) and How questions in both a newspaper and/or a feature story.
5. distinguish between an editorial, an editorial cartoon, and a letter to the editor.
6. describe at least one distinguishing characteristic of a news story, a feature story, and an editorial.
7. analyze a classified ad and a display ad.
8. name the major sections of the newspaper and summarize the purpose of each.
9. give examples of at least three special features most commonly found in the newspaper.
10. The student will describe five different types of leads to be used in news and feature stories.
11. The student will create an original front page of a newspaper, applying futuristics concepts.

Futuristics Objectives

The student will be able to . . .

1. define a minimum of eight futuristic terms.
2. examine at least one trend and be able to give three implications or effects of that trend for the future.
3. make inferences about the role of current developments in science and technology on future trends.
4. study his or her role as an important ingredient of the future.
5. evaluate technologies and their impact on the future.

GLOSSARY OF TERMS FOR THE UNIT

There are two basic sets of terms to be learned as part of this interdisciplinary unit. Again, one set of vocabulary words is essential to a study of the newspaper while the other set is important to the understanding of futuristics.

Newspaper Terms

Balloon: in a comic strip, the line surrounding a statement to make it look as though the words are coming from a person's mouth.

Banner Headline: a large front-page headline which sometimes spans the full width of the page.

By-line: a line at the head of an article giving the writer's name.

Caption: the explanatory copy which accompanies a photograph or illustration.

Classified Advertising: brief advertisements which are divided into categories or classes and run together in the newspaper.

Copy: news and other written textual matter which will be typeset and printed in the newspaper.

Dateline: the line at the beginning of a non-local news story giving its date and place of origin.

Display Advertising: advertising that is set off from newspaper text by larger display typefaces, rules, incorporated white spaces, and illustrations.

Ear: box or space in upper corner of front page usually containing advertising of the paper itself or a weather forecast.

Editorial: opinionated material which states the viewpoint of a particular newspaper according to its publisher and/or editors.

Editorial Cartoon: a cartoon which illustrates a newspaper's editorial stance on an issue.

Feature: newspaper material that is not news-oriented.

Index: a list of major topics in newspaper plus their page numbers.

Inverted Pyramid: the journalistic format for organizing and writing straight news articles in which details are reported in descending order of importance.

Lead: the first paragraph of a news story which summarizes the chief news to follow.

Lead Story: most important news story of the day, usually placed at top of front page.

Futuristics Terms

Automation: the coupling of computers with machines to perform services previously accomplished by people.

Clone: an asexually-produced offspring of a life form which contains the exact genetic coding of the parent.

Cybernetics: the study of communications and control mechanisms in living things and in machines.

Electronic Cottage: the cottage-industry concept moved into the computer/electronic age. Alvin Toffler, in *The Third Wave*, describes the possibility of a low-cost work station in any home containing a "smart typewriter," a facsimile machine or computer console, and teleconferencing equipment. Using these machines, he contends, would radically extend the possibilities for home-based work.

Forecast: a conditional statement about a future possibility based on research.

Futuristics: the field of study that deals with possible future developments.

Information Age: also called the Age of Technology, the Post-Industrial Age, and the Computer Age. An outgrowth of the success of the Industrial Era. Information is considered the key product including the development, storage, and retrieval of that information.

Organ Transplant Network: a communication system that matches available donor organs with candidates needing those organs.

Robot: a machine capable of performing human functions.

Space Colony: colonies of people, primarily space technicians, that live and work on artificial satellites or in protected environments in space.

Trend: a pattern of events which has occurred over an extended period of time in the past, indicating a tendency or direction that might be repeated. Used with caution by futurist researchers.

ORGANIZATION OF THE UNIT

This interdisciplinary unit consists of twelve different activities with each activity having three major sections. The first section is a short Information Section that requires students to read and learn about an important newspaper concept. The second section is a Scrapbook Section requiring students to examine the local newspaper and cut out applications of the newly learned concept for inclusion in personal scrapbooks. The third section is a Futuristics Section which requires students to write original pieces of newspaper copy for their king-size futuristics front pages. The final component of this interdisciplinary unit is a "How Much Did You Learn?" test that uses Bloom's Taxonomy as the structure for completing two sets of tasks—one based on the newspaper objectives and one based on the futuristics objectives.

ASSESSMENT OF THE UNIT

Each student will successfully complete three different products for this interdisciplinary unit—a scrapbook of newspaper application tasks, a king-size newspaper of original articles about the future, and a take-home test.

ADVANCED PREPARATION FOR THE UNIT

It is suggested that the teacher arrange to have multiple copies of the local newspaper delivered to the classroom on a daily basis for a three-week period. These will be read and cut up by the students as they complete their scrapbook assignments. Students should bring blank scrapbooks to school or construct them from supplies of large manila drawing paper and poster board. In addition, the teacher should provide each student with a long piece of shelf paper approximately five feet in length for his or her king-size, future-oriented newspaper. Finally, the teacher and students should begin collecting a wide variety of resource materials on both the newspaper and futuristics and use these books, periodicals, artifacts, and audiovisual items to set up a Newspaper/Futuristics Learning Center for the classroom.

1. ACTIVITY ONE: WHAT MAKES NEWS?

Information Section (Four Purposes of a Newspaper)

There are four principal purposes or duties of a newspaper. The first duty of a newspaper is to *inform* its readers who need to know what is going on locally, in the state, in the nation, and internationally. The most important story of the day becomes the banner story. This story, along with its banner headline, occupies the place of greatest importance on the front page of the paper. It is usually placed at the top right corner of the page.

The second duty of a newspaper is to offer many *services* to its readers. Some of the services: women's pages, family pages, social news pages, financial or business pages, special columns, movie and television guides, and advertising.

A newspaper prints not only news, but also explains important issues which affect its readers. This is called *interpretation* and is found on the editorial page.

Finally, there are the parts of the newspaper included for fun and *entertainment*. Advice columns, amusing feature stories, and comic strips are a few examples.

Six Criteria Of What Makes News

1. *Timeliness:* People do not want to read about old news. Instead, they want to learn about events that have just happened.
2. *Important Names:* People like to know about everything that happens to a superstar, a hero, or an important figure in the government, movies, sports, or television.
3. *Nearness:* People love to read about news that occurs in their own neighborhood or community.
4. *Discovery:* People are often interested in stories of achievement, adventure, or discovery. They like to read about such events as a kidney transplant or a space exploration or some new scientific technique because these stories are full of mystery and wonder.
5. *The Unusual:* People are intrigued by anything that could be classified as rare or unusual because it stirs curiosity and personal interest.
6. *Struggle or Conflict:* People are fascinated by such activities as combat, struggle, violence, conflict, and showdowns. Struggle attracts readers because it involves emotion and opposing forces, whether it be in the areas of crime, sports, wars, elections, or government.

Scrapbook Section

Browse through your local newspaper and find at least one example each of a newspaper article intended to inform, to interpret, to serve, and to entertain its readers. Paste these in your scrapbook and label each article with its purpose.

Futuristics Section

Think up a creative title for your Futuristics newspaper. Some starter ideas include: *The Interplanetary Gazette, The Galaxy Glamour, The Daily Cosmic Blast,* and *The Moony Meteorite.* Print your title in big, bold letters at the top of your piece of shelf paper which will now become your futuristic newspaper's king-size front page!

2. ACTIVITY TWO:
ANATOMY OF A FRONT PAGE

Information Section (Newspaper Layout)

Study the layout of the front page below. Use unit's glossary (page 325) to help you learn the definitions of each of the key parts of the front page.

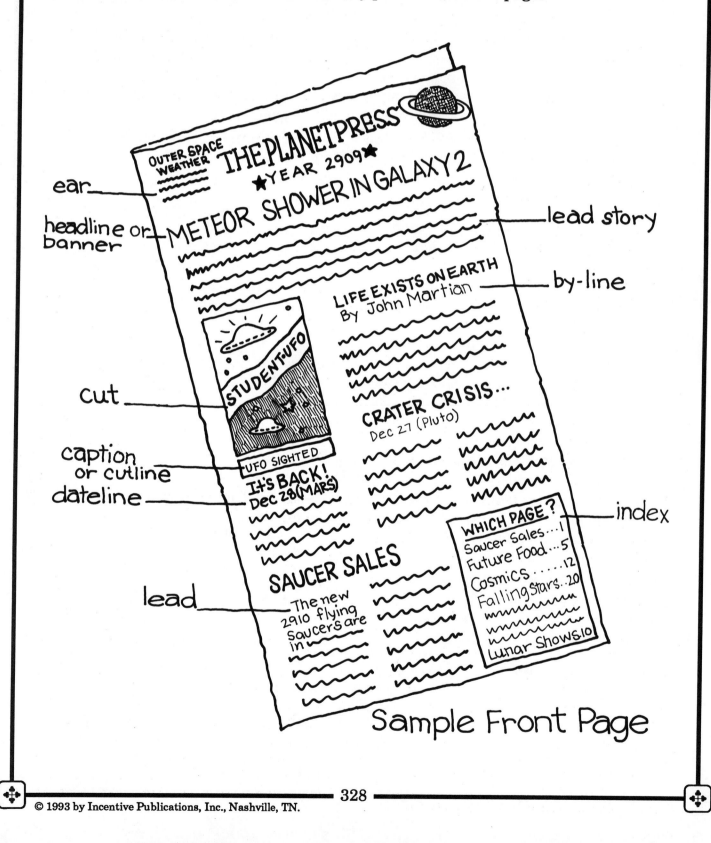

Sample Front Page

Scrapbook Section
1. What is the headline of today's top story on page one of your newspaper?
2. Find the datelines of the front page articles. Where did the stories take place? List the locations and find them on a map.
3. How many writers have a by-line on the front page? Write down their names.
4. Select the cut (photo on the front page) and rewrite the cutline (information below the picture).
5. List the titles of the articles and the wire services that supplied the news.
6. How many news stories can you count on page one of this edition of the newspaper?
7. Find an article that contains what you believe to be the best lead paragraph. Write down its 5 W and How questions.
8. In addition to the headline, stories, and index, what other kinds of information can you find on your front page? Explain.

Futuristics Section
Choose one of the following topics (or think up a better one of your own) and write a lead story for your Futuristics newspaper. Be sure to include a lead that contains the five W and How questions: Who, What, Where, When, Why, and How. What banner/headline will you invent to grab your readers' attention?
1. Computers to replace Mother Nature and control weather
2. Chemical control of the aging process so that people can live to be several hundred years old
3. Sustaining the human body in frozen storage
4. Control of people's behavior by radio stimulation of the brain
5. Building of enclosed cities in outer space or under the sea
6. Development of robots to do unpleasant jobs
7. Educating children totally with machines
8. Occupations becoming obsolete every five years
9. Discovery of life far superior to ours on other planets
10. Use of mental telepathy as a mode of communication
11. Genetically controlling the gender and traits of unborn children
12. Using your sixth sense of clairvoyance (telepathy)
13. The laser energy beam of the future
14. A house run by a computer
15. Growing up in an undersea city
16. Settling in space colonies
17. Super chickens and other future foods
18. Space parts for people
19. Discovery of nationwide wrist-radio network
20. UFOs and communicating with aliens
21. Mining the moon for resources

3. ACTIVITY THREE: DISCOVERING NEWS STORY STRUCTURE

Information Section (The Who, What, When, Where, Why, and How of a Story)

A short story writer often presents the minor facts first and then builds up to the story's climax or high point. The most important information is given at the story's end. The diagram on the left below shows the organization of such a story.

The news reporter does not organize a story in the same way. Because newspaper readers want to be able to know immediately what a story is about, the reporter begins the news story with the important information first and ends with the lesser facts. The diagram on the right below represents the structure of a typical news story and is often referred to as the inverted pyramid or summary lead news story.

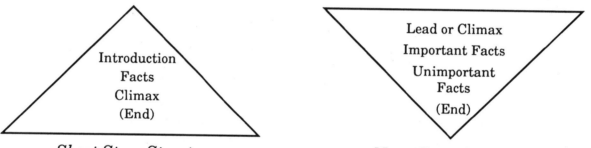

Short Story Structure   *News Story Structure*

There are other types of leads that we should learn to recognize. The SHOCKER LEAD is intended to shock the reader with a simple statement. *Example: Teenage AIDS cases will triple in the next two years!* The QUESTION LEAD simply asks a question designed to arouse curiosity in readers. *Example: Is your privacy being violated?* The QUOTATION LEAD quotes a speaker. *Example: "Nerds. That's all they are."* A final type of news lead is the CONTRAST LEAD which makes two statements that seem to be opposite in meaning or contradict each other. *Example: Nolan Ryan pitched the best game of his career Monday night—and got beaten.*

Scrapbook Section

Find a news story with a summary lead in your local newspaper and paste it in your scrapbook. Next to the story, write out the five W and How questions. Label each phrase or group of words that tells what, when, where, why, who, and how.

Find examples of news stories for each of the other types of leads. Paste these stories in your scrapbook and label each one.

Futuristic Section

Select another topic from those listed as part of Activity Two's Futuristics Section. Write four different leads for a possible news story on this topic. Include a shocker lead, a question lead, a quotation lead, and a contrast lead. Can you develop one of these leads into a short, yet informative, news article for your futuristics newspaper using the inverted pyramid model? Go ahead and try it!

4. ACTIVITY FOUR: "HUMAN SIDE OF THE NEWS"

Information Section (Feature Stories)

Feature and human interest stories add excitement, novelty, and spice to the newspaper menu. They are similar to short stories in that they use colorful words, build to an exciting climax or high point, and are designed to entertain the reader by developing an emotional appeal. Unlike the straight news story, the feature story follows a pattern much like that of a short story: the incidents are developed in chronological order or in the order of their occurrence. There are four basic types of feature stories.

1. Historical Features: describe events related to a particular celebration or that highlight events of today similar to those of the past.
2. Descriptive Stories: describe any place of interest, adventure, excitement, or interesting people.
3. Explanatory Stories: explain the "why" or "how" of an event such as a hobby, game, or special skill.
4. Entertainment Stories: describe adventure, odd or funny events, travel or anything else that appeals to human interest or feeling.

Scrapbook Section

Use the local newspaper to make a collection of human interest and feature stories that include elements of laughter, anger, pride, or sympathy. Cut out these stories, paste them into your scrapbook, and label each with the appropriate emotion that is evoked. Study the vocabulary of each story, paying particular attention to the emotional words used. Underline those words designed to appeal to the readers' emotions. Beneath each article, summarize the main idea or theme in one or two sentences.

Futuristics Section

Pretend you are a reporter interviewing one of the following individuals about their futuristic activities.

1. The leader of a colony on Mars
2. A scientist who has just created the first authentic cyborg
3. Bobby, the all-new model 2025 upstairs/downstairs robot servant
4. Mollie, the mechanical teacher
5. The inventor of a nuclear-powered vehicle
6. A space farmer
7. The first interplanetary citizen

Write down a list of interview questions and possible answers that might take place in such an interview. Use this list to write a human interest story. Remember that feature stories use highly descriptive, colorful, and powerful words which evoke some emotional response in the reader such as tears, fear, anger, humor, excitement, or hostility.

5. ACTIVITY FIVE: ANALYZING THE OPINION PAGE

Information Section (The Editorial Section)

The editorial page is very important because it is here that we find the opinions of the newspaper as stated by the editor and readers of the newspaper. Most of the other pages contain straightforward news reporting, but the editorial page is the place for presenting different points of view and different interpretations of ideas and facts. Editorials are written by the editors who give their opinions on important issues. These are most often printed in the upper left-hand corner of the editorial page. In addition to editorials, you will also find a section of "Letters to the Editor" where readers can express their opinions on current topics. Another feature of the editorial page is the political cartoon. These cartoons are drawn by experts in political affairs who want to express their opinions of the latest political developments. An editorial cartoon is created to inform, entertain, or anger readers. The editorial cartoonist uses symbolism in his or her drawings just as a poet uses figures of speech in poetry.

Scrapbook Section

Use your local newspaper to find examples of an editorial, a letter to the editor, and a political cartoon. Paste these in your scrapbook and label each one. Next to the editorial, write a short paragraph that outlines the editorial's main points. Tell why you agree or disagree with the editor's viewpoint.

Futuristics Section

Write an editorial for your futuristics newspaper on the subject of cloning. Try to cover these questions or points in your discussion:
1. What are the advantages of cloning?
2. Who gets cloned? Who doesn't?
3. Who decides? Who controls cloning?
4. Do the advantages of cloning outweigh the disadvantages?
5. How do you know whether or not cloning is successful?
6. What happens when a clone is defective? How often is a defective clone made? What do you do with defective clones?

6. ACTIVITY SIX: THE ATTENTION GRABBERS

Information Section (Photographs, Captions, and Headlines)

Photographs are an important part of any newspaper. They break up the monotony of the printed pages and make these pages more interesting and appealing to the reader. Photographs also convey the facts, emotions, and events of a happening in ways that a news story cannot. The idea that one picture is worth a thousand words is often the case with a news event. Photographs are often used for a specific purpose: to make the viewer angry, to attract sympathy for a cause, or to move a reader to some type of action. Captions are included with most photographs. (Captions are headings used with pictures.) Captions should be brief, summarize the content of the accompanying news story, be clever and attract the readers' attention, and be varied and bold in letter design.

Scrapbook Section

Use the local newspaper to cut out several photographs that accompany news stories. By using these photographs and their captions alone, develop a photo essay that tells an imaginary story. Paste the photos into your scrapbook.

Futuristics Section

Browse through some newspapers or magazines until you find a picture of something that is futuristic in nature. Perhaps it might be an illustration of a rocket ship, a robot, a computer, a mechanical part, or a transportation vehicle. Cut it out and paste it in your futuristics newspaper. Write a clever caption for the picture. Try to develop a short news or feature story to accompany it.

7. ACTIVITY SEVEN: THAT'S FUN AND LAUGHS

Information Section (The Entertainment Section)

Some parts of the entertainment section, such as the comics and puzzle sections, actually do the entertaining themselves. This section also contains some articles which are written about the entertainment world itself. Book and play reviews, television, movie, and radio guides, feature stories about people or places in the entertainment industry, and travel stories are a few examples of news stories meant primarily to entertain the reader.

Scrapbook Section

Use the local newspaper to plan a week's worth of entertainment. Clip out television schedules, restaurant ads, movie blurbs, book reviews, and descriptions of community events to use to write a one-week diary describing what you did and what you saw.

Futuristics Section

You are to create a vacation package for the entertainment section of your futuristics newspaper. Write a feature story on any one of the following travel activity options. Where will you stay? How long will you be gone? What will you see and do? What will it cost?

1. 30 days on Saturn
2. Five days on a cloud
3. A perfect vacation on planet Azonk
4. Nine days with King Robot
5. Come to Utopia—30 days in Heaven

8. ACTIVITY EIGHT: NEWSPAPERS MEAN BUSINESS

Information Section (The Business and Financial Section)

Another vital part of the daily newspaper is the business section and, in particular, the financial columns. Business people and stock owners read this section of the newspaper very carefully. Probably the most widely read part of the financial section is the daily stock exchange transactions.

In addition to the stock market report, the financial section includes many news stories about the business world. If a company plans to build a new plant, for instance, the financial page would probably carry a news story about it. If the government changes a law that affects business, the newspaper would certainly print a news story on this topic in the financial section.

Illustrations of all kinds frequently appear on the financial or business pages. Photographs, drawings, diagrams, and charts or graphs are used regularly to illustrate news stories about big business.

Scrapbook Section

Use the local newspaper to study the stocks from the New York Stock Exchange. For our purposes in this assignment, you will be concerned with only the last four columns of figures labeled "High," "Low," "Last," and "Net Chg."

The column labeled "High" tells the highest price at which a particular stock sold on that day. The column labeled "Low" tells the lowest price at which each stock sold during the day's trading. The column labeled "Last" indicates the price when the stock exchange closed for the day, and the final column "Net Chg." means the net change in today's price from the price of the stock on the previous day.

Divide a page in your scrapbook into six columns. Label the first column "Stock" and list the names of ten stocks from the New York Stock Exchange that interest you. Label the next five columns "Abbreviation" (for stock name), "High," "Low," "Last," and "Net Chg." Circle the stock which is worth the most per share. Underline the stock which is worth the least per share. Put a box around the stock which recorded the greatest gain from the previous day and a triangle around the stock which recorded the least gain from the previous day.

Futuristics Section

With the great technological progresses made in the world today, new business and occupations are developing constantly. Make up a business, a service, or a profession of the future. Attach a name to this new occupation and explain what service will be performed. Some possible business ventures to consider might be: space shuttle pilot, manufacturer of spare human parts, robot repair service, moon mining company, space station designer, or international peacekeeper. Write a short news story about your new enterprise for your futuristics newspaper.

9. ACTIVITY NINE: SUPERSPORT STORIES

Information Section (The Sports Section)

Detailed averages, scores, standings, and competitive results are an important part of the sports section. Sports writers have strong feelings about the sports, and they use powerful, descriptive language to capture the excitement of whatever games they are covering. Sports writing is always packed with colorful action verbs!

Scrapbook Section

Use the local newspaper to find a sports story that appeals to you. Cut it out and paste it into your scrapbook. Underline the colorful verbs in the article (e.g. whipped, roared, smash, fought, etc.) and copy down the sentences that include these verbs. Rewrite the sentences, substituting the figures of speech and action verbs with their literal or regular meanings. See how ordinary the sentences are without them!

Futuristics Section

You are to invent a new sport or athletic contest that can be played by two persons in an enclosed 8' x 8' x 8' space. All rules, playing-area design, equipment, and scoring strategies must be explained in an article. Since there is a shortage of space and land in our world today, this type of athletic game may indeed become a necessity in the future. What special vocabulary will have to be created and used for this sport? Can you write a play-by-play description of this new sport for your futuristics newspaper?

10. ACTIVITY TEN: WEATHER WONDERS

Information Section (The Weather Section)

The weather always makes good news. Many newspapers print a summary of the weather forecast on the front page. These summaries are always brief and usually forecast the weather for the upcoming twenty-four to forty-eight hours. For a more detailed story about the weather, a reader would have to look for the official weather map from the U.S. Weather Bureau.

The U.S. Weather Bureau supplies newspapers with a detailed alphabetized list of United States cities and their current weather conditions. Usually included is a one-word description of the weather in each city, the high temperature recorded, the low temperature recorded, and the amount of precipitation in inches.

Scrapbook Section

Use the local newspaper to find the weather information from the U.S. Weather Bureau. Paste this information in your scrapbook and state five weather facts which this information provides for you.

Futuristics Section

Write a simple weather summary for your futuristics newspaper. Will it be about a meteor storm, a skyquake, a lunar eclipse?

11. ACTIVITY ELEVEN: CREATIVE CARTOONS

Information Section (The Comic Section)

The most frequently read section of any newspaper is the comic section. Cartoonists use many devices to make their work interesting to the reader. They may exaggerate situations or events, use forms of language that reflect various localities or various cultural characteristics, or draw witty illustrations of people and places. Cartoonists also make their work more easily understood by using particular graphic techniques. When a new or difficult word is used, a character's actions often explain its meaning. Balloons are used to depict conversations between characters. To avoid monotony of appearance, picture panels are divided into sections. Even photographic techniques, such as close-ups, long shots, unusual angles, and dramatic lighting, are used for emphasis.

There are different styles of comic strips. Some comics are intended to be purely humorous, while others convey some sort of social or political message. Comic strips can also be serialized, which means that the story line continues from day to day. "Dick Tracy" is an example of a serialized comic strip. Other comic strips tell a complete story each day.

Scrapbook Section

Look through the local newspaper to find your favorite comic strip. Cut it out, remove the word balloons from the strip, and paste it in your notebook. Then, write your own comic strip by coming up with your own dialog for the comic strip's characters. Write your new words beneath the comic strip using correct punctuation for quotations as well as proper indentations for changes of speaker. Try to add words or phrases of explanation to convey the actions or expressions of the cartoon figures. *Example: "Lucy, come here at once!" hollered Charlie angrily.*

Futuristics Section

Choose your favorite comic strip character. Change his or her lifestyle through the use of language, clothing, daily adventures, occupations, activities, setting, and problems encountered to reflect a future-oriented environment. You might want to do this by having your cartoon strip feature an interview, flashback, or chance meeting between people of today and people of tomorrow. What will you name your cartoon character? How about Roberta Robot, Charlie Clone, Cy Cyborg, or Bionic Bonnie? Put your cartoon strip in your futuristics newspaper.

12. ACTIVITY TWELVE: MARKETPLACE OF THE NEWSPAPER

Information Section (The Advertising Section)

There are two basic types of advertisements in a newspaper—classified ads and display ads. Classified ads, sometimes called want ads, contain no art work and are usually placed in a special section of the newspaper. Classified ads deal with the buying and selling of goods and services. These ads are brief and to the point, containing only the essential details of the service, job, or merchandise advertised. These ads are usually placed in the newspaper by individuals.

Display ads are typically used by local merchants such as large department, furniture, and grocery stores, as well as by national advertising accounts. Display ads tend to be large, often using a quarter, half, or full page in the newspaper, and contain elaborate artwork.

Advertising is important to the consumer because it provides information about new products and techniques in the marketplace as well as current prices of available goods and services. It also allows the individual to shop from home. For people in the business world, newspaper advertising provides an effective medium for promoting their goods and services. Advertising is important to the newspaper itself because it provides revenue for the paper. It is the money received from advertisers that allows the paper to be produced each day.

Scrapbook Section

Look through the classified ads of your local newspaper. Read through some of the ads and pick out one that makes you think of a story or an incident. Is the ad sad, happy, funny, or serious?

Paste the ad in your scrapbook and write a story that tells what you think the ad is about. What do you think the purpose of the ad is? Who placed the ad? What do you think will happen if the ad is successful or unsuccessful?

Futuristics Section

Make up a futuristics classified ad for each of the following situations: Help Wanted, Personal, Item for Sale, Lost and Found, Real Estate, and Special Services Available.

Next, design a display ad to advertise one of the following future-oriented products:

1. Youth Pill
2. Robot
3. Picture Phone
4. 100-speed Bicycle
5. Instant Fortune-Telling Machine
6. Portable Weather Station
7. Inflatable Furniture
8. Artificial Organ
9. Miniaturized Television
10. Wrist Radio Satellite

How Much Did You Learn?

Directions: This is a take-home test which will help you determine how much you have learned about the newspaper and the world of futuristics.

Newspaper Tasks To Complete

Knowledge (5 points)
1. List the major sections of the local newspaper. _____
_____
_____

Comprehension (10 points)
2. In your own words, briefly describe the four purposes of a newspaper and give an example of at least one feature item commonly found in a newspaper that serves this purpose. _____
_____
_____

Application (15 points)
3. Construct a set of headlines that would meet any five of the six criteria for what makes a good news story. Label each one._____
_____
_____

Analysis (20 points)
4. Compare and contrast each of the following items:
   a. A display ad with a classified ad_____
_____

   b. A feature story with an editorial_____
_____
_____

Synthesis (25 points)
5. Pretend that you are a newspaper reporter in your community. Your assignment is to write a feature story about your class and this recent study of the newspaper with its futuristic application. On another piece of paper, write the feature from your own perspective.

Evaluation (25 points)
6. Determine which section of the newspaper would be most beneficial to the mayor or city council of your community. What criteria will you use and what alternatives will you consider? Write your answers on another piece of paper. Be sure to defend your choice with 3 to 5 reasons one section is of greater benefit that any of the other options.

How Much Did You Learn? (continued)

Futuristic Tasks To Complete

Knowledge (5 points)
1. Briefly define each of these terms: clone, robot, trend, automation, and futuristics.

_____

_____

_____

_____

_____

Comprehension (10 points)
2. Describe one possible advantage and one possible disadvantage of each of these potential discoveries/inventions for future populations: the widespread use of electronic cottages and the widespread use of genetic engineering. _____

_____

_____

_____

Application (15 points)
3. Make a list of five quality interview questions that you would like to ask the head of a major organ transplant hospital. Make sure that your questions address the complex issues associated with the controversy surrounding transplants in today's society. _____

_____

_____

_____

_____

_____

Analysis (20 points)
4. If you had one day to show an alien the best of our country, where would you go and what would you do? Write your answers on another piece of paper.

Synthesis (25 points)
5. Global interdependence and respect for cultural diversity are important to our future. On another piece of paper, write your own special pledge for people to sign to become world citizens and share in the rewards of an international economy.

Evaluation (25 points)
6. If you could clone a plant, animal, insect, natural resource, and a person, which ones would you choose to clone and why? Write your answers on another piece of paper. Be certain to defend each of your choices with logic and reasons.

TEACHER'S INTERDISCIPLINARY INSTRUCTION WRAP-UP, À LA BLOOM

KNOWLEDGE
Identify the essential elements of a high-quality interdisciplinary unit.

COMPREHENSION
Give examples of appropriate themes for interdisciplinary instruction.

APPLICATION
Construct a set of interview questions you could use to evaluate the effectiveness of an interdisciplinary unit with students.

ANALYSIS
Determine ways interdisciplinary instruction compares to the interrelatedness of learning in work and everyday life.

SYNTHESIS
Imagine how interdisciplinary instruction will influence and could change the schooling process over the next ten years.

EVALUATION
Judge the value of research available to teachers supporting the need for integration of subject matter in the classroom.

BIBLIOGRAPHY

INDEX

Bibliography

NUTS AND BOLTS

Arth, A.A., Johnston, J.H., Lounsbury, J.H, Toepfer, C.F. and Melton, G.E. *Developing a Mission Statement for the Middle Level School.* Reston, VA: National Association of Secondary School Principals, 1987.

Arth, A.A., Johnston, J.H., Lounsbury, J.H, Toepfer, C.F. and Melton, G.E. *Middle Level Education's Responsibility for Intellectual Development.* Reston, VA: National Association of Secondary School Principals, 1989.

Cochran, J. *What to Do With the Gifted Child in the Regular Classroom.* Nashville, TN: Incentive Publications, 1992.

Eichhorn, D.H. *The Middle School.* New York, NY: The Center for Applied Research in Education, Inc., 1966.

Smith, D.D., Executive Director. *This We Believe.* Columbus, OH: National Middle School Association, 1992.

"Structuring Schools for Student Success: A Focus on Ability Grouping." The Massachusetts Department of Education, January, 1990.

Van Hoose, J. and Strahan, D. *Young Adolescent Development and School Practices: Promoting Harmony.* Columbus, OH: National Middle School Association, 1988.

INTERDISCIPLINARY TEAMING

Epstein, J.L. and MacIver, D.J. *Education in the Middle Grades: Overview of National Practices and Trends.* Columbus, OH: National Middle School Association, 1990.

Erb, T.O. and Doda, N.M. *Team Organization: Promise, Practice and Possibilities.* Washington, DC: National Education Association, 1989.

George, P. and Lawrence, G. *Handbook for Middle School Teaching.* Glenview, IL: Scott, Foresman and Company, 1982.

George, P., Stevenson, C., Thomason, J. and Beane, J. *The Middle School—and Beyond.* Alexandria, VA: Association for Supervision and Curriculum Development, 1992.

Irvin, J.L. *Transforming Middle Level Education: Perspectives and Possibilities.* Needham Heights, MA: Allyn and Bacon, 1992.

Lounsbury, J.H., ed. *Connecting the Curriculum Through Interdisciplinary Instruction.* Columbus, OH: National Middle School Association, 1992.

Merenbloom, E.Y. *The Team Process: A Handbook for Teachers.* Columbus, OH: National Middle School Association, 1991.

Miller, R. *Team Planning for Educational Leaders: A Training Handbook.* Philadelphia, PA: Research for Better Schools, 1987.

ADVISORY

Cole, C. *Nurturing a Teacher Advisory Program.* Columbus, OH: National Middle School Association, 1992.

Farnette, C., Forte, I., and Loss, B. *People Need Each Other (Revised).* Nashville, TN: Incentive Publications, 1989.

Forte, I. *The Me I'm Learning to Be.* Nashville, TN: Incentive Publications, 1991.

Forte, I. and Schurr, S. *Advisory: Middle Grades Advisee/Advisor Program,* Nashville, TN: Incentive Publications, Inc., 1992.

Forte, I. and Schurr, S. *Operation Orientation.* Nashville, TN: Incentive Publications, Inc., 1991.

James, M. *Adviser-advisee Programs: Why, What and How.* Columbus, OH: National Middle School Association, 1986.

COOPERATIVE LEARNING

Beane, James A. and Lipka, Richard P. *Self-Concept, Self-Esteem, and the Curriculum.* New York, NY: Teachers College Press, 1986.

Breeden, T. and Mosley, J. *The Cooperative Learning Companion.* Nashville, TN: Incentive Publications, 1992.

Breeden, T. and Mosley, J. *The Middle Grades Teacher's Handbook for Cooperative Learning.* Nashville, TN: Incentive Publications, 1991

Cohen, E.G. *Designing Groupwork: Strategies for the Heterogeneous Classroom.* New York, NY: Teachers College Press, 1986.

Forte, I. *Cooperative Learning Teacher Timesavers.* Nashville, TN: Incentive Publications, 1992.

Forte, I. and MacKenzie, J. *Pulling Together For Cooperative Learning.* Nashville, TN: Incentive Publications, 1991.

Forte, I. and Schurr, S. *The Cooperative Learning Guide & Planning Pak for Middle Grades.* Nashville, TN: Incentive Publications, 1992.

Graves, Nancy B. and Graves, Theodore, D. "The Effect of Cooperative Learning Methods on Academic Achievement: A Review of the Reviews," *The International Association for the Study of Cooperation in Education, NEWSLETTER,* Volume 5, Numbers 3 and 4, December 1984, p. 5.

Hill, S. and Hill, T. *The Collaborative Classroom.* Portsmouth, NH: Heinemann, 1990.

Johnson, D.W. *Circles of Learning (2nd edition).* Edina, MN: Interaction Book Company, 1986.

Johnson, D.W. and Johnson, R.T. *Leading the Cooperative School.* Edina, MN: Interaction Book Company, 1989.

Johnson, D.W. and Johnson, R.T. *Learning Together and Alone: Cooperation, Competition, and Individualization (2nd edition).* Englewood Cliffs, NJ: Prentice-Hall, 1987.

Kagan, S. *Cooperative Learning Resources for Teachers.* Riverside, CA: Resources for Teachers, Inc., 1989.

Schniedewind, Nancy and Davidson, Ellen. *Cooperative Learning, Cooperative Lives.* Dubuque, IA: Wm. C. Brown Company Publishers, 1987.

CREATIVE AND CRITICAL THINKING SKILLS

Brown, Marilyn. *Effective Questions to Strengthen Thinking.* Hawthorne, NJ: Educational Impressions, Inc., 1989.

Collins, C. *Time Management for Teachers.* West Nyack, NY: Parker Publishing, 1987.

Costa, A.L., ed. *Developing Minds: A Resource Book for Teaching Thinking.* Alexandria, VA: Association for Supervision and Curriculum Development, 1985.

Costa, A.L. *The School as a Home for the Mind.* Palatine, IL: Skylight Publishing, 1991.

DeBono, E. *Six Thinking Hats.* Boston, MA: Little, Brown and Company, 1985.

Forte, I. *Think About It! Middle Grades.* Nashville, TN: Incentive Publications, 1981.

Forte, I. and Schurr, S. *Science Mind Stretchers.* Nashville, TN: Incentive Publications, Inc., 1987.

Frender, G. *Learning to Learn.* Nashville, TN: Incentive Publications, Inc., 1990.

Kincher, J. *Psychology for Kids: 40 Fun Tests that Help You Learn About Yourself.* Minneapolis, MN: Free Spirit Publishing, Inc., 1990.

Lazear, D. *Seven Ways of Knowing: Teaching for Multiple Intelligences (Second Edition).* Palatine, IL: Skylight Publishing, 1991.

Lazear, D. *Seven Ways of Teaching: The Artistry of Teaching with Multiple Intelligences.* Palatine, IL: Skylight Publishing, 1991.

Lyman, F. "The Thinktrix: A Classroom Tool for Thinking in Response to Reading," *Reading: Issues and Practices.* College Park, MD: University of Maryland Press, 1987.

Schurr, S. *Dynamite in the Classroom: A How-to Handbook for Teachers.* Columbus, OH: National Middle School Association, 1989.

Wiederhold, C. *Cooperative Learning and Critical Thinking: The Question Matrix.* San Juan Capistrano, CA: Resources for Teachers, Inc., 1991.

Williams, Frank. *Creativity Assessment Packet.* Austin, TX: Pro-Ed Publishers, 1980.

ASSESSMENT

Brandt, R.S. *Performance Assessment: Readings from Educational Leadership.* Alexandria, VA: Association for Supervision and Curriculum Development, 1992.

Forte, I. and MacKenzie, J. *Writing Survival Skills for the Middle Grades.* Nashville, TN: Incentive Publications, 1991.

Griswold, P. *Assessing Relevance and Reliability to Improve the Quality of Teacher-Made Tests, NASSP Bulletin.* Resont, VA: National Association of Secondary School Principals, February 1990.

Herman, J.L., Aschbacher, P.R. and Winters, L. *A Practical Guide to Alternative Assessment.* Alexandria, VA: Association for Supervision and Curriculum Development, 1992.

Holt, D. and Eison, J. "Preparing Freshmen to Take Essay Examinations Successfully," *Journal of the Freshman Year Experience,* Vol. 1, No. 2, 1989.

Paulson, F., Paulson, P., and Mayer, C. "What Makes a Portfolio a Portfolio?" *Educational Leadership 43, 3:30–33.* Association for Supervision and Curriculum Development, 1991.

Schurr, S. *The ABC's of Evaluation: 26 Alternative Ways to Assess Student Progress.* Columbus, OH: National Middle School Association, 1989.

Schurr, S. *How to Evaluate Your Middle School: A Practitioner's Guide for an Informal Program Evaluation.* Columbus, OH: National Middle School Association, 1989.

Stenmark, J. *Assessment Alternatives in Mathematics: An Overview of Assessment Techniques that Promote Learning.* Berkeley, CA: Equals and Assessment Committee of the California Mathematics Council, Regents University of California, 1989.

Wiggins, G. "A Response to Cizek," *Phi Delta Kappan,* 729, May 1991.

INTERDISCIPLINARY INSTRUCTION

Beane, J.A. *A Middle School Curriculum: From Rhetoric to Reality.* Columbus, OH: National Middle School Association, 1990.

Fogarty, R. *The Mindful School: How to Integrate the Curricula.* Palatine, IL: Skylight Publishing, 1991.

Integrated Learning: What-Why-How, Instructional Services Curriculum Series, No. 1, pp. 3–4. Raleigh, NC: North Carolina Department of Public Instruction, 1987.

Jacobs, H.H. *Interdisciplinary Curriculum: Design and Implementation.* Alexandria, VA: Association for Supervision and Curriculum Development, 1989.

Lewbel, S. *Interdisciplinary Units in New England's Middle Schools: What and Why?* Rowley, MA: New England League of Middle Schools, 1991.

Lounsbury, J.H., ed. *Connecting the Curriculum through Interdisciplinary Instruction.* Columbus, OH: National Middle School Association, 1992.

Vars, G.F. *Interdisciplinary Teaching in the Middle Grades: Why and How.* Columbus, OH: National Middle School Association, 1987.

Index

Ability grouping (assumptions and research), 65–66
Academic, defined, 119
Adolescence, defined, 119
Advisor
  dos and don'ts, 132–133
  responsibilities of, 130
  ways to prepare for advisory role, 131
Advisory, 115–156
  activities in addition to curriculum, 148
  children's books for students in transition, 143–144
  decisions to be made, 128–129
  defined, 19
  definitions, 119–120
  discussion starters, 147
  dos and don'ts for advisors, 132–133
  investigation tasks for model program, 139
  journal writing, 147
  model program, 136–142
  overview, 117
  overview of model advisory program, 136–142
  preparing for role of advisor, 131
  program characteristics, 127
  program scheduling, 134–135
  questions to find answers for, 118
  research findings, 121
  sample instrument for evaluating program's effectiveness, 152–154
  sample lesson plans, 140–142
  sample student interest inventory, 150
  sample student questionnaire, 151
  scope and sequence charts for three levels, 137
  table of contents for model program, 138
  teacher's wrap-up à la Bloom, 156
Advisory program
  characteristics, 127
  decisions to be made, 128–129
  instrument for evaluating effectiveness of, 152–154
  investigation tasks for three levels, 139
  overview of one model, 136–142
  scheduling, 134–135
  scope and sequence charts, 137
  student interest inventory, 150
  student questionnaire, 151
  table of contents for three levels, 138
Affective, defined, 119
Analyze, defined, 195

Assessment, 257–298
  authentic tests, 262, 279
  Bloom's Taxonomy, 278
  classroom, 297
  defined, 262
  definitions, 262
  essays, 274–276
  evaluating lesson plans, 270
  gathering data, 287–289
  overview, 259
  performance testing in core curricular areas, 285
  portfolios, 280–282
  questions to find answers for, 260–261
  research findings, 263–266
  sample student study guide, 291
  student products, 283
  student self-evaluation, 286
  student understanding, 292–296
  study group, 290
  teacher's wrap-up à la Bloom, 298
  testing, 267–269, 271–273, 277, 285
At-risk students, 28
Auditory learners, 254
Authentic assessment, defined, 262
Authentic tests, characteristics of, 279
Bee sharp, project planning, 180
Biographical beginnings (Bloom's-based research activity), 178
Block schedule
  advantages, 49, 50
  defined, 19
  flexible, defined, 77
  reasons to flex, 50
  ways to flex, 51–53
Bloom's Taxonomy, 207–210
  action verbs, 208–210
  defined, 207
  project chart, 284
  use in assessment, 278
Boning up on botany, 242–244
Brainstorming, defined, 195
Brainstorming web, 213
Bulletin boards, 40
Chart for making quality decisions, 215–216
Children's books
  in advisory program, 143–144
  used to develop appreciation of differences, 146
  used to explore behaviors, 145

Cognitive, defined, 119
Common planning time
  defined, 19, 77
  ways to use, 100
Communication, defined, 120
Comprehension, defined, 195
Consistency, defined, 119
Convergent thinking, defined, 195
Cooperative learning, 157–190
  behavior checklist, 184
  definitions, 161
  global education and, 168
  group plan at a glance, 182
  groups, 169, 171–175, 186
  overview, 159
  pitfalls, 170
  post-test, 188–189
  questions for assessing social skills, 185
  questions to find answers for, 160
  sample warmup activities, 176–181
  social/process skills, 172
  student evaluation, 188
  student planning worksheet, 183
  student's role, 161, 169
  teacher's role, 161
  teacher's wrap-up à la Bloom, 190
Core curriculum, defined, 19
Creative and critical thinking skills, 193–256
  Bloom's Taxonomy, 207–210
  characteristics of intellectual growth, 201
  definitions, 195–196
  fostering a creative classroom climate, 227
  journal writing, 205
  learning styles, 254–255
  mini-lecture, 202
  overview, 193
  promoting, 203, 204, 206, 207–225
  questions to assess creativity, 226
  questions to develop thinking skills, 225
  questions to find answers for, 194
  research to document the need for, 197–200
  selected models, 207–224
  simulation games, 206
  smuggling skills into subject area, 228
  teacher's wrap-up à la Bloom, 256
Creative thinking, defined, 195
Creativity
  fostering a creative classroom climate, 227
  questions to assess, 226
Critical thinking, defined, 195
Curriculum, defined, 303
Curriculum matrix, defined, 303
Curriculum priorities, 43

Decision making, defined, 195
Definitions
  advisory, 119–120
  assessment, 262
  cooperative learning, 161
  creative and critical thinking skills, 195
  interdisciplinary instruction, 303
  interdisciplinary teaming, 77
  nuts and bolts, 19
Developing criteria, defined, 195
Different drummer (reaction groups), 180
Differentiating instruction, 41–42
Discipline, 68
Disciplines, defined, 303
Discussion sparkers
  advisory, 147
  advisory, selected resources, 155
  quotations from well-known figures, 149
Divergent thinking, defined, 195
Early adolescence, defined, 19
Egocentric, defined, 120
Elaborate, defined, 196
Essay direction words, 274–276
Evaluation, defined, 196, 262
Exploration, defined, 19
Exploratory offerings, 63
Face-to-face interaction, defined, 161
Facility requirements, 38, 39
Findings from the published literature
  advisory, 121-126
  assessment, 263–266
  cooperative learning, 162–167
  higher-order questioning and thinking skills,
      197–200
  interdisciplinary instruction, 304–307
  interdisciplinary teaming, 78–81
  nuts and bolts, 21-25
Flexibility, defined, 196
Flexible block schedule, defined, 19, 77, 107
Fluency, defined, 196
For good measure (content-based discussion
    and demonstration), 181
Future is news to me (interdisciplinary unit),
    324–339
Futuristics, 324–339
Games
  in pursuit of trivia, 179
  simulation, 206
  thinking skills strategies, 253
Gifted students, indicators of giftedness, 29
Global education, cooperative learning and, 168
Group plan at a glance, 182
Group processing skills, defined, 161

Grouping students, 171
Heterogeneous grouping, defined, 20, 161
Homogeneous grouping, defined, 20, 161
IDU's, defined, 303
In pursuit of trivia (game) 179
Incorrect answers, 46, 204
Individual accountability, defined, 161
Informing parents and caregivers, 71
Inquiry, defined, 196
Instruction, defined, 303
Instruction, differentiation of, 41–42
Instructional materials, selection of, 44
Integrated learning, defined, 303
Intellectual growth, characteristics of, 201
Interdisciplinary instruction, 299–340
    defined, 20, 77
    definitions, 303
    integrated curriculum, 321
    integrating disciplines, 311–312
    interdisciplinary units, 315–339
    myths, 308
    overview, 301
    planning matrix, 314
    points to ponder, 313
    questions to find answers for, 302
    reasons to integrate disciplines, 309
    teacher's wrap-up à la Bloom, 340
    unit themes, 310, 315
Interdisciplinary planning matrix, 314
Interdisciplinary team, defined, 20
Interdisciplinary team identity, tools for
    building, 93
Interdisciplinary team test, 323
Interdisciplinary teaming, 73–114
    advantages, 75
    assignment data sheet, 108
    barriers to overcome, 96, 97
    characteristics of effective, 104
    check-up à la Bloom, 114
    common planning time, 100
    defined, 77
    definitions, 77
    development of teams, 82–86, 92
    flexible block master schedules, 54–62, 107
    functions and activities, 94, 95
    great, 94–95
    leadership, 91
    questions to find answers for, 76
    self-assessment, 88–90
    teaching dilemmas, 87
    team discipline rules, 101
    team evaluation report, 109
    team handbook, 98 –99
    team identity, 93
    team interview, 110
    team meetings, effective, 103
    team self-evaluation checklist, 111–113
    terms, 77
    varying team sizes, 105, 106
Interdisciplinary teams, development of, 82–86
Interdisciplinary unit
    essential elements of, 316
    evaluating, 322
    student comments, 317
    themes, 318
Interpersonal and small group skills, defined,
    161
Interscholastic, defined, 20
Intramural, defined, 20
Intrascholastic, defined, 20
Journal writing for thinking skills, 205
Junior high school
    contributions to middle school, 32
    distinguished from middle school, 31
Kinesthetic learners, 254
Knowledge, defined, 196
Learning styles, 254–255
Lecturette, 202
Left-brain learners, 255
Lesson planning, 45, 69
Lesson plans, evaluating, 270
Master block schedules, 47, 48, 49, 54–62, 107
Metacognition, defined, 20, 262
Middle school mission statement, 34
Middle school philosophy, 17, 22
Middle school programs
    balance in, 43
    Carnegie report recommendations, 33
    contributions from junior high, 32
    curriculum priorities, 43
    discipline, 68
    distinguished from junior high, 31
    exemplary, 30, 35
    exploratory offerings, 63
    mini-courses, 64
    planning, 69
    positive climate, 36, 37, 39, 67
    schedules, 47–62
    transformation of, 33
Middle schools, facilities, 38, 39
Mini-courses, 20, 64
Mini-lecture, 202
Mission statement, steps in developing, 34
Models, thinking skills, 207–224
    Bloom's Taxonomy, 207–210
    Chart for making quality decisions, 215–216

Problem-solving pattern, 221
Research, write, and create, 214
Starter statements, 223–224
Thinking on your feet, 219–220
Thinktrix, 217–218
Web, 213
Why model, 222
Williams' Taxonomy, 211–212
Needs and characteristics of young adolescents, 21–27
Negative, defined, 120
Newspaper interdisciplinary unit, 324–339
Nuts and bolts, 15–72
    definitions, 19
    overview, 17
    questions to find answers for, 18
    terms, 19
    wrap-up à la Bloom, 72
Off to a good start (student planning worksheet), 183
Organ transplants (content-based unit) 246–253
Originality, defined, 196
Outcome-based education, defined, 262
Overviews
    advisory, 117
    assessment, 259
    cooperative learning, 159
    creative and critical thinking skills, 193
    interdisciplinary instruction, 301
    interdisciplinary teaming, 75
    nuts and bolts, 17
Parents and caregivers, 71
    effective parent conference, 102
Performance assessment, defined, 262
Planning a lesson, 45
Planning strategies, 69
Portfolio assessment, defined, 262
Portfolios
    decisions, 282
    power of, 280–281
    reasons to consider, 282
Positive, defined, 120
Positive climate in middle schools, 36, 37, 39, 67
Positive interdependence, defined, 161
Problem solve, defined, 196
Problem-solving pattern, 221
Product assessment, defined, 262
Questions
    gathering assessment data, 287–289
    to use during a team interview, 110
Questions to find answers for
    advisory, 118

assessment, 260–261
cooperative learning, 160
creative and critical thinking skills, 194
interdisciplinary instruction, 302
interdisciplinary teaming, 76
nuts and bolts, 18
Reasoning, defined, 196
Relationship, defined, 120
Reliability, defined, 262
Research findings
    assessment, 263–266
    cooperative learning, 162–167
    early adolescence, 21–25
    higher-order questioning and thinking skills, 197–200
    interdisciplinary instruction, 304–307
    interdisciplinary teaming, 78–81
    nuts and bolts, 21–25
Research, write, and create (thinking skills model), 214
Responding to incorrect answers, 46, 204
Right-brain learners, 255
Sample behavior checklist, cooperative learning, 184
Sample cooperative learning post-test, 188–189
Sample cooperative learning warmups, 176–181
    Bloom's-based research activity, 178
    content-based discussion and demonstrations, 181
    content-based unit, 246
    creative construction, 177
    reaction groups, 180
    games and game construction, 179
    interdisciplinary unit, 324
    project planning and implementation, 180
Sample instrument for evaluating advisory program's effectiveness, 152
Sample interdisciplinary team assignment data sheet, 108
Sample interdisciplinary team evaluation report, 109
Sample interdisciplinary units
    futuristics, 324–339
    measurement, 319–320
Sample lesson plans
    advisory, level one, 140
    advisory, level three, 142
    advisory, level two, 141
    using picture book to develop appreciation of differences, 146
    using picture book to explore behaviors, 145
Sample schedules, 54–62
    adjusting for special events, 54

daily rotation, 56
special week, 57
team rotation, 61
team teaching patterns, 55, 58, 61
three grade levels, 59
variations, 60–62
Sample student advisory questionnaire, 151
Sample student interest inventory, 150
Sample student planning worksheet, 183
Sample team self-evaluation checklist, 111–113
Schedules
block schedule, 49
flexing the block, 50–53
master schedule, 47, 48
samples, 54–62
Scheduling, 47–62
advisory program, 134–135
flexible, 78
School mission statement, 34
Selecting instructional materials, 44
Self-esteem, defined, 120
Self-evaluation, benefits for students, 286
Send the message (creative construction), 177
Simulations, defined, 303
Springboard for discussion starters and journal
writing, 147
Starter statements, 223–224
Strategies, thinking skills, 228–253
commercial posters, 234–235
desktop learning stations, 239–240
fact and activity file folders, 241–244
games, 253
investigation kits, 238
learning logs and dialogue diaries, 245
reports, 236–237
think smart task cards, 228–231
Stress reducers, 70
Structured cooperative learning, defined, 161
Student products, 283
Student study group, 290
Sample student study guide, 291
Synthesize, defined, 196
Teacher time wasters, 70
Teacher timesavers, 70
Teacher's wrap-up à la Bloom
advisory, 156
assessment, 298
cooperative learning, 190
interdisciplinary instruction, 340
interdisciplinary teaming, 114
thinking skills, 256
nuts and bolts, 72
Teaching dilemmas, 87

Team handbook, 77, 98–99
Team identity, 77
Team leaders, roles and responsiblities, 91
Team meetings
defined, 77
effective, 103
Team rules and discipline plan, defined, 77
Team teaching, defined, 77
Terms
advisory, 119–120
assessment, 262
cooperative learning, 161
creative and critical thinking skills, 195
interdisciplinary instruction, 303
interdisciplinary teaming, 77
middle school success, 19
nuts and bolts, 19
Testing
Bloom's Taxonomy, 278
commandments of, 267
essay tests, 277
preparing students for, 277
questions to answer before, 267
teacher-made tests, 269
using time wisely, 267
writing objective test items, 272–273
writing quality items for, 271
Theme, defined, 303
Themes for interdisciplinary unit, 318
Thinking matrix, 217–218
Thinking on your feet, 219–220
Thinking skills (see creative and critical
thinking skills)
Thinking, defined, 196
Thinktrix, 217–218
Thomason, Julia, 81
Time wasters, 70
Timesavers, 70
Transcescence, defined, 20
Validity, defined, 262
Visual learners, 254
Web, 213
Webbing, defined, 303
Why model, 222
Williams' Taxonomy, 211–212
aggressive, 212
cognitive, 211
defined, 211